AGE OF KINGS

TIME LIFE BOOKS ®

GREAT AGES OF MAN

A History of the World's Cultures

AGE OF KINGS

by

CHARLES BLITZER

and

The Editors of TIME-LIFE BOOKS

TIME-LIFE BOOKS, NEW YORK

THE AUTHOR: Dr. Charles Blitzer is Director of the Smithsonian Institution's Institute of Education and Training. Prior to this assignment, he was Executive Administrator of the American Council of Learned Societies, and from 1950 until 1961 taught political science at Yale. He is the author of *An Immortal Commonwealth*, the editor of a book of documents, *The Commonwealth of England*, and co-author with Carl J. Friedrich of *The Age of Power*.

THE CONSULTING EDITOR: Leonard Krieger, University Professor of History at the University of Chicago, was formerly Professor of History at Columbia and Yale universities. He is author of *The German Idea of Freedom* and *The Politics of Discretion* and co-author of *History*, which was written in collaboration with John Higham and Felix Gilbert.

THE COVER: The dominant personality of the 17th Century, the French King Louis XIV, holds a military baton in this detail from a tapestry he commissioned.

The following individuals and departments of Time Inc. gave valuable aid in the preparation of this book: photographer Dmitri Kessel; Editorial Production, Norman Airey; Library, Benjamin Lightman; Picture Collection, Doris O'Neil; Photographic Laboratory, George Karas; TIME-LIFE News Service, Murray J. Gart; Correspondents Maria Vincenza Aloisi (Paris), Barbara Moir, Margot Hapgood and Anne Angus (London), Ann Natanson (Rome), Elisabeth Kraemer (Bonn), Traudl Lessing (Vienna), Franz Spelman (Munich), Andrzej Glowacz (Cracow).

CONTENTS

INTRODUCTION 7

1 "'TIS ALL IN PIECES" 10
Picture Essay: HOUSES OF CARDS 19

2 THE THIRTY YEARS' WAR 30
Picture Essay: IN BATTLE'S WAKE 43

3 THE SUN KING 54
Picture Essay: THE GLORIOUS MONARCH 63

4 TUMULT IN THE ARTS 76
Picture Essay: TITAN OF THE BAROQUE 85

5 A RECONSTRUCTED UNIVERSE 96
Picture Essay: THE NEW SCIENTISTS 107

6 PATTERNS OF REASON 116
Picture Essay: THE BIRTH OF BALLET 127

7 ROYALTY VS. PARLIAMENT 138
Picture Essay: SAMUEL PEPYS'S LONDON 149

8 A WORLD IN BALANCE 164
Picture Essay: THE ORDER OF THE DAY 173

Chronology, 184
Bibliography, credits and art notes, 186
Acknowledgments, 187
Index, 188

INTRODUCTION

The Age of Kings was a great age. Today, we are more willing to admit this than our ancestors were, for they had to fight and eventually to destroy the monarchies that were the 17th Century's distinctive product. Louis XIV and Peter the Great were towering figures whose achievements included far more than the triumph of monarchial absolutism. This was the epoch in which the secular state, such as England, France or Russia, finally won its independence from ecclesiastical supervision and interference.

Sometimes the period treated in this fine volume has been called the Age of the Baroque, a style much favored by the great secular monarchs even though it was originally created by and for the ardently missionary Society of Jesus. Style is often the most telling hallmark of an age, and there was, as Charles Blitzer recognizes, a strong link between the Age of Kings and the Baroque. The link was the startling new experience of power—power of the mind over nature, power of the army and the state over man. In art, this new sense of power led to an "art of the impossible" that dared to defy all the familiar canons of form and taste. It was an age of demonic urges, symbolized by the figure of Satan —a Satan, in the words of John Milton, "aspiring to set himself in glory among his peers" and rebelling "against the throne and monarchy of God."

Herein lies the key to the renewed appreciation of this remarkable age. Once more man is overwhelmed by a new sense of power—and of impotence: the space age and the nuclear age are also the age of totalitarian dictatorship. Just as Europeans in the 17th Century fought to control the partitioning of Europe, so men of today are fighting to control the whole globe. Just as emergent nations clashed in the 17th Century, so emergent cultures clash now. The ever higher towers in our cities, the ever faster planes that link continent with continent, the ever more refined methods of mass communication testify to a new age of power. So too do our explorations of the infinitely small and the incomprehensibly vast; our search for an understanding of the subconscious by psychoanalysis, and for a means to manipulate power with the help of political science.

It would be a mistake, of course, to stress these similarities too much. Nevertheless, they do help to explain the new and deeper interest in the 17th Century, an interest well served by this book. In sketching the essential traits of the Age of Kings, Charles Blitzer has marshaled those facts that allow us to perceive the century's character in all its strength and weakness. He thus enables us better to understand and appreciate the strengths and weaknesses of our own times.

CARL J. FRIEDRICH

Eaton Professor of the Science of Government

Harvard University

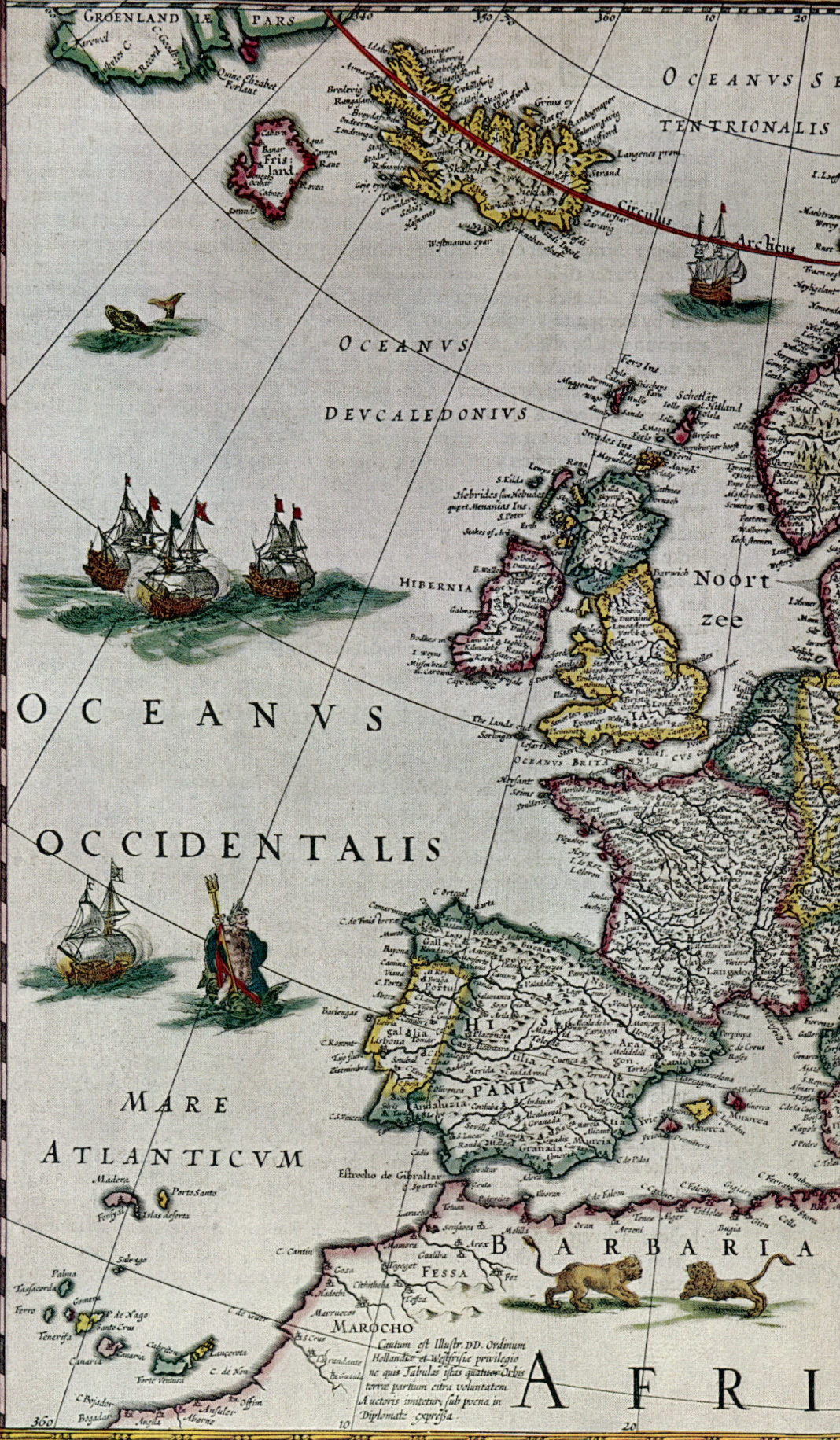

EVROPA
recens descripta
à
Guilielmo Blaeuw.

Germani

Hungari

Bohemi

Poloni

Greci

1

"'TIS ALL IN PIECES"

In 1611, the English poet John Donne composed "An Anatomie of the World," and put into words feelings that troubled many of his contemporaries. Traditional beliefs about mankind and the universe were being destroyed, Donne lamented, by the new ideas of science and philosophy:

And new Philosophy calls all in doubt,
The Element of fire is quite put out;
The Sun is lost, and th'earth, and no man's wit
Can well direct him where to looke for it.
And freely men confesse that this world's spent,
When in the Planets, and the Firmament
They seeke so many new . . .

In the same plaintive tone of disapproval, Donne went on to regret the shattering of the old order of things, and simultaneously to reveal a new and challenging aspect of this development—the heady notion that man was unique and possessed of unlimited creative capacities:

'Tis all in pieces, all coherence gone;
All just supply, and all Relation:
Prince, Subject, Father, Sonne, are things forgot,
For every man alone thinkes he hath got
To be a Phoenix, and that there can bee
None of the kinde, of which he is, but hee.

Between these two extremes of feeling—dismay at the destruction of the old order, pride in the ability to create a new one from its ruins—the 17th Century played out its magnificent drama. The very discoveries that Donne deplored were hailed by his contemporary, Francis Bacon, on the ground that they would "extend more widely the limits of the power and greatness of man." And Bacon's hopes, as it turned out, proved to be better founded than Donne's fears.

In the course of the century, man's limits were indeed extended to lengths scarcely dreamed of by previous ages. The result was the creation, nothing less, of the modern world. But this was not a foregone conclusion when the century began, nor was it achieved by a process of gradual and orderly evolution. There were formidable obstacles to be overcome, and overcoming them was a matter of tension and conflict, violence and turmoil.

When the century dawned, the medieval world was dead, shattered beyond repair by Renaissance humanism and the Protestant Reformation. But the constituent parts of the medieval world were still

UNITING TWO HOUSES, *a royal banquet culminates the marriage of first cousins in the Habsburg dynasty: Leopold I of Austria, Holy Roman Emperor, and Margaret Theresa, daughter of the King of Spain, at left rear. Through such marriages Europe was linked in a network of monarchial power.*

11

very much alive. The Catholic Church remained powerful, even though it was no longer the unquestioned arbiter in matters of faith throughout Latin Christendom. The feudal nobility clung tenaciously to its traditional privileges, even though feudalism itself was destroyed. The ancient view of the universe as earth-centered was gravely challenged, but men continued to believe that the planets moved according to the theories laid down by Aristotle.

To confuse matters further, new institutions, new beliefs and new theories had sprung up to exist side by side with the old. Protestant sects of varying size, strength and fanaticism were aggressively active in virtually every country except Italy, Spain and Portugal. An increasingly prosperous merchant class was everywhere encroaching upon the rights of the old aristocracy. A new generation of scientists, armed with sophisticated instruments, was learning things about nature that made nonsense of existing theories. In a very real and painful way, the world had lost its coherence. Everything from the place of the earth in the universe to the place of the individual in society was suddenly open to question—and it was not at all clear where men should turn for answers. For what was most in doubt of all was the source of authority itself—in religion, in government, in science, in thought. The men of the 17th Century found themselves living not so much between two worlds as in two worlds at once, subjected simultaneously to the conflicting values, beliefs and institutions of both.

The great men of the 17th Century were those who took this loss of authority as a challenge, and dared to create a new kind of order out of the materials at hand. The key to their success was power, the ability to master the unruly forces in men and nature, and shape them into patterns and harmonies of a new kind. The motto for these men might well have been a single sentence written by Thomas Hobbes, the century's most penetrating political philosopher, in the *Leviathan*: "So that in the first place, I put for a general inclination of all mankind, a perpetual and restless desire for Power after Power, that ceaseth only in death."

Yet power unchecked by traditional beliefs and institutions could reduce the world to anarchy and chaos, and this was precisely the specter that haunted the 17th Century. Shakespeare, in *Troilus and Cressida*, drew an unforgettable picture of what could happen when an established order is destroyed:

> *Take but degree away, untune that string,*
> *And hark, what discord follows! Each thing meets*
> *In mere oppugnancy. The bounded waters*
> *Should lift their bosoms higher than the shores*
> *And make a sop of all this solid globe.*
> *Strength should be lord of imbecility,*
> *And the rude son should strike his father dead.*
> *Force should be right, or rather, right and wrong,*
> *Between whose endless jar justice resides,*
> *Should lose their names, and so should justice too.*
> *Then everything includes itself in power,*
> *Power into will, will into appetite;*
> *And appetite, an universal wolf,*
> *So doubly seconded with will and power,*
> *Must make perforce an universal prey,*
> *And last eat up himself.*

Often, during the 17th Century, and particularly during its first decades, it did seem that Europe would consume itself in the forces unleashed by the collapse of traditional order. Conflicts of every kind, from the bloodiest of wars to the bitterest of religious disputes, raged over the continent. Kingdoms and communities were torn apart; untold numbers of people lost their lives and property; Europe was threatened with a new Dark Age. Yet along with conflict, there was also creativity. Names such as Velasquez and Rembrandt, Milton and Molière, Galileo and Newton, Cromwell and Louis XIV, suggest the range and degree of achievement in every sphere of human activity.

The problems encountered in working out a relationship between restless motion and enduring order created in the 17th Century a unique quality of mind, a style. The word for the style was Baroque, which in a narrow sense labeled the century's art, but in a broader sense characterized the century's whole approach to life. Baroque art was a heroic attempt to transcend the contradiction between order and motion. Its twisted columns, endlessly elaborate forms, intensely dramatic changes and contrasts, were all expressions of a new kind of order—one that took into account the dynamic, ever-changing quality of nature and human emotions. Baroque artists were inventing a new artistic language, suitable to their new world.

In other fields, other men were preoccupied with precisely the same problem: how to find a pattern, an order, within the apparent disorder of a changing world. In science, the crucial discoveries of the age stemmed without exception from the quest to account for motion—motion in planets, motion on earth, motion within the blood stream of living creatures. Dynamics, the modern science that explains why moving bodies move as they do, is a creation of the 17th Century. Calculus, the foremost mathematical achievement of the age, is an algebraic means of expressing motion. In every field of physical science, men were learning that nature's apparently chaotic processes had pattern and regularity, and that they could be controlled.

But the search for order was most pressing of all in the field of politics. Unlike the artist, who cultivated discontent, or the scientist, whose success required a natural curiosity, ambitious rulers and their fearful subjects sought order for the sake of survival. Nations and individual human beings were threatened by anarchy, civil war and foreign aggression. Conspiracies, assassinations and insurrections

spread across the whole of Western Europe in a virtual epidemic:

In 1605, a band of Roman Catholic extremists gained access to the cellar of Britain's Westminster Palace and filled it with more than a ton of gunpowder, intending to blow up the King and the Houses of Parliament and seize control of the government; their plot was discovered and thwarted only at the last moment.

In 1610, Henry IV, the beloved French King who coined the phrase, "A chicken in every peasant's pot every Sunday," was murdered by a religious fanatic who claimed that Henry was preparing to destroy the Catholic Church.

In 1648, after six years of civil wars, Oliver Cromwell and his rebellious Puritans seized control of the English government and, on January 30, 1649, chopped off the head of Charles I before a multitude of spectators and "divers companies of foot . . . and troops of horse. . . ."

In France, between 1648 and 1652, in a series of outbreaks known as the Fronde, disgruntled noblemen, their authority diminished by the policies of Richelieu, threatened to take over the powers of state and rule the country themselves.

Behind these outward signs of civil unrest lay a much deeper disorder, a disintegrating political system. Europe's traditional machinery of government had been designed to manage the affairs of an essentially static society—feudal, agrarian, bound together by the ties of religious uniformity. It could not cope with the tensions and problems of an expanding commercial society whose members were sharply divided over questions of religion. The religious issue in particular aroused violently partisan feelings, confronting every country with an apparent choice between anarchy and absolutism. Midway through the century one perceptive Englishman, James Harrington, warned his countrymen of the danger to England in delaying the choice:

APOTHECARY

"Look you to it, where there is tumbling and tossing upon the bed of sickness, it must end in death, or recovery. . . . If France, Italy and Spain were not all sick, all corrupted together, there would bee none of them so, for the sick would not bee able to withstand the sound, nor the sound to preserve her health without curing the sick. The first of these Nations (which . . . will in my minde bee France) that recovers the health of ancient Prudence, shall assuredly govern the world. . . . I do not speak at randome."

His prediction was remarkably accurate. In the course of the century, France did recover first from its political sickness and did come close to governing the world. The French state created by Louis XIV was based on a new kind of political order, absolutism, and for one glorious moment absolutism dazzled Europe. Its essential elements were supreme royal power and an administrative bureaucracy responsible solely to the king. Louis reigned not on the sufferance of his vassal princes, but because he controlled the machinery of state. Absolutism, as he practiced it, brought France political stability and national power. It also touched off an astonishing outburst of intellectual and artistic creativity.

The reign of Louis XIV was unquestionably the high-water mark in French culture and a landmark in Western civilization. All the immense energies of the age were for a brief time harnessed and shaped by the power of Louis' state into a magnificent spectacle. The French monarchy was admired and envied by other monarchs; the French language became the language of diplomacy; French art and architecture were slavishly imitated even in courts as far from Versailles as imperial Russia, where Peter the Great hired one of Louis' architects to design his capital city, St. Petersburg. Frederick III of Brandenburg-Prussia was so eager to emulate Louis that he installed a royal mistress at his court,

BUTCHER

BLACKSMITH

CLOCKMAKER

BAROQUE EXUBERANCE *is expressed in the playful style of these 17th Century French engravings. The artist has constructed four tradesmen from tools of their trade: an apothecary with flasks and jars, a butcher with chopping blocks and oxhide, a blacksmith with bellows and anvil, and a clockmaker with clockwork.*

even though, as a pious man and faithful husband, he never used her services.

But power, the key to Louis' grandiose achievements, was also his nemesis. His much admired and copied government soon proved to have grave weaknesses. Louis coped with the unruly forces within his kingdom by subjugating them utterly to his will. Rebellious nobles were crushed; Protestant dissenters were forced to become Catholic or were driven into exile; businessmen, merchants and farmers were regulated down to the minutest detail; artists and intellectuals were made servants of the state. Similarly, Louis used the power of his army to attack and intimidate France's neighbors.

By the end of Louis' 72-year reign, these policies had become self-defeating. An excess of order and authority destroyed the very vitality that had been France's glory. Deprived of any responsible role in government, the French nobility became increasingly dissolute and corrupt. The French economy faltered under too-meticulous regulations and the ever-increasing demands of the military for funds. French industry lost the skilled hands of thousands of Protestant artisans, and French art, tied to the artificialities of Louis' court, substituted the refinement of rococo for the vigor of Baroque. Finally, when the other great powers of Europe united to resist French military might, Louis found that he had sacrificed his country's spirit upon the altar of order and authority.

Nevertheless, absolutism, as a concept, remained very much alive. In England, the Stuart kings tried to force absolutism upon their island realm, despite the considerable power of Parliament. They failed, but in failing they laid the foundations for a novel system of political order. An alternative to both anarchy and absolutism, it came to be called constitutionalism. Unlike the foes of absolutism elsewhere in Europe, the English resisted absolute authority not because of old ideas about aristocratic rights, but for an entirely new reason. After generations of unrest and decades of civil war, the English developed a true national community, one strong enough and structured enough to participate in the affairs of government. The leaders of this community, far from opposing centralized authority, worked with their rulers to achieve it.

Thus, England and France, by the close of the century, had gone far toward defining a new system of political order. For France, that order, in recognizing the supreme authority of a secular ruler, foreshadowed the modern secular state. For England, in establishing that kings ruled only by consent of the governed, it laid the groundwork for modern democracy.

But if the century ended on a note of hope, it also ended with a residue of political confusion. The 17th Century was notable in Germany for the Thirty Years' War, and a peace that left the Holy Roman Empire of the German Nation in much the same condition that it found it—a political entity without political coherence. Voltaire's famous statement that the Holy Roman Empire was neither holy nor Roman nor an empire only begins to convey some notion of the confusion that reigned in this curious political survival from another age.

By the beginning of the 17th Century, the Empire—once a mighty union of Christian states, led by an emperor who was one of the most powerful rulers in Christendom—had become a kind of political monstrosity, a chaotic patchwork of conflicting authorities torn by internal dissensions. Even the Empire's exact boundaries are impossible to define, because of the uncertain status of the various territories it was supposed to include. In the 15th Century its ancient and resounding title had been amended, rather apologetically, with the words, "of the German Nation," and for all practical purposes its boundaries were defined by language—its people were largely Germanic. With its

population of some 21 million, it could have been one of the most powerful states of 17th Century Europe—if it had been a state. But it was not, and what it was defies description.

To begin with, the Empire contained something on the order of 2,000 separate territorial authorities —principalities, free imperial cities, bishoprics and fiefs. Some of these consisted of little more than a castle and its surrounding land. Through a series of complicated overlapping alliances, these 2,000 local autonomies were reduced to about 300 political units; it was often said that the Empire contained a sovereign ruler for every day of the year.

The most powerful of these rulers were the seven princes who chose the Emperor, the Electors of the Holy Roman Empire. Three of the Electors were Catholic prelates, the Archbishops of Mainz, Trier and Cologne; three were secular princes, the rulers of Saxony, Brandenburg and the Rhineland region known as the Palatinate (from palatine, the medieval title of a prince who held a royal fief). One Elector was not a prince at all, but a king, the monarch of the kingdom of Bohemia.

None of the seven Electors was as powerful in practice, however, as the princes of the Austrian house of Habsburg, whose lands included all of Austria and part of Hungary—by far the largest landholdings in the Empire. The Austrian Habsburgs, furthermore, were the junior branch of the dynastic family that ruled Spain, Portugal, much of Italy and the southern Netherlands—to say nothing of the Spanish colonies overseas. By the 17th Century the Austrian Habsburgs were tacitly acknowledged to be the hereditary owners of the crown of the Holy Roman Empire.

But the title carried with it little real authority. For one thing, the office of emperor was still elective, even though the chief function of the Electors had lost some of its significance. Theoretically, it was still possible for them to choose someone other than the Habsburg heir, and they did not hesitate to use this power to gain concessions from the hereditary "candidate." Even more damaging, the Emperor was forced to act through an extraordinary legislative body, the Reichstag, an assembly of all the princes of the Empire from Electors down to the lowliest knight whose feudal properties entitled him to a voice in imperial affairs.

The Reichstag was the sole authority for laws applying to the whole Empire, and for taxes of a similar nature. But many of its members took their duties so lightly that they did not bother to appear in person, choosing instead to send deputies. And many of the Reichstag meetings were spent in endless disputes over who was entitled to vote, and how many votes each member possessed. Even more serious, the membership of the Reichstag included a number of foreign princes whose lands extended into the Empire, and a number of imperial princes with extensive foreign holdings. The King of Denmark, for instance, held ancient fiefs within the Empire that entitled him to sit on the Reichstag. With interests alien to those of the Empire, and especially to the Habsburg Emperor's dynastic ambitions, these princes frequently caused the Reichstag to register opinions completely opposed to those of the Emperor.

The Emperor's authority was also thwarted by a series of military governments within the Empire that in effect were local autonomies. A century before, the Empire had been divided into 10 defensive zones, or imperial circles. Each circle had its own governor and assembly, and its own treasury. Each was responsible for training and recruiting men for an imperial army, ostensibly for use on imperial business—to keep peace and ward off aggression. In practice, however, the circles' policies and actions represented the individual interests of their governors, who were inevitably the leading local princes. By some curious circumstance, al-though they were theoretically subject to the Emperor's orders, the circles could and did make war on their own initiative, without consulting him.

All of this made effective central government difficult, but not impossible. What finally made the situation hopeless was the division of religious belief. With the Reformation's shattering of Christian unity, the one force that might have united the Empire's disparate parts became instead an insuperable barrier to the creation of a German state. In a sense, the Empire's fate had been sealed the century before, in 1555, at the Peace of Augsburg, when the Emperor Charles V, after a futile attempt to oust Lutheranism from his Empire, acknowledged the right of each German prince to impose his own religion on the inhabitants of his territory.

Proclaimed as a triumph of liberty, the Peace of Augsburg was in fact a license for each prince to practice the most severe religious repression. Under its guise princes tyrannized over their subjects brutally. The conversion of a prince from one religion to another—and such conversions were not uncommon—had particularly horrible consequences. They were inevitably followed by the prince's wholesale seizure of Church lands within his territory and by the persecution of "heretic" subjects who failed to follow his religious lead.

The same "liberties" that cast the princes in the role of tyrants also established a pattern of conflict between princes and Emperor that guaranteed the fragmentation of the Empire for centuries to come. As one distinguished historian, C. V. Wedgwood, has put it, "Two battles were being fought, one between the princes and the Emperor, another between the princes and the peoples, and the princes bore the brunt in both, facing both ways, carrying the torch of liberty in one hand and the tyrant's sword in the other."

Early in the 17th Century, the Empire's utter fragmentation began to give way to tentative groupings along religious lines. At first, these alliances were temporary in nature. Other interests besides religion prevented the co-religionists from forming strong bonds. For a brief moment in 1608, for instance, it seemed that Protestant Germany might unite against the Emperor. A riot broke out between Catholics and Protestants in the free city of Donauwörth, on the Danube, when the Catholics, in defiance of the city's Protestant majority, held a religious procession. To punish Donauwörth for this disorder, the Emperor placed it under imperial ban, ordered it to accept a predominance of Catholics on its city council.

To the Protestant princes, this seemed clearly a transgression of religious freedom, and boded ill for their own beliefs. Accordingly, they banded together and walked out of the Reichstag, threatening to arm and defend themselves against such measures. But the threats came to nothing. Lutherans quickly found themselves at odds with Calvinists, whose religious views they considered dangerously radical; Protestant princes were reluctant to risk their power and prestige within the Empire for the sake of a city whose problems, however grave, did not threaten their "liberties."

Nevertheless, the incident at Donauwörth helped to crystallize Protestant sentiment, and the princes did unite into a Protestant Union. Their action was followed almost immediately by a similar union of Catholic princes, organized by Maximilian of Bavaria—the Catholic League. Within these alliances, however, there continued to be divergent opinions not only about religious matters, but also about politics. Some Catholic princes, for instance, supported the League's religious position but disagreed with its anti-imperial bias—Maximilian, the League's guiding spirit, mistrusted the Emperor's dynastic ambitions.

Thus the Empire was divided not into two camps, but four: Lutherans, Calvinists, Catholic princes

and the party of the Habsburg Emperor. Of these, two were primarily religious in their outlook, concerned with the propagation of the True Faith, whichever it happened to be. These were the Calvinists and the party of the Emperor. The other two, the Lutherans and the Catholic princes, were more concerned with politics and the future of the German nation. Between the intricate interweavings of these complex forces, the fate of Germany was soon to be determined.

In the second decade of the century, these forces coalesced with dramatic suddenness. The Habsburg relatives of the Emperor Matthias—who was middle-aged, unambitious and childless—decided to make one of their number, the Archduke Ferdinand of Styria, Matthias' successor. Ferdinand, an able and intelligent ruler, was also a stubborn and devout Catholic. His selection did not please the Protestant princes. In particular, it did not please the young Elector Palatine, Frederick—or, to be exact, Frederick's chief advisor, Christian von Anhalt, who believed it might be possible for the first time to elect a Protestant Emperor.

Of the seven imperial Electors, Christian assumed that three—the Catholic Archbishops of Mainz, Trier and Cologne—would vote for Ferdinand. But he thought that the three Protestant Electors might be persuaded to vote for another candidate, if that candidate had some chance of winning. The key vote would be that of the King of Bohemia, who was usually a Habsburg and who held his office, like the Emperor himself, by election. If the people of Bohemia, who were predominantly Protestant, could be encouraged to elect a Protestant king, the vote of that king could put a Protestant on the imperial throne. Christian's candidate for the Bohemian crown was young Frederick of the Palatinate. Out of his scheme to bring off this coup grew the most hideously destructive war Europe had ever known.

HOUSES OF CARDS

In their degrees of rank and power, the noblemen of the 17th Century resembled the pasteboards in one of the era's favorite pastimes: card playing. Highest in rank were the kings who headed Europe's great ruling houses; their game was power, their board the map of Europe. Below the kings, members of each court contended for their own positions of prestige in the hierarchy of court life, a hierarchy as rigidly defined as the ranking of cards within a suit. Occasionally an ambitious gambler very nearly brought the whole house down.

Card playing was such a passion at court that fortunes changed hands in an evening of play. Even the decks used caught the spirit of the game: face cards bore dashing figures from far-off lands; the lower ranks carried their numerical values like the fruit of fanciful trees. One of the most decorative decks (*above and following pages*) was made in 1628 for England's Charles I, who lost more at politics—his head—than he ever did at cards.

THE KINGS:
FOUR FACES
OF MONARCHY

A king, proclaimed France's Louis XIV with his customary lack of modesty, "is of superior rank to all other men . . . occupying, so to speak, the place of God." And indeed the four monarchs portrayed at right, next to the kings of the four suits of cards, did possess a power that was almost godlike. Theirs were the great ruling dynasties and coalitions of Europe: the Bourbons of France, the Habsburgs of Catholic Germany and Spain, the Stuarts of England, the Protestant houses of Northern Europe. Louis reigned omnipotent as an absolute monarch. Leopold I, the Habsburg ruler of a declining Holy Roman Empire, still managed to turn his hereditary lands in Austria into the cornerstone of a new imperial state. William III of Orange, who gained the English throne by marrying a Stuart princess, and Gustavus Adolphus of Sweden, wielded great power in their own countries in partnership with their parliaments.

LOUIS XIV *of France, Europe's pre-eminent monarch, is seen besi the King of Hearts, highest face card in the 17th Century dec*

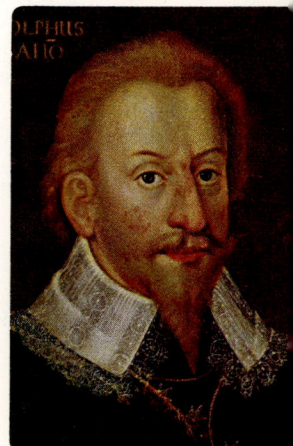

LEOPOLD I, *the Habsburg emperor, is shown costumed for court theatricals, as elaborately clad as the King of Spades at the left.*

WILLIAM III *of Orange, whose reign ended more than half a century of civil strife, ruled as England's first constitutional monarch.*

GUSTAVUS ADOLPHUS *of Sweden, by military conquests, turned his country into one of the leading Protestant nations of Europe.*

THE QUEEN OF HEARTS, *Madame de Maintenon became the wife of Louis XIV after serving more than 10 years as governess for some of his illegitimate children. She used her favored new position to improve court morals. Operas and plays were forbidden during Lent, plunging necklines rose demurely and piety became the fashion of the day.*

A JOKER AND A KNAVE, *the Grand Dauphin (left) and the Grand Condé (right) were as different as two men could be. The Dauphin, called "Grand" partly because he was so fat, stayed in favor with his father, Louis XIV, by avoiding politics; he spent his time hunting and going to parties. The Prince de Condé, a relentless politician, led a revolt against the Royal Family in 1652 and later defected to Spain to command an army. The Prince's military talents were so great that Louis eventually restored him to honor, deciding that he would be less dangerous as a friend than as an enemy.*

CLERICAL GAMESMEN, *Cardinals Richelieu (right of the Nine of Hearts) and Mazarin (below card) played politics as prime ministers of France before Louis XIV gained power; their regimes laid the foundations of Louis' omnipotence. Louis' foremost apologist was Bishop Bossuet (at top), who claimed that absolute monarchy was God's will. But Archbishop Fénelon (left of card), tutor to Louis' grandson, disagreed, calling such power "barbarous."*

LEADING LADIES of the French court played an ever-diminishing role in the game of power politics as the 17th Century wore on. Machiavellian gambits marked the seven-year regency of Marie de'Medici (left), the grandmother of Louis XIV; but her schemes failed, and she died in exile. During Louis' reign, the ladies learned to stay out of politics. The rich and intellectual Madame de Sévigné (below card) confined herself to court gossip, preserved in some 1,500 letters to her daughter. Mlle. de La Vallière (bottom), like Louis' other mistresses, learned that the best way to stay in favor with the King was to keep her opinions to herself. A contemporary described her as having "a lovely complexion, blonde hair . . . no ambition, no points of view."

A DOUR BANKER, Jean Baptiste Colbert completely revamped the French economy in order to pay the debts of the court. In ten years as Louis XIV's finance minister, he doubled national revenues.

A DOUBLE DEALER, Nicolas Fouquet amassed a fortune of his own while serving as finance minister. His take was so impressive that Louis became jealous, and had him imprisoned for embezzlement.

CATHOLIC PARTNERS *fought side by side during the Thirty Years' War to help preserve the Habsburgs' imperial power. Albrecht von Wallenstein (far left), the Habsburgs' most brilliant general, won resounding victories over the Protestants in the war's early days, but he was assassinated by political enemies in 1634. The empire's most powerful ally was the army of the Catholic League, commanded by Count Johann Tilly (near left) and financed by Maximilian of Bavaria (center), a man of such rigid morals that he banned dancing among his peasants and decreed a death penalty for adulterers.*

HABSBURG QUEENS, *the successive wives of Leopold I were strategic cards in the Emperor's struggle to maintain his power. Leopold's first marriage, to his cousin Margaret Theresa (far left), daughter of the King of Spain, was a political maneuver by which Leopold hoped, in vain, to inherit the Spanish crown. Following the death of Margaret, and of Leopold's second wife Claudia of Austria, the Emperor married a German princess, Eleanor of Neuburg (near left)—a choice calculated to pacify the German noblemen in the empire, who had been demanding more and more independence from imperial rule.*

A PLAYER AGAINST ODDS, *Ferdinand II was elected in 1619 as the eighth Habsburg ruler of the Holy Roman Empire. From his first day in office, he had to deal with a revolt of Protestant Bohemians, which had challenged Habsburg rule and precipitated the crippling Thirty Years' War. Shown here with his wife, Maria of Bavaria, Ferdinand battled ruthlessly to keep the power of his dynasty.*

A PAIR OF LOSERS, *these Spanish Habsburgs were cleaned out in the political games of the 17th Century. Under Philip IV (below left), the Spanish army suffered a defeat by the French from which it never recovered. Philip hoped to preserve his dynasty through his first son, Don Baltasar Carlos (below card), but Carlos died at age 16. Philip's only other son, Charles II, was half-witted and sickly; at his death in 1700, the Spanish line became extinct.*

A VULNERABLE HEIR, *Ferdinand III acquired the many political problems of his father, Ferdinand II, along with his title as Holy Roman Emperor. Unrest at home and invasions from abroad continued to threaten him. To consolidate the two Habsburg dynasties, Ferdinand married his cousin, Maria Anna of Spain, shown here holding their son Ferdinand. Maria had never seen her husband before the engagement; she found him handsome and clever, a fluent linguist and a gifted musician.*

THE PEOPLE'S TRUMP, *Oliver Cromwell led England from 1649 to 1658. He commanded the Puritan army that swept Charles I from power and temporarily established Parliament as the country's sole ruler. But soon Cromwell himself took on dictatorial powers as sweeping as any king's. He suspended Parliament in 1653, saying, "Come, come, I will put an end to your prating."*

A FAVORITE QUEEN, *Mary II was presented with the English crown amid popular rejoicing after her father, James II, had been deposed in the Glorious Revolution of 1688. She ruled jointly with her husband, William III, in newly found harmony with Parliament. Unlike most of her Stuart relatives, Mary was rather modest and unassuming, but a capable administrator of state affairs.*

BUNGLING HIS HAND, *Charles I (extreme right) plunged England into civil war by his clumsy attempts to increase his power over the people and Parliament. He imposed illegal taxes, dissolved Parliament four times during his reign and arrested its leaders. These moves cost Charles both his crown and his head; Cromwell captured and executed him in 1649. Charles' daughter, Henriette (near right), fared better. She escaped the turmoil of English politics by marrying Philippe d'Orléans, Louis XIV's brother, and living in France, where she became one of Louis' earliest loves.*

A QUEEN WITH HER CHAMPION, *Anne (left) followed William III and Mary, her sister, to the English throne in 1702. Though dowdy, dull and gout-ridden, she gained distinction by naming the Duke of Marlborough (right) as her chief general. Because of Marlborough's victories over the French army, Parliament voted that he had "retrieved the ancient honor and glory of the English nation."*

A KING AND HIS COMPANIONS, *Charles II (left, at bottom) and his retinue of lady friends brought a fresh atmosphere of frivolity and extravagance to England. Charles had met his first mistress, Lucy Walter (extreme left, holding a portrait of their son), while in exile in Holland when they were both 18. Later, as king, he installed another mistress, Barbara Villiers (near left), as lady-in-waiting to his queen, Catherine (next to Barbara). But the most flamboyant of his ladies was the comic actress Nell Gwyn (portrayed here nude), described as "the indiscreetest and wildest creature that ever was in court."*

A DISCARDED MONARCH, *the Stuart James II (far right) assumed the throne in 1685 with all the pride and pomp of a great king, but left it ignominiously during the Glorious Revolution three years later. James, who had succeeded his brother Charles II, earned the hatred of his people through his outspoken claims to absolute power. "I am above the law," he once stated. His ill-timed efforts to impose his own Roman Catholic religion upon his Protestant subjects prompted the revolt that brought his downfall.*

CLUBS: THE MARTIAL PROTESTANTS OF NORTHERN EUROPE

A WILD QUEEN, *Christina of Sweden, daughter of Gustavus Adolphus, shocked Europe with her bizarre conduct. She rode—and swore—like a trooper, and studied philosophy, considered a most unladylike diversion. In 1654 she impulsively abdicated, became a Catholic and departed for Rome, dressed as a man.*

FIVE OF A KIND, *the wily Hohenzollerns and their top general built the small territories of Brandenburg and Prussia into the foundations of a German state. When Frederick William (top row, with his wife, Louise Henriette) began his reign in 1640, he was so destitute that the roof of his palace was caving in. But Frederick William brought prosperity to his lands and organized a victorious army led by George von Derfflinger (right). His formula for success was opportunism: "Be like the bee which sucks the sweetest juice from all the flowers," he told his son, the ambitious Frederick I of Prussia (bottom row, with his wife, Sophie Charlotte).*

WINNERS FOR A HAND, *Frederick, the Elector Palatine (far left), and his wife, Elizabeth Stuart (near left), ruled as the Protestant King and Queen of Bohemia during the first winter of the Thirty Years' War. But they were unable to pay their general, Ernst von Mansfeld (center); he deserted, and they were quickly overthrown by the Habsburgs.*

A TOUGH OPPONENT, *Christian IV of Denmark briefly commanded the Protestant army during the Thirty Years' War. A vigorous leader, he inspired his men to deeds of great heroism in battle.*

FOLLOWING A ROYAL LEAD, *two Swedish noblemen continued the policies of Gustavus Adolphus. Count Axel Oxenstierna (above) served as his level-headed chief minister ("If everyone were as cool as you," the King once said, "we should all freeze to death"); he was regent after Gustavus' death. Charles X (right), like Gustavus, was a soldier; he conquered parts of Poland and Denmark between 1655 and 1660.*

A STRONG SUIT, *The House of Orange dominated politics in the Netherlands. Their elected leader, Prince William II of Orange (far right), was an astute politician with a taste for regal power. He married Mary Stuart (near right), the prideful sister of England's Charles II and sired William III, who was to become King of England in 1689.*

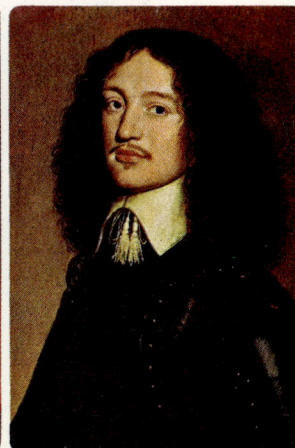

29

2

THE THIRTY YEARS' WAR

Of all the lands within the Holy Roman Empire, none was more valuable to the Empire's Habsburg rulers than the kingdom of Bohemia. More than half of the Empire's operating expenses came from the taxes on Bohemia's prosperous farms and mines and commerce. In addition, the King of Bohemia was a key figure in imperial politics. As one of the seven Electors of the Empire, his vote was crucial in the choice of an Emperor—and for almost a century the King of Bohemia had been a member of the Habsburg family.

Early in the 17th Century, the Habsburgs' control of the Bohemian throne was gravely threatened. The forces that threatened it were political and religious, and existed not only in Bohemia, but in other European countries as well. In Bohemia, however, the forces were more intense, and created a climate of conflict and tension that could be resolved only by violence—a violence that ultimately spread to all of Europe, and enveloped the continent in the Thirty Years' War.

Bohemia, like many other European countries, was ruled by an elected monarch, acting in concert with an assembly representing the three Bohemian estates—the nobles, the townsmen and the peasants. They met together, the King and the estates, like ambassadors of hostile powers rather than partners in a joint enterprise. Instead of seeking some accommodation with the others' opposing interests, they directed their efforts far more often to frustrating each other's designs.

Significantly, the documents that defined the relations of these kings and estates were often called "treaties," and by the 17th Century the uneasy peace they embodied was clearly doomed. Ambitious monarchs were seeking to rid themselves of the cumbersome machinery that prevented them from imposing their wills upon their subjects, while their subjects clung tenaciously, and sometimes belligerently, to their traditional rights.

In Bohemia this situation was aggravated by two additional sources of conflict: a sharp sense of Bohemian nationalism, and sharp divisions of religious belief. Increasingly, the Czech population of the country resented being ruled by an Austrian prince, especially—as usually happened—by one who could not even speak their language. Also, a

THE AGONY OF DEATH *contorts the face of a soldier in one of 22 "warrior masks" carved in stone by Germany's greatest Baroque sculptor, Andreas Schlüter. Each mask shows one phase of man's struggle with war and death.*

EUROPE IN 1618

Legend:
- Catholics
- Protestants
- Austrian Habsburgs
- Spanish Habsburgs
- Brandenburg–Prussia
- Swedish Empire
- Boundary of the Holy Roman Empire

Map labels:

NORWAY · SCOTLAND · NORTH SEA · SWEDEN · RUSSIA · BALTIC SEA · DENMARK · IRELAND · ENGLAND · UNITED PROVINCES · POMERANIA · EAST PRUSSIA · BRANDENBURG · POLAND · Osnabrück · Lutter · Münster · Dessau · WESTPHALIA · Breitenfeld · SPANISH NETHERLANDS · Cologne · Lützen · SILESIA · Trier · Mainz · SAXONY · Prague · PALATINATE · BOHEMIA · ATLANTIC OCEAN · FRANCHE-COMTÉ · Donauwörth · Vienna · HUNGARY · BAVARIA · AUSTRIA · SWISS CONFEDERATION · TYROL · STYRIA · TRANSYLVANIA · FRANCE · SAVOY · MILAN · PORTUGAL · SPAIN · ADRIATIC SEA · OTTOMAN EMPIRE · BALEARIC IS. · SARDINIA · NAPLES · MEDITERRANEAN SEA · SICILY

Miles
0 100 200 300 400 500

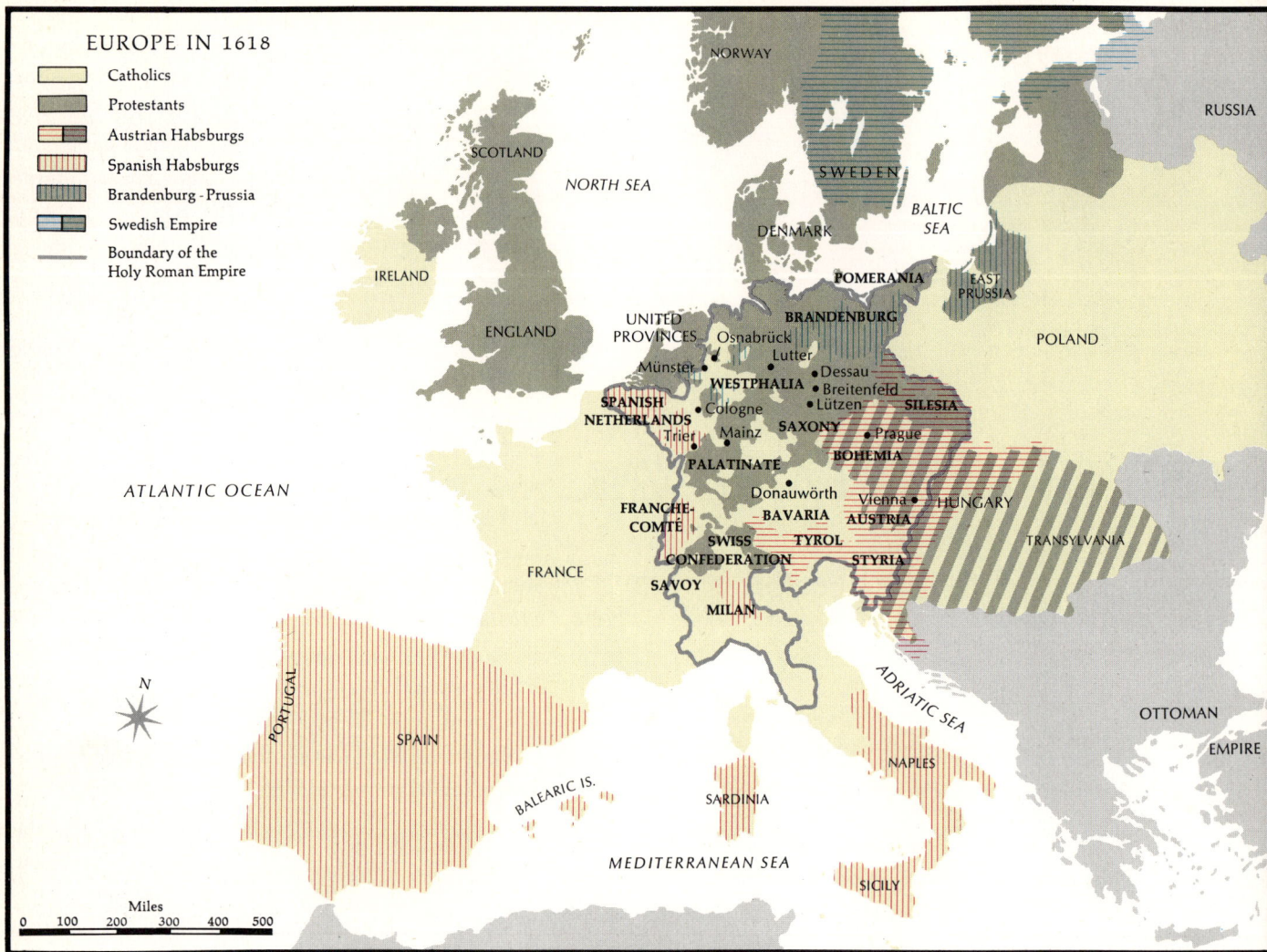

substantial number of the Protestants who made up the bulk of Bohemia's population resented the rule of a Catholic. In particular, they looked with foreboding upon the Habsburg Prince who was destined to be their next king (as well as the next emperor), the ardently Catholic Ferdinand of Styria.

If the two forces for political liberty in Bohemia, nationalism and Protestantism, could have united behind a single candidate for the Bohemian throne, they might very well have succeeded in electing him, and thus have upset the Habsburgs' position of power in central Europe. In fact, however, they simply canceled each other out. Motivated partly by mutual jealousy and suspicion, partly by common timidity and conservatism, the Bohemians gave up any thought of resisting Ferdinand and on June 17, 1617, elected him their king.

In less than a year, Ferdinand succeeded in doing for the opposition what it had been unable to do for itself. His repressive measures against Protestantism within his new kingdom united his Bohemian enemies into a single coalition, opposed to Habsburg rule.

On May 21, 1618, a great assembly of Bohemian Protestants met in Prague to decide upon a course of action. Ferdinand was absent from his kingdom, but in his place two deputy governors ordered the assembly to dissolve. Instead, the angry rebels threatened to murder the deputies and install a provisional Protestant government. On the morning of May 23, the leaders of the rebellion set out for the royal castle of Hradčany, high on the bluffs above the River Moldau, dominating the city of Prague. They were followed by an immense crowd

—into the castle, up the broad staircase, through a series of anterooms, and finally into a council chamber where the two royal deputies and their secretary stood barricaded between a table and a window overlooking the courtyard, 50 feet below.

Surging forward uncontrollably, the angry crowd seized the screaming deputies and their secretary and threw them out the window. Miraculously, none was seriously injured—a circumstance attributed by Catholics to divine intervention and by Protestants to the fact that the three had landed on an immense pile of rubbish. Nevertheless, the intention was clear. The Defenestration of Prague, as the event came to be known, was Bohemia's declaration of independence from Habsburg rule. The question was now whether the Bohemians could maintain their independence against the mightiest power in Christendom. To do so, they would have to attract help from outside—from other Protestant nations and perhaps from Catholic powers who might find it in their own self-interest to reduce the influence of the Habsburgs.

Within four months of the Defenestration, two Habsburg armies had crossed the Bohemian borders to crush the rebels. One, financed by the Spanish Habsburgs, came from Spain's territories in Flanders. The other, in the pay of the Austrian Habsburgs, marched from Vienna. They met on the road to Prague on September 9, 1618. The Bohemian rebels' own army, under Count Heinrich Matthias Thurn, numbered only 16,000 hastily recruited men and was quite inadequate to meet this threat. At the last minute, however, another Protestant army arrived on the scene, sent by the Elector Palatine, Frederick V, and Charles Emanuel, the Duke of Savoy. It was a professional army of 2,000 battle-seasoned men under the command of Ernst von Mansfeld, one of the greatest mercenary soldiers of the day.

With the appearance of Mansfeld's army, the imperial army withdrew, and the Bohemian cause was momentarily saved. But Bohemia's fate was now irretrievably linked to the politics of the rest of Europe, and so, too, was the fate of the young Elector Palatine. Frederick V was then only 21 years old and had succeeded to the Palatine throne eight years before. He was amiable, attractive, honorable and weak willed, and his main interest was to enjoy life. He played tennis, hunted and swam, and was devoted to his vivacious young wife, Elizabeth, the daughter of England's King James I. He seemed scarcely the sort of character for the role in which history, and an ambitious chancellor, now cast him: champion of European Protestantism.

The scheming chancellor was Christian von Anhalt, and Anhalt's plan was to get the Bohemian rebels to elect Frederick their king. Frederick, who addressed his chancellor as *"Mon père,"* willingly agreed; devoutly Calvinist by upbringing if not by temperament, he sincerely believed it was his duty to rescue Bohemia from Catholicism. Also, he was captivated by the visions that Anhalt conjured up. As Elector Palatine and King of Bohemia, he could cast two votes in the next imperial election and assure the Empire a Protestant emperor. As leader of the Empire's Protestant Union and son-in-law to England's Protestant King, he would head a grand alliance that stretched across Europe, a permanent bulwark against Habsburg power and the Roman Catholic Church.

The plan was not wholly farfetched. Unfortunately for Frederick, however, it was based upon two false suppositions. It assumed that the Protestant powers of Europe were prepared to work together in the name of reformed religion, whereas in fact they were deeply divided by sectarian jealousies and rival political ambitions. Calvinists and Lutherans were hostile to each other's ideas of religious reform; and Frederick was not the only Protestant prince to covet the Bohemian crown (one of the other contenders was Charles Emanuel, the Duke of Savoy). It also assumed that Frederick possessed the talents needed to construct a confederation of European states, when in fact he was not even able to organize his own affairs.

On August 26, 1619, in Prague, the Bohemian rebels elected Frederick their king. Two days later, in Frankfurt, another election turned his victory into a tragedy. While the Empire had been occupied with events in Bohemia, the Emperor Matthias had died, and in August the seven Electors or their deputies met in Frankfurt to choose his successor. The man they chose, on August 28, was Ferdinand—and the vote was unanimous. The three Catholic Electors voted for him automatically, and Ferdinand, as Elector of Bohemia, also cast his vote for himself, leaving the three outnumbered Protestant Electors (including Frederick) little choice but to follow suit. Consequently, when the news of the Prague election of Frederick reached Frankfurt, his position was ridiculous. Two days before, it appeared, he had deposed as king the man whom he had just helped to elect emperor. Instead of standing before the powers of Europe as a sovereign prince at war with another prince, he was a vassal rebelling against his master.

Almost overnight, Christian von Anhalt's great dream of a pan-European Protestant alliance collapsed. Arrayed against Frederick, now, were not merely Catholics and supporters of the Habsburgs, but all those who believed in monarchial legitimacy and in the constitutional integrity of the Holy Roman Empire. The princes of the Protestant Union voted to recognize Frederick's claim to the crown of Bohemia, but refused to send him aid. Protestant cities in the Empire acknowledged his need for money, but never supplied it. Frederick's father-in-law, the King of England, denied any part in his son-in-law's activities—even though the English people were enthusiastically Protestant.

The King of Denmark urged others to help Frederick, but did not do so himself, while the King of Sweden, busily at war with Poland, asked Frederick instead to help him.

Most crushing of all, Frederick was abandoned even by those who feared and mistrusted Ferdinand. Maximilian, the Duke of Bavaria, allied himself with the Emperor, even though he feared Ferdinand's political ambitions. So too did John George, the Elector of Saxony, tempted by the promise that he would share in a defeated Frederick's lands and titles. Of all the Protestant powers in Europe only two genuinely rallied to Frederick's cause: Transylvania, under the Calvinist prince Bethlen Gabor, and the Calvinist government of the United Provinces in the Netherlands. Bethlen Gabor sent his troops against Habsburg forces in Hungary; the United Provinces voted Frederick a monthly subsidy of 50,000 florins and sent a few troops to join his Bohemian army. Only this army, Bethlen Gabor's troops, and Mansfeld's army stood between Frederick and the combined forces of the Habsburgs and their allies.

Then, as the final crisis approached, Mansfeld deserted Frederick. To understand why, it is necessary to understand the phenomenon of the 17th Century mercenary army. These armies-for-hire came into being as a consequence of two unrelated but interacting causes. One was a fact of military life: warfare had become a matter for professionals. The other was a flaw in the structure of 17th Century politics: governments were not equipped to create this professionalism. The development of artillery and the musket had revolutionized not only strategy and tactics, but also the composition of armies. Bands of peasants with homemade weapons and dashing knights in armor could not stand against the fire of a steady line of musketeers and their pikemen.

Neither, on the other hand, could musketeers

and pikemen function without discipline and drill. A muzzle-loading musket five feet long was not an easy thing to handle. Its barrel had to be rested on a forked wooden support while the charge was set off, and the pikemen had to protect the musketeers after each shot while they reloaded. In the classic battle formation, a line of musketeers would advance and fire, then fall back behind a row of pikemen to reload, repeating the process over and over with the greatest precision. It was a business calling for organization and a high degree of competence.

Business, in fact, was what warfare had become. Unable to devise a satisfactory system for conscripting and maintaining such an army, states turned to the great entrepreneurs of warfare—to professionals who sold the services of their armies to the highest bidder.

Ernst von Mansfeld was such a man. The bastard son of a nobleman, who raised him but refused to recognize him as his son, Mansfeld was attached to no place, no party, no cause. An adventurer by disposition, he turned to the battlefields for fame and fortune, and became one of the great military commanders of his age. His talents for strategy and tactics were no better than those of any other good general of the time, but his gifts for organization and finance were extraordinary. He was superb at the job of recruiting soldiers and officers to train and lead them. He fed, clothed and quartered his army, provided it with military supplies and equipment, and produced it on order, ready for battle, at the proper time and place.

The men who comprised the raw material of such an army were drawn from all over Europe and were tough professionals, desperados and adventurers who hired themselves out to anyone who would pay them. Their business was killing, and it mattered little to them whether their victims were Frenchmen, Englishmen or Germans; Catholics, Lutherans or Calvinists. If they were captured, they often enlisted in the army of their captor. If they were not paid, they deserted. If they were not fed, they looted. The sheer task of maintaining discipline in such an army—bound by no sense of loyalty, no common language or nationality, no devotion to cause—was staggering.

To make the problem of control even more severe, every army soon gathered around itself an enormous number of civilians—servants, dependents, camp-followers. Colonels were said to be accompanied into the field by as many as 18 servants apiece; lieutenants by five. In one such army, employed by the Habsburgs, six or seven children were born each week. At the very least, an army of 25,000 men must have carried with it a civilian population of some 50,000. The men, women and children were in effect displaced persons, utterly dependent for their sustenance upon the army—and ultimately, upon its commander.

The character of these great marauding mercenary armies was primarily responsible for the peculiar horror of the long succession of military engagements, beginning with those in Bohemia, that made up the Thirty Years' War. Marching and countermarching across the face of central Europe, the armies carried with them violence, destruction and disease, and left behind nothing but desolation. With no fixed base of operations to return to between battles or periods of employment, they roamed the continent in search of plunder, lived off the land, and practiced the most hideous tortures on helpless civilians who could not, or would not, supply their needs. Even the presence on his land of a friendly army—especially in the wintertime when food was scarce—was a nightmare to a ruler. Much of the grand strategy of wars, in fact, revolved around where to establish winter quarters.

When money was not available to pay these armies, the kings and princes who hired them—and indeed even their own generals—were unable to bridle their savagery. It was for this reason that Mansfeld abandoned Frederick. "Neither they nor their horses can live on air," he wrote in defense of his action. "All that they have, whether it be arms or apparel, weareth, wasteth and breaketh. If they must buy more, they must have money, and if men have it not to give them, they will take it where they find it, not as part of that which is due unto them, but without weighing or telling it. This gate being once opened unto them, they enter into the large fields of liberty. . . . They spare no person of what quality soever he be, respect no place how holy soever, neither Churches, Altars, Tombs, Sepulchres nor the dead bodies that lie in them."

The loss of Mansfeld's army sealed Frederick's doom. In the summer of 1620, the forces of his united foes marched out to destroy him. In the east, Maximilian of Bavaria headed across Austria for Bohemia with the 25,000-man mercenary army of the Catholic League. In the west, the Spanish Habsburgs recruited a 25,000-man mercenary army in Flanders, and set out for Frederick's homeland, the Rhenish Palatinate. By the end of September, the Flemish army had occupied most of the Palatinate almost without opposition. On November 8 Maximilian's army crushed the combined armies of Frederick and Bethlen Gabor at the Battle of the White Mountain, just outside Prague. The very next day, Prague surrendered, and the hapless Frederick fled with his queen to the Dutch Republic, where he never ceased to dream of a new Protestant confederation, and spent the rest of his short life (he died at 36, of the plague) in fruitless schemes to regain his lost lands and titles.

The Bohemian phase of the Thirty Years' War was over. Ferdinand took back the Bohemian crown, and gave part of Frederick's lands and his Electoral vote to Maximilian in return for his services. The

Emperor's revenge against the Bohemian rebels was swift and savage: he hanged their leaders in the great square of Prague and spitted their heads on the railings of the Charles Bridge. Much of Bohemia's land was sold or given to the Emperor's supporters, and Protestantism was wholly eradicated in the first country in Europe whose people had dared to oppose Rome (a hundred years before Luther, the Czech reformer Jan Hus had questioned the doctrines of the Roman Catholic Church).

But the forces unleashed by Frederick and Ferdinand were to rage on, unchecked, for almost three decades, desolating Germany and completely rearranging the political order of Europe.

Politically, the most immediate and fateful outcome of the Bohemian rebellion was Ferdinand's determination to strengthen his own position in the Empire by making the German princes more subservient to his will.

Surveying his victory and the success of his postwar measures in Bohemia, he had reason to congratulate himself on his prospects. There was, however, one problem. All his triumphs so far had been won by the arms of others—by his Spanish Habsburg cousins and, in particular, by Maximilian and his Catholic League. If he intended to subjugate Germany, he could hardly hope to do so with the army of one of the very princes he meant to bend to his will. He needed an army of his own, and in the spring of 1625 he was offered one by a man who was one of the most mysterious and fascinating figures in history.

More than 1,600 books and pamphlets have tried to unravel the character of Albrecht von Wallenstein, but none has wholly succeeded. He was born in 1583, the son of a minor Bohemian nobleman, and was raised as a Protestant. In his twenties he became nominally a Catholic (although his real religion seems to have been astrology). After his conversion, Wallenstein attached himself to the

Habsburgs—in particular, to Ferdinand, while Ferdinand was still Archduke of Styria. He married well, inherited a considerable fortune when his wife died, and managed it shrewdly, gaining the reputation of being an uncommonly gifted administrator. At the end of the Bohemian war, Ferdinand rewarded Wallenstein for his loyalty to the imperial cause by making him governor of Prague.

Thereafter Wallenstein's fortunes soared. He profited enormously from the confiscation of Bohemian lands, accumulating, in all, 66 estates—more than a quarter of Bohemia, including the entire Bohemian province of Friedland. In 1625 the Emperor named him Duke of Friedland. But wealth, security and a noble title were not enough. Although no one has ever really discovered the object of his ambition, some of his biographers suggest that he wanted to be King of Bohemia, some that he even aspired to succeed Ferdinand on the imperial throne. Oddly enough, the most illuminating analysis of this complex man comes from a horoscope cast for him by the great 17th Century astronomer, Johannes Kepler:

"Of this gentleman, I may in truth write that he has a character alert, lively, eager and restless, curious of every kind of novelty, unsuited to the common manner and behavior of mankind, but striving after new, untried or extraordinary ways; moreover he has much more in his head than he allows to be expressed or perceived . . . melancholy though luminous thoughts, a bent toward alchemy, magic and enchantment, community with spirits, scorn and indifference toward human ordinances and conventions and to all religions, making everything proposed by God or man to be suspected and despised. . . . Likewise he will be unmerciful, without brotherly or nuptial affection, caring for no one, devoted only to himself and his desires, severe upon those placed under him, avid, covetous, deceitful, inequitable in his dealings, usually silent, often violent . . . not to be browbeaten."

Clearly not an attractive man, but a formidable one, Wallenstein seems to have deliberately exploited his personality. He dressed his tall, thin frame always in black with a single startling touch of vivid red, and surrounded himself with mystery and drama. This was the man who, in 1625, offered to recruit for Ferdinand at his own expense an army of 50,000 men. The Emperor, suspecting quite rightly that Wallenstein had ulterior motives, was nevertheless unwilling to forego the opportunity. He agreed to let Wallenstein raise an army of 20,000 men, but only on condition that it be kept within the borders of the Habsburg lands except on the Emperor's orders. Within three years, Wallenstein was marching through northern Germany with an army of 125,000 men, ostensibly in the service of the Emperor but actually functioning as an independent force in the politics of Europe.

The combination of Ferdinand and Wallenstein —still supported by the arms of the Spanish Habsburgs and Maximilian's Catholic League—proved irresistible. In 1625, King Christian IV of Denmark took over Frederick's role as champion of the Protestant cause in the Holy Roman Empire; he soon suffered a similar fate. Christian's two allies were Christian of Brunswick, a minor German prince whose army was practically useless (it was composed mostly of peasants armed with iron-bound sticks) and—far more formidable—the Protestant English King, James I, who now had in his service the veteran commander Ernst von Mansfeld.

On April 25, 1626, Mansfeld's army met the army of Wallenstein at Dessau, on the River Elbe. By nightfall one third of Mansfeld's army was destroyed. The great commander, his fortunes on the wane, fled across Europe to the east—with what scheme in mind, no one knows; he died within the year on the Dalmatian coast. As for Christian of Denmark, his army was completely routed at the village of Lutter, in central Germany, by the army of Maximilian's Catholic League. Thus, in little more than a year, Denmark's part in the Thirty Years' War was over.

To Ferdinand, the path to his dream of a united, Catholic Germany seemed cleared of obstacles, and so, on March 6, 1629, he promulgated his Edict of Restitution, "concerning certain Imperial grievances calling for settlement." The Edict proclaimed that all lands seized from the Catholic Church since the Peace of Augsburg in 1555 were to be returned to it; and that the return was to be supervised by an imperial commission from whose judgments there would be no appeal. In addition the Edict outlawed all Protestant faiths except Lutheranism, leaving Calvinists, in effect, with no legal right to practice their religion.

The Edict had two important consequences, one economic, one political. According to the Peace of Augsburg, each German prince had been permitted to determine the state religion of his own territory. In the course of doing so, many Protestant princes illegally had seized and distributed—or sold —Catholic lands within their domains. Consequently, Ferdinand's Edict, by restoring these lands to the Church, threatened hundreds of German property holders with economic ruin. More ominous still, the Edict laid down a new and dangerous principle of imperial authority: it asserted Ferdinand's right to overturn the decisions of local authorities by imperial decree.

Now, at last, the rest of Europe—Protestant and Catholic alike—awoke to the menace of the Habsburgs. Within Germany, princes of every religious persuasion finally realized that they had unwittingly allowed Ferdinand to subvert their constitutional rights. Outside Germany, other rulers —and even the Pope himself—looked with trepidation at the power rising in their midst. A sense of this danger was in the air in the summer of 1630, when

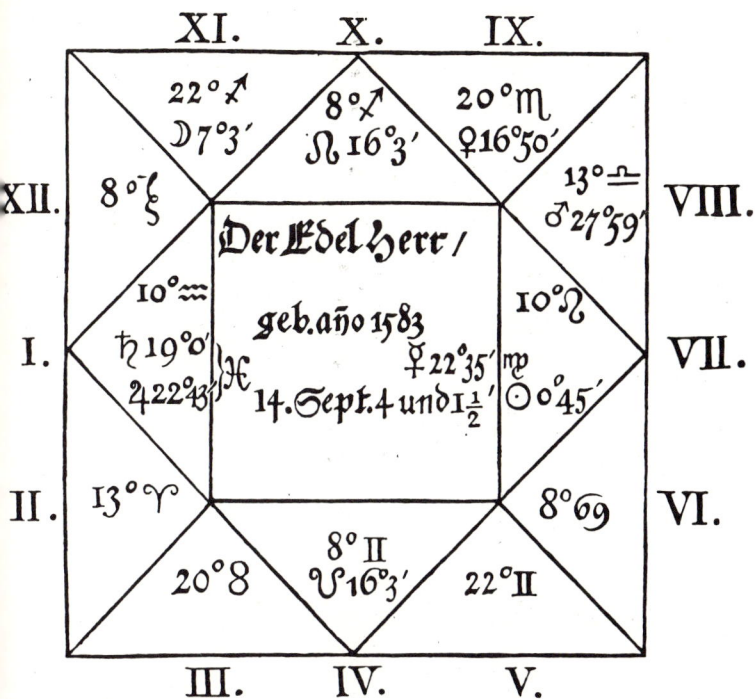

A GENERAL'S HOROSCOPE, *cast for Albrecht von Wallenstein when he was 25 by the astronomer Johannes Kepler, accurately fore-told a life of ambition and violence. The center square gives the date and time of his birth and identifies him in German as "The Noble Man"; the figures in the triangles note the positions of various heavenly bodies that influence 12 areas of his personality.*

Ferdinand and the German Electors met at Regensburg to discuss imperial business. Ferdinand had come to the meetings with two demands: he wanted the Empire to declare war on the Dutch, who were fighting with his Spanish cousins; and he wanted the Electors to name his son King of the Romans, a title which, like that of England's Prince of Wales, designated the imperial successor. The first goal proved impossible to fulfill; Ferdinand refused to meet one of the Electors' main conditions, withdrawal of the Edict of Restitution. For the second he had to pay a formidable price: the princes forced him to dismiss Wallenstein (and then, it should be added, never kept their part of the bargain regarding Ferdinand's son).

Ferdinand's difficulties at Regensburg resulted in large measure from the presence there of an extraordinary diplomat, the Capuchin Father Joseph de Tremblay, sent by Cardinal Richelieu to represent the anti-Habsburg interests of France. It was Father Joseph who engineered the German princes' resistance to Ferdinand's demands.

Humble of manner, dressed in a stained and ragged robe that was quite out of character with the pomp and circumstance that surrounded him, Father Joseph was nevertheless an aristocrat and one of the most adroit statesmen in Europe. Like Ferdinand, Father Joseph also dreamed of a united Catholic continent. But the union of his dream would be dominated by France, and it would have a purpose beyond power: Father Joseph wanted to mount a crusade of all Christendom against the infidel Turks who were encroaching on Eastern Europe. To this purpose he bent a brilliant mind, exquisite manners and an intensity of religious spirit unique even for a Capuchin, an order ruled by the strict precepts of St. Francis: poverty, penance, fasting. Father Joseph, observed one of his superiors, was "the perfect Capuchin and the most consummate religious of his province, indeed of the whole order." At the same time, reported a contemporary, "his conversation was ravishing, and he treated the nobility with infinite dexterity."

Richelieu, chief minister to Louis XIII and the virtual ruler of France, realized that the time had come for France to profit from the tension and disorder within the German Empire. His goal was less idealistic than Father Joseph's: he wanted to sap Habsburg power. Disposing of Wallenstein was the first step in this direction. The next one, soon to follow, altered the character of the Thirty Years' War for the second time. From a local Bohemian war it had become a national German war. Now, in its twelfth year, it became a power struggle between the two great dynastic families of Europe and their respective states, the Habsburgs and the Bourbons, rulers of Austria and France. Although religion continued to provide the banner under which men fought, it was largely a pretext: the real issue was who should control Europe.

Richelieu proposed to wear down the Habsburgs by prolonging the war in Germany, and he found the perfect instrument for this purpose in Gustavus Adolphus, the Protestant King of Sweden. For a long time Gustavus Adolphus had made no secret of his willingness to be the next champion of the Protestant cause in Germany, but he was prevented from acting by his interminable war with Poland (the same war that had stood in the way of his helping Frederick, some 11 years before). French diplomats stepped in and quickly arranged a truce, and on July 6, 1630, the Swedish King and an army of 13,000 troops landed on the northern coast of Germany. Europe had never seen its like before.

The Swedish army, soon to be more than doubled in size, thanks to French subsidies, was the best equipped, best trained, best disciplined fighting force since the Roman legions. Gustavus outfitted his men in fur cloaks and gloves, woolen stockings, and waterproof boots of Russian leather. Their muskets were flintlocks, with a built-in sparking device, a vast improvement over guns that had to be fired by a match. Their artillery was light and mobile. Mobility, in fact, was one of the key principles in Gustavus' military strategy. He divided his men, both infantry and cavalry, into small units that could alter direction at a moment's notice and attack the enemy from any quarter.

The discipline within this army was remarkable. Gustavus forbade his troops to attack hospitals, churches and schools, and they obeyed him. When he turned them loose to rape, loot and kill—which he did on occasion, to punish his enemies—they wrought this devastation at his will, not their own. Their fanatical loyalty was inspired partly by his qualities as a person, partly by his abilities as an administrator (he had, among other things, made Sweden one of the best governed countries in Europe). A man of towering stature and majestic bearing, Gustavus was truly a warrior-king—as

few kings of his time were. He accompanied his men into battle, fought by their side, shared their hardships, and above all, infected them with his supreme self-confidence. "He thinks," commented one contemporary, "the ship cannot sink that carries him."

Richelieu made the mistake of viewing Gustavus as a cat's-paw; in fact the King of Sweden, although he cheerfully accepted the French subsidies, was no man's agent. He had come to Germany to achieve two related goals: to conquer the southern coast of the Baltic Sea for Sweden, and to rescue the Protestant princes of Germany from Catholic rule. Later he expanded this rescue operation to include a larger goal—the creation of a new Protestant confederation in central Europe of which he would be the head. In a succession of quick victories, Gustavus made himself the master of northern Germany. Then, on September 17, 1631, he met the combined forces of the Empire and the Catholic League in the village of Breitenfeld, outside Leipzig. Gustavus' tactical brilliance and the superb performance of his army carried the day; the imperial troops lost nearly 20,000 men and, with a single stroke, the tide of Habsburg domination of Europe was checked and turned.

All of Germany now lay open to Gustavus. As he marched south, Protestants hailed him as their deliverer and hastened to join him. Soon he commanded a combined force of seven armies totaling 80,000 men, and when he spoke of recruiting 120,000 more, the figure seemed quite within the realm of possibility. Ferdinand, his imperial fortunes in extreme peril, turned to the only man who could save him: Wallenstein. But that gentleman, still angry over his dismissal, took his time about replying. Only after months of negotiation did he finally heed the Emperor's urgent pleas and agree to raise an army. On the morning of November 16, 1632, the two greatest commanders of the Thirty

Years' War faced each other across a flat, misty plain outside the town of Lützen. By evening, the army of Sweden was victorious, but Gustavus Adolphus himself lay dead. With his death, the war lost what little remained of its religious character, and Germany lost its last champion of unity. Fourteen years of fighting had produced only one result, and a negative one at that. It had demonstrated that Germany could be united neither by Catholics nor by Protestants, neither by Germans themselves nor by outsiders. The time had come for the nation to compose its differences and repair as best it could its ravaged lands. Accordingly, in Prague in May 1635, the Emperor and the Protestant princes signed a treaty of peace annulling the Edict of Restitution and returning the Empire to essentially what it had been when the war began.

If this seemed a pitiful end to so much bloodshed, it was nothing compared to the tragedy ahead —for the war, far from being over, was to continue for another decade. On May 21, 1635—in the very same month that the Peace of Prague was signed— France, having meddled more or less covertly in German affairs for years, finally came out in the open and declared war on the Habsburgs. The last and dreariest phase of the Thirty Years' War had begun, a dynastic power struggle—fought on German soil, often with German soldiers—between France and Sweden on the one side and the Habsburgs of Spain and Austria on the other.

From this phase of the war, through force of arms and diplomatic intrigue, France emerged the victor—if such a war can be said to have a victor. About the identity of the war's victims, there can be no such doubt. The German people, Catholic and Protestant alike, suffered the most unspeakable horrors and privations.

Some large areas lost as much as half of their population, and the number of people in Germany as a whole probably dropped about one third. More deadly even than the swarms of soldiers were starvation and disease. Plague littered the countryside with unburied bodies. Starvation drove people to desperate extremes. Dead men, women and children were found with grass stuffed in their mouths; at times there was even cannibalism.

By 1644 Germany lay exhausted, and the main characters in the Thirty Years' War were dead. In a suitably dramatic end to his baroque career, Wallenstein was murdered in 1634 by a group of his own officers—perhaps at the instigation of Ferdinand, who is thought to have suspected his commander of treason. In 1637, Ferdinand himself was dead, of natural causes. Five years later, Richelieu sickened and died, nursed briefly by his King; Louis XIII in the days just before the Cardinal's death had come to his bedside to feed him nourishing egg yolk.

With these men gone, peace at last became possible, and Europe embarked on the first international peace conference in its history. The conference, held simultaneously in two cities, Münster and Osnabrück in Westphalia, lasted four years, from 1644 to 1648. Its length and its double location were the result of the diplomatic complexities arising from 25 years of warfare and political maneuvering involving almost every country in Europe. Six months alone were spent in settling matters of protocol, precedence, etiquette and legal terminology. The question of who should precede whom into a room, the representative of the King of France or the representative of the King of Spain, might not seem a proper question to occupy men's minds in the midst of a war that was killing thousands—but in fact it was. The 135 assembled ambassadors and diplomats were engaged in a new and dangerous game, power politics. Until they established ground rules, relations between the newly emerging secular states of Europe would be chaotic, and settlement of the issues impossible.

One of the first of the conciliatory measures was the agreement to meet in two places: Sweden refused to concede superiority to France, and so the two countries conducted their negotiations with the Habsburgs separately, France in Münster, Sweden at Osnabrück. But this did not help matters much. After nearly a year of meetings the delegates were still not agreed on the all-important *subjecta belligerantia:* who was at war with whom over what? Then, when they had finally picked their way through this tangled web and faced the serious business of bargaining, they encountered another obstacle. Because the war was still going on, the bargaining positions of the various parties changed from week to week; every time a battle was fought, the victor would raise his demands. Considering the difficulties, it is surprising that the Peace of Westphalia was ever concluded at all.

The most critical question that faced the diplomats at Westphalia was deciding what sort of political order to establish in the Empire: should Germany be governed by some unifying authority, or should the German princes retain their divisive "German liberties"? When France, backed by the German princes, insisted over Habsburg objections that each of the German states be separately represented at the peace conference, the question became academic. The fragmentation of Germany, challenged for 30 years by the efforts of Ferdinand, Frederick and Gustavus Adolphus, was enshrined in international law. Each of the hundreds of German principalities was guaranteed the right to conduct its own foreign affairs, exchange ambassadors and make treaties—and Sweden and France, as the official "guarantors," gained a permanent right to interfere in German affairs. With splendid irony, the government of France, which was then engaged at home in an effort to curtail the powers of its own nobility, was cast in the role of protector of the ancient rights of German noblemen.

This was only one of many ironies in the Peace of Westphalia. While it seemed to consolidate the rights of German princes, it also transferred suzerainty of some of their lands. Sweden, for example, was awarded a substantial piece of northern Germany, and France acquired certain holdings in the German Rhineland (the first of many Franco-German exchanges of lands between the Moselle and the Rhine). But the ultimate irony was that the Peace perpetuated the very conditions that had caused the war. It reaffirmed each German prince's right to determine the religion of his subjects; it recognized the seizure of Catholic lands up to the year 1624, five years before the Edict of Restitution; it officially sanctioned Calvinism as one of the legitimate religions of the Empire, along with Lutheranism and Catholicism. At the same time, it confirmed the Habsburgs' hereditary claim to the Kingdom of Bohemia and Bavaria's control of Frederick's Palatine Electorship (although, to appease Frederick's heirs, it created an eighth Electorship —of the Lower Palatinate).

It is not fair to blame the foreign diplomats at Westphalia for the inconsistencies of the Peace. The fatal mistakes had been made years before, by the German princes, whose inability to work together to solve their country's problems made foreign intervention inevitable. Nevertheless, the result was very nearly the worst of all possible worlds. The Peace, instead of either guaranteeing religious toleration or imposing religious unity, settled for something in between—and sacrificed freedom without achieving order. The same was true of politics. Instead of guaranteeing local liberty or imposing national authority, the Peace settled for a compromise—and left Germany a chaotic collection of petty autocracies. In the long run, the terms of the Peace of Westphalia were to have even more disastrous consequences for Germany, and for Europe, than the Thirty Years' War.

IN BATTLE'S WAKE

The mercenary armies of the Thirty Years' War swept over the cities and farms of central Europe like plagues of locusts—plundering, torturing, murdering, leaving the countryside barren of crops and the towns in smoking ruins. The commanders of these forces were ambitious entrepreneurs, their officers unscrupulous fortune seekers, and even the more principled men serving in their ranks were soon corrupted by the harsh conditions of army life. To the peasants on whose land the armies were quartered, a soldier—any soldier—was an enemy, and these oppressed civilians retaliated when they could with a violence equal to the soldiers' own. In 1633 the French artist Jacques Callot, who saw much of the conflict at first hand, completed a series of etchings called the *Miseries and Misfortunes of War*, in which he showed, in harsh detail, war's brutality and waste

A GILDED PROMISE OF GAIN AND GLORY

At first, when the war was young and still seemed glamorous, commanders attracted men to their ranks with recruitment drives that featured waving banners and rattling drums. Farm boys and youthful apprentices, trapped in the boredom of everyday life, flocked to join an enterprise that promised so much—adventure, glory, good pay.

But the new recruits were quickly disenchanted. Warfare, they learned, was a bloody business in which the enemy was not always the opposing army. Bad officers failed to provide for their men and often put their subordinates' wages in their own pockets. Disease stalked the camps and battlefields, taking more lives than guns and cavalry charges. Hunger and cold turned men into thieves and plunderers. By the time the war was a few years old, recruitment had become such a problem that commanders signed up vagabonds, conscripted men against their will, and even raided one another's ranks with offers of better pay. One of the more efficient generals, Albrecht von Wallenstein, put together an army for the Habsburgs by erecting a gallows outside each town and offering reluctant candidates a grim choice—enlistment or the noose.

DRUMMING UP ENTHUSIASM for army life, a commander's crack troops run smartly through a military drill outside the walls of a provincial town. At the far left, a seated officer enrolls recruits while another distributes muskets to the new men.

COLLECTING HIS ALLOTMENT, an officer who has signed up a company of men turns in a list of their names to his superior officer, seated at right. In return, he is being given money for their wages and provisions—plus a generous cut for himself.

THE HOLOCAUST OF BATTLE

In the smoke and dust of actual combat, like the cavalry charge shown below, a soldier received his first lessons in the facts of military life. "Awful music," was the verdict of one soldier, the not-so-simple hero of the 17th Century novel, *Simplicius Simplicissimus*. Simplicius described the "music" in detail: "the cruel shots, the clashing of armor plates, the

spintering of pikestaffs, the screams of the attackers as well as the wounded . . . the blare of trumpets, the roll of drums, the shrill sound of fifes." When it was all over he observed, "the earth that is accustomed to covering the dead was herself now covered with corpses."

The soldier who came out of such a battle alive could be

grateful, but what lay ahead might be worse than death itself. If he was wounded, the impromptu medication he received from his companions was rough and cursory. One of the common ways to stop bleeding was to sprinkle a wound with gunpowder and set it afire. The flaring powder successfully cauterized the wound—but occasionally it killed the man

AFTER THE BATTLE
AN ORGY OF LOOTING

Customarily an army was given the right to assess the peasants of a prince's territory for its food and provisions, but famine and greed turned this practice into wholesale plunder. With or without their officers' approval, roving bands of soldiers terrorized the countryside. They robbed peasants of their household goods, attacked their women, carried off their livestock, burned their homes and barns. Anyone suspected of having hidden money or jewelry was subjected to the most hideous kind of torture.

By the end of the war, peasants had become so demoralized by the constant passage and repassage of armies across their lands that they did not bother to reap or sow—and the appearance of any army, whether its colors meant friend or foe, was a catastrophe. "We have had blue-coats and red-coats and now come the yellow-coats," lamented the citizens of one Alsatian town. "God have pity on us."

SACKING A VILLAGE (above), marauding soldiers pile stolen goods on carts and set fire to two cottages and a church. In the left foreground, able-bodied villagers are herded away to perform forced labor for the army.

PLUNDERING A FARMHOUSE, soldiers gorge themselves on the farmer's food and wine, while their companions kill his servants, make sport with his womenfolk—and roast the poor farmer himself on his own hearth.

HARSH JUSTICE
FOR PLUNDERERS

Occasionally a commander would make an attempt to discipline his troops for their ferocious behavior. It was not that he disapproved of looting; the gathering of spoils was one of the recognized fringe benefits of war. But when the practice got out of hand, so did the army's military effectiveness; entire companies often wandered off to become freebooters.

To curb such tendencies, commanders staged scenes like the one at the right, partly as punishment but also as an object lesson. Here a band of soldiers, tried and convicted of pillaging, is being executed by hanging in full view of the rest of the regiment. One of the condemned men, properly contrite, kneels at the foot of the ladder to receive absolution from a priest, but two others, unrepentant, toss dice on a drum on the other side of the tree, to decide which will go up the ladder next.

Most of the troops watching this grisly ceremony were no doubt guilty of the same crimes, and silently thanked St. Dismas, patron saint of thieves, for protecting them. Most of them, too, would continue to go absent without leave and even to desert entirely when another regiment offered richer booty. One English mercenary summed up his army career at war's end by admitting, "I wandered . . . I knew not whither and followed I knew not whom."

SOLDIERS' PAY

When the last gun had been fired, the victorious commanders collected lands and titles awarded by their princely employers, but their troops got no share in the glory. Mustered out far from home, often without pay, they made their way back to their native lands as best they could. Many of them, with no means of support, ended their days as beggars and vagabonds. So, too, did the huge armies of servants, women and children that had followed them. "I was born in war," said one camp follower, "I have no home, no country and no friends; war is all my wealth and now whither shall I go?"

HOMEWARD-BOUND VETERANS *dying by the roadside (top) receive communion from a priest; some of the luckier wounded men apply for admittance to one of the 17th Century's few charity hospitals (bottom).*

A VICTORIOUS COMMANDER *(right) kneels before his enthroned sovereign to receive a medal and, no doubt, other rewards. The brilliant General Wallenstein garnered 66 landed estates and the Duchy of Friedland.*

3

THE SUN KING

The lesson of the Thirty Years' War was clear to every statesman and political philosopher in Europe. The same forces that had torn apart the Holy Roman Empire existed to a greater or lesser degree in other countries, too. Each had its militant religious groups, determined to defend their particular orthodoxies to the death—and also prepared, should the occasion arise, to impose these orthodoxies on others. Each had its great nobles and aristocrats, fighting the growing royal power that threatened their traditional privileges. Each had its autonomous cities and provinces, jealously guarding their historic local rights against any attempt at centralization.

Faced with these powerful divisive forces, how could any country hope for order and national unity? Yet order and national unity were imperative. In the middle of the century, with the memory of the war still fresh in his mind, Thomas Hobbes set down his classic description of the fate of men doomed to live together without effective government.

"During the time men live without a common power to keep them all in awe," Hobbes wrote in the *Leviathan*, "they are in that condition which is called war; and such a war, as is of every man, against every man. . . . Whatsoever therefore is consequent to a time of war . . . the same is consequent to the time, wherein men live without other security, than what their own strength, and their own invention shall furnish them. . . . In such condition, there is no place for industry; because the fruit thereof is uncertain: and consequently no culture of the earth; no navigation, nor use of the commodities that may be imported by sea; no commodious building; no instruments of moving, and removing, such things as require much force; no knowledge of the face of the earth; no account of time; no arts; no letters; no society; and which is worst of all, continual fear, and danger of violent death; and the life of man, solitary, poor, nasty, brutish, and short."

To many men of the 17th Century, the surest way to escape this fate lay in absolutism—the concentration of power in one supreme authority. This awesome power, which went under the name of "sovereignty," was needed precisely because the forces of disunity—local and class privilege, tradition, religious schism—were themselves so strong. The only

A GILDED PORTAL, *Versailles' massive entrance gate marks the point at which the broad Avenue de Paris sweeps into the vast parade ground that fronts the Sun King's palace. Glimpsed across this cobbled plain, where Louis' resplendent guards often marched in review, is the Royal Chapel he built.*

way to subdue these forces was to impose on them a superior force, a new and rational political order, which Hobbes christened "the great *Leviathan.*" Absolutism became, in theory and practice, the century's clearest answer to the problem of order. At a deeper level, it was also the earliest form of a much more significant development: the modern state.

A state may be defined as an authority which, recognizing no earthly superior, rules over the inhabitants of a given territory. Within that territory, it monopolizes the use of force and the administration of justice. Monarchy is the state's simplest, most obvious form. It embodies in a single person the state's supreme authority. It is not, of course, the only form, and some of the variants began to appear even in the 17th Century. In a constitutional monarchy, the sovereignty of the state lies in a contract between ruler and ruled, by which each agrees not to exercise its full powers. And in a modern democracy the sovereignty of the state, in theory at least, lies in the will of the people.

Nothing better expresses sovereignty in its simplest form than Louis XIV's apocryphal remark, "I am the State." Nothing better reveals the changes that lay ahead than Frederick William I of Prussia's remark, two generations later, when the Age of Kings was over, "I am the State's first servant." In that short time, the state had begun to have a life of its own, independent of the man who happened at the moment to rule it. The great monarchs of the 17th Century, the men whose authority was absolute, were thus the architects of an institution that overshadowed their individual accomplishments. Unquestionably, the greatest of them was Louis XIV, during whose 72-year reign the modern state emerged.

Louis ascended the throne of France in 1643, when he was five years old. But he did not begin to rule his country until the death of his powerful prime minister, Cardinal Mazarin, in 1661. Mazarin, who had succeeded Richelieu as first minister, may actually have been the young Louis' step-father: it was rumored in court that the Cardinal had secretly married Louis XIII's widow. In any case, he dominated the youthful King, and kept him on short rein. On the day after Mazarin died the Archbishop of Rouen approached 23-year-old Louis, seeking to know the name of the next prime minister. "Your majesty," he inquired, "to whom shall we address ourselves in the future?" "To me," Louis replied, giving notice of his intentions. "It was," Louis confided in his memoirs, "the moment for which I had waited and which I had dreaded."

For the next 54 years, Louis devoted himself singlemindedly to the task of ruling France. Ultimately, his achievement was both practical and symbolic. On the one hand, he perfected the machinery of government, the elaborate bureaucracy through which he imposed his will upon France. On the other hand, he made himself the focus of his subjects' loyalty, the living embodiment of the majesty of the state.

Louis' first step was to staff his government with men who would obey him unquestioningly. In the past, the major posts had been filled by great nobles who looked upon these positions as due them by right, and who might or might not act in accord with the King's wishes. Louis set out to correct this. The official minutes of his Council for March 9, 1661, note that the King assembled "all those whom he customarily called—and dismissed them most civilly with the statement that, when he had need of their good advice, he would call them."

In fact, he called them almost not at all. Instead he appointed advisers drawn largely from the middle class, men with no claim to power except what the

King was pleased to entrust them with. Both he and they knew that what the King was pleased to give he might also, at any moment, be pleased to take away. Such men had no illusions about the source of their greatness, or the terms on which they were suffered to enjoy it.

But even with men who were wholly his creatures, Louis determined to keep the reins of government firmly in his own hands. Although he was not a man of extraordinary intelligence, he made up for this shortcoming in devotion to his job. All decisions, he insisted, were to be his decisions. No detail was too small to escape his attention. "Never as long as you live send out anything in the king's name without his express approval," wrote Jean Baptiste Colbert, one of Louis' most trusted and hard-working ministers, to his son and successor.

There had been a time, not long past, when keeping track of all the actions of the government of France would not have been a burdensome task. Many of the functions normally associated with government —the administration of justice, the maintenance of order, the control of revenue—were either not performed at all, or tended to be the prerogatives of local governments: of guilds, of nobles, of provincial law courts. As recently as the time of Louis' grandfather, the entire bureaucracy of the national government could easily accompany the King on his travels —and often did.

Now, Louis proposed to expand the activities of the central government, and become in practice as well as theory the master of his kingdom. Consequently, the number of state servants grew enormously. The 600 people who surrounded Louis at court at the beginning of his reign soon became 10,-000. More than that, there now appeared a new species of royal officials, called *intendants*, who ranged throughout the length and breadth of France, gathering information for the King and supervising the enforcement of his decisions. No one was too exalted to be immune from the attentions of these omnipresent royal servants. Acting as Louis' eyes, ears and hands within the various ministries of state, they brought a new kind of order to France.

The most significant features of this new order were the reorganized French army and the coordination of the French economy. The first was the work of Louis' Secretary of State for War, Michel le Tellier, and later of Le Tellier's son, the Marquis de Louvois, who succeeded his father in the office; the second was the work of the great Jean Baptiste Colbert. The problems these men faced, the methods they used and the results they achieved reveal how these familiar elements of the modern state were born.

Between 1643, when Michel le Tellier took office, and 1691, when his son Louvois died, the two men created not only a fighting force bigger and better than that of any other country in Europe, but also a military establishment quite without precedent. The army of Gustavus Adolphus, for instance, was essentially a personal army, trained and led by its warrior-king. But Louis went into battle more or less as a spectator. His army was a complex military machine of more than 400,000 men, managed for him by ministers and led for him by generals.

Of all the hierarchical organizations in the world, none seems more rigidly stratified than an army. Yet in the 17th Century, even so simple a device as a regular chain of command was regarded as an innovation. A military command was a personal possession, a prerogative of nobles or a commodity to be bought and sold—along with the armies that went with them. The semi-feudal leaders of the time had gone forth to battle only when it pleased them to do so, or when it served their own interests. They recognized no special allegiance to the King; in fact, they fought against him almost as often as for him. Furthermore, they did not command their armies in any real sense. The officers who served under them—like the commanders themselves—held their commissions through inheritance or purchase, a system calculated to produce neither effective subordination nor professional expertness.

All of this Le Tellier and Louvois set out to change by establishing a regular, pyramidal structure of responsibility and authority. At its apex was the Secretary of State for War, a civil servant rather than a military officer. Under him were the Marshals of France, who in turn gave orders to the army's numerous generals. Below these were the captains and colonels who traditionally "owned" their commissions—and who posed a problem. Because the purchase of commissions was an important source of state revenue, and because these officers were likely to resist any attempt to dismiss them, Le Tellier and Louvois were forced to outflank them in order to supplant their authority with the state's. To each colonel they attached a lieutenant colonel, to each captain a lieutenant—literally, in French, one who acts in lieu of another. These trained, professional officers, integrated into the army's regular chain of command, in effect directed the troops, leaving the colonels and captains free to enjoy their empty honors.

But neither Louis nor his ministers were naïve enough to believe that giving the army a formal structure would automatically ensure order and discipline. They recognized that the conduct of both officers and men needed constant surveillance. The office of *intendant de l'armée* was created and soon scores of these royal inspectors were scattered through the army, watching over its obedience and honesty. One of their most persistent problems was the practice of *passe volants:* captains, who were the paymasters of their troops, frequently collected money for a full complement of men when in fact they were short-handed; then, just before the *intendant* appeared, they hired extra men to stand for review. The punishment for this deception was flogging and branding for the hireling, fine and imprisonment for the officer—and the *intendants* enforced it vigorously. It is no accident that the name of the first inspector-general, Martinet, stands to this day for rigid discipline.

Neither did Louis and his ministers neglect the material side of warfare. In keeping with the times, they laid great stress on science and technology, and assembled an extraordinarily gifted group of experts. Marshal Sebastian Vauban, an engineer, developed the science of fortification to a level not exceeded until the 20th Century, and surrounded France with an impenetrable ring of fortresses. The Marquis de Chamlay, the army's chief topographer, allegedly knew every foot of ground, every hill and stream in France. "Monsieur de Chamlay can camp without me," wrote Marshal Turenne, the century's finest military strategist, "but I cannot camp without Monsieur de Chamlay."

Louis' impressive military machine suffered, however, from two grave defects. It was essentially a mercenary army, an army of the French state but not an army of France. Despite the brilliance of its leadership and the effectiveness of its discipline, it lacked the final dedication of an army whose men are personally committed to the cause for which they fight. A century earlier, the wars of religion had produced such armies, and two centuries later, when fervent nationalism swept Europe, they were to be the norm. But the armies of the 17th and 18th Centuries were composed in the main of dispassionate professionals. Although fanatical armies, in human terms, are not always desirable, the absence of fanaticism, in strictest military terms, is often considered a drawback.

The French army's other defect, far more serious, was its chronic lack of sufficient funds to support such a vast establishment. The man who wrestled with this problem was Louis' Controller-General of Finance, Jean Baptiste Colbert.

Colbert was in many ways the ideal bureaucrat, and the perfect instrument for carrying out Louis' policies. The son of a bourgeois draper from Reims, he had served both Le Tellier and Mazarin as a financial expert before becoming Louis' Minister of State. Coldly efficient, enamored of order, he devoted his life to making France solvent and self-supporting. It was an impossible task. Between Louis' extravagant châteaux and palaces, and his never-ending wars, the monarchy's demands for money brought the country to near bankruptcy. Nevertheless, Colbert's accomplishments were substantial.

Colbert operated according to a clear and precise economic doctrine, mercantilism. His object, always, was to foster industry and industrial exports. Along with other mercantilists, he believed that wealth consisted ultimately of gold and silver. Since these metals were finite in supply, one nation was bound to prosper only at the expense of another. "The increase of any estate must be upon the foreigner," wrote Francis Bacon, the British philosopher, "for whatsoever is somewhere gotten is somewhere lost." The more of its products a nation could export in exchange for gold and silver, the better off it would be.

Later economists have pointed out that mercantilism becomes a travesty when—as may happen—entire nations find themselves reduced to the plight of King Midas, starving in the midst of vast wealth. Nevertheless, it was an effective doctrine in its time. Seventeenth Century mercantilism was designed not to benefit the citizens of a state, but to increase the state's war-making potential—and for this end served admirably. It may not have helped the people, but it did supply the government with revenue. It is also important historically for two concepts that are now firmly rooted in economic thought. It conceived of the economy of a state as a unified whole, and it treated the economic ac-tivities that went on within a state as matters of vital concern to the national government.

The situation Colbert set out to make sense of was one of appalling complexity. France was divided into scores of separate economic units. Each regional government collected customs at its borders, had its own internal system of tariffs, its own peculiar methods of doing business. Many even had their own weights and measures and currencies. Medieval guilds of craftsmen and artisans still operated much as they had always done. They deliberately restricted production in order to maintain high prices, and jealously guarded access to their professions in order to prevent competition. A wildly inequitable system of taxation exempted all nobles, placing the tax burden on those least able to pay, the peasants. In short, the economic disorder of France was formidable.

Colbert began by setting the King's own affairs in order. He instituted a regular system of bookkeeping and audits, so that the government would have accurate records of its income and expenditures. He ferreted out corrupt officials, especially dishonest tax collectors, so that all the money collected would in fact end up in the royal treasury. He established a bureaucracy of clerks and a corps of *intendants* to carry out these tasks, placing them under the close supervision of a supreme council on finance. With this apparatus, he set out to give France a thriving national economy.

Every new order built upon an old order involves destruction as well as creation—and so it was with Colbert's work. He destroyed internal tariff barriers in order to free internal commerce, and built a great system of roads and canals to facilitate the movement of goods and people. He disrupted local commercial practices by giving the kingdom a single, uniform commercial code. He undermined the traditional functions of guilds by incorporating them into his bureaucracy and giving them the

INLAID DESK WITH CLOCK

task of regulating not quantity, but quality. He changed the very shape of the French economy by discouraging unprofitable enterprises and introducing new ones that seemed likely to increase French exports and swell the royal treasury.

At his prompting, the state established the great Gobelins tapestry workshop and school, assuring France of pre-eminence in this important craft. He brought Italian artisans into France to teach his countrymen how to blow glass and make lace. He published government pamphlets on such subjects as the dyeing of wool, and granted government subsidies to such industries as shipbuilding and furniture manufacturing (hoping, in the case of the former, to build France a navy and merchant marine). Gradually, under Colbert's watchful eye, France acquired a more rational economy in every area except one. Neither he nor the King, despite repeated efforts, ever succeeded in correcting the basic evils of the tax system. The forces of centuries of tradition and privilege were too strong. Peasants continued to bear the tax burden, and nobles to be immune from taxation. Public finance remained the Achilles' heel of the French monarchy.

However impressive the practical accomplishments of Louis' brilliant ministers, their will was in the last analysis the King's will. The authority they wielded was Louis' authority. Like planets, they shone with the reflected glory of his sun. Louis, for his part, clearly recognized his role as the symbol of the state, the embodiment of power, and he endowed his every act and gesture with superhuman significance, surrounding himself at all times with the spectacle of majesty.

As a setting for this spectacle, he created the palace of Versailles, choosing for its site—as if to deliberately demonstrate his limitless power—a totally undistinguished, dusty plain a few miles outside Paris. Here he decreed a residence to rise, fitting for the mightiest of monarchs, and tens of thousands of workmen labored for decades to produce it. An enormous sum of money, possibly as much as half a billion dollars, was spent to assemble the finest materials, the most skilled craftsmen, the greatest architects, artists, sculptors and gardeners. Engineers even attempted to divert the River Eure to fill lakes, pools and fountains; they failed to change the river's course, but they built pools and fountains that are still without equal.

When the task was finished, Louis had indeed the largest, most magnificent building ever created for a purely secular purpose. Versailles is overwhelming in size alone. Standing before its 1,361-foot façade or within its 240-foot-long Hall of Mirrors, the ordinary mortal is forcefully reminded of his own insignificance. Contemplating the endless vistas of the vast formal gardens, with their precisely arranged shrubs, paths and lawns, he tends to feel that nature itself has been reduced to a rational order by the irresistible will of the King.

Against this overwhelming background, Louis acted out his chosen role. Other individuals might be dwarfed by Versailles; Louis gave it meaning and focus. He imposed on his court an etiquette as rigorous and intricate as that of an oriental despot. Even his most intimate acts were surrounded by elaborate ceremonial. His rising in the morning and retiring at night were public spectacles at which the greatest nobles of France vied for the privileges of assisting him in dressing and undress-

PEDESTAL CLOCK

SIDE TABLE WITH MOSAIC MARBLE TOP

ARMCHAIR WITH LOUIS MONOGRAMS

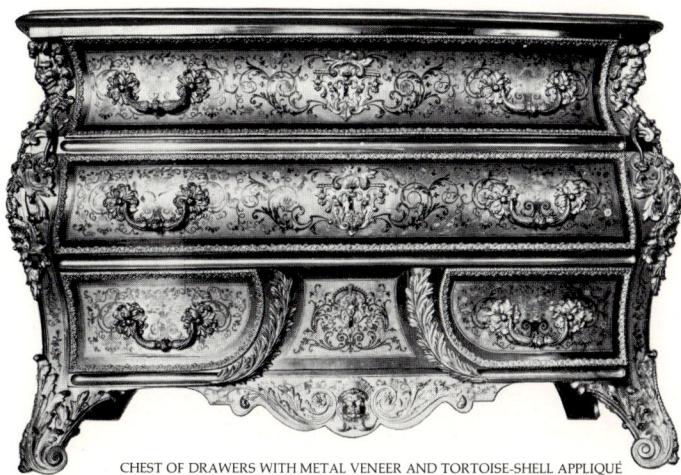
CHEST OF DRAWERS WITH METAL VENEER AND TORTOISE-SHELL APPLIQUÉ

FURNISHINGS FOR A KING, *elaborate pieces such as these were picked by Louis XIV for his new palace at Versailles. The style, which became known by the French monarch's name, is characterized by heavy, squarish lines, deep, ornate carving, lavish use of metal inlays and gilt, and a general emphasis on magnificence of appearance rather than comfort.*

ing. Men whose ancestors had made the kings of France tremble now accounted themselves honored to hold the sleeve of the royal nightshirt.

Since no one was worthy to eat with him, Louis dined alone; favored members of his court looked on in fascination—partly because Louis declined to use a fork, then a modern invention. His love affairs and his royal mistresses were the court's most important topic of conversation; his most trivial remarks were faithfully reported and endlessly discussed. To live in the awesome presence of the Sun King, one contemporary remarked, was like living in the presence of God.

Actually, life at Versailles left much to be desired in the way of amenities. The palace was designed more for display than human comfort. One disgruntled nobleman, the Duc de Saint-Simon, composed a lengthy report on life at court that is probably more accurate than the usual panegyrics. "The royal apartments," he wrote, "suffer from the most dreadful inconveniences, with backviews over the privies and other dark and malodorous offices. The astonishing magnificence of the gardens is equalled only by the bad taste with which they are designed. . . ."

"To reach the coolness of the gardens' shade one is forced to cross a vast, scorching plain at the end of which there is no alternative at any point, but to climb upwards or downwards, and the gardens end with a very small hill. The flint surface burns one's feet, but without it one would constantly be plunged into soft sand or black mire. The violence done to nature everywhere is repellent and disgusting. The innumerable water-courses, pumped or otherwise guided in from all directions, make the water itself green, thick and muddy; it provokes an unhealthy and perceptible humidity, and gives off a vile odor . . .''

Within the palace, courtiers and servants alike were crowded into a vast, sprawling rabbit warren of tiny, dark, unventilated rooms. Distances were formidable; it was sometimes necessary to walk through miles of corridors in the course of a single day, and the service facilities were so far removed from the halls of state that the King's meals generally arrived at the table cold—although 498 servants were occupied in preparing them. Plumbing was inadequate and inconvenient; even the most fastidious nobles resorted to urinating on the stairs. As this indicates, the level of personal cleanliness was abysmal, and baths were almost unheard of. In their place, men and women alike doused themselves liberally with perfume.

The atmosphere of pettiness and intrigue that pervaded the palace was even more dispiriting. However much the Duc de Saint-Simon might profess to disdain everything he saw around him at Versailles, he nevertheless brooded over the possibility that he might have to walk five steps behind the Duc de Luxembourg in the royal procession. Nobles and prelates of most exalted rank plotted to introduce their daughters and nieces, and even their wives, into the royal bed—for to be related to the King's mistress was a source of inestimable prestige. For those who had only sons, there were similar favors to be gained from the King's homosexual brother, Philippe d'Orléans.

Boredom led the courtiers into every sort of vice, from reckless and ruinous gambling to sexual promiscuity and perversion. No mere noble could hope to match the $25 million diamond-encrusted robe that Louis wore to a reception for the ambassador from Siam, but many a wealthy family bankrupted itself to meet the court's standards of dress.

And yet, despite the expense and the tedium,

the inconveniences and the squalor, French aristocrats fought for the privilege of living at Versailles. A century earlier, the departure of a noble from the court was an ominous sign—it meant that the nobleman had withdrawn his allegiance from the King. Now, it was a sign that the nobleman was, socially speaking, dead. Louis' most casual, ''We have not seen him,'' amounted to the end of a man's courtly career.

Louis made Versailles the center of European culture—partly through his own good taste, partly through his lavish patronage of the arts. But the attraction of Versailles went far beyond the pleasures of watching a comedy by Molière in the Hall of Mirrors, or listening to the operas of Lully in the glorious gardens. The attraction of Versailles was Louis himself, and it was very like the attraction of the sun he made his symbol. Knowing—perhaps better than any ruler had ever known before—the importance of appearances, Louis deliberately and with deadly seriousness created the mystique of the State.

''Those who imagine that these are merely matters of ceremony are gravely mistaken,'' he wrote. ''The peoples over whom we reign, being unable to apprehend the basic reality of things, usually derive their opinions from what they can see with their eyes.'' For nearly three quarters of a century, Louis XIV supplied Europe with dazzling visual proof of the power and majesty of his state.

But, as the English historian Lord Acton once observed, power tends to corrupt, and absolute power corrupts absolutely. In the later years of his reign, Louis overstepped the bounds and pursued power as an end in itself. In doing so, he gravely injured his own and his country's reputation, and aligned all Europe against him. He demonstrated that absolute power could bring order to a divided nation—but he also demonstrated that absolute power needed to be checked.

A TAPESTRY PORTRAIT *of Louis XIV holding a general's baton and riding to a battlefield in Flanders shows the French ruler at age 29.*

THE GLORIOUS MONARCH

"My dominant passion is certainly love of glory," wrote Louis XIV when he was 30, and throughout the 72 years of his reign, the longest in European history, he remained faithful to that passion. Everything about the King was glorious—or so, at least, the King thought—and his court hastened to agree. When he entered his chapel at Versailles, the courtiers turned their backs on the altar and knelt to their monarch instead. When his mistresses quarreled, poets compared their wrangling to the battles of goddesses fighting over the affections of Jupiter. Even on the battlefield, where Louis usually bungled, his exploits were invariably likened to those of Caesar or Alexander the Great. Typical of Louis' unquenchable self-esteem is a series of tapestries, made for him by his own royal Gobelins factory, illustrating, for all posterity to see, the many aspects of his genius.

GREETING HIS FATHER-IN-LAW, *Louis XIV doffs a plumed hat to Philip IV of Spain three days before his wedding to Philip's daughter, Marie Thérèse, show*

HUSBAND AND FATHER

Although Louis fancied himself an excellent family man, his interpretation of what that meant was broad indeed. His "family," toward the middle of his reign, included his wife, Queen Marie Thérèse, their son, the Dauphin, as well as his mistresses of the moment and a throng of illegitimate children. To preserve the appearance of domestic peace, Louis forced the mistresses to pay calls on the Queen, and the entire brood had to attend mass together every day with the King.

anding behind her father. BAPTIZING HIS SON, *the King proudly stands to the left of the font, two officiating bishops, and the Dauphin's godparents.*

Marie Thérèse quietly accepted the King's promiscuity, but she never learned to like it. Born a Princess of Spain, she had been married to Louis to create a political bond between the two countries. For her part, she never looked at another man —partly because she was madly in love with her husband, partly because she considered all other men beneath her station. When a French courtier asked her if, as a girl, she had found any of the men in Spain attractive, she replied in astonishment, "How could I possibly? There was no other king there except the King my father."

Such remarks earned the Queen an enduring reputation for naïveté at Versailles. The sophisticated courtiers laughed at her bad French, her old-fashioned gowns, her childlike love of dwarfs and little dogs. If the King shared their amusement, he never let on. In fact, at her death he graciously remarked, "This is the only annoyance she has ever caused me."

LOUIS THE
HAPPY WARRIOR

Louis loved war so much that he had miniature battle scenes painted on his high heels and insisted on giving a military flavor even to nonmilitary events. The tapestry at left shows his triumphant entry into Dunkirk—a city he did not conquer, but bought from the English in 1662.

Louis the Warrior was a character that existed only in Louis' imagination. When he retreated at Heurtebise in 1676, to avoid a battle he feared to lose, he announced that the battle was unnecessary: "I have shown that my mere presence is enough to embarrass the enemy." When one of his generals scored a victory, Louis took the credit, claiming that the success was due to "that happy genius which has never yet been lacking in me."

In his later years Louis conducted many of his campaigns from his desk at Versailles, and suffered defeat after defeat. After one particularly stunning loss to the British general, Lord Marlborough, the King indignantly complained, "God seems to have forgotten all I have done for Him."

HIS NATION'S MASTER DIPLOMAT

During most of his reign Louis served as his own prime minister, and in his dealings with foreign princes proved himself a shrewd statesman. In his major power struggle, with the Habsburg rulers of Austria and Spain, he bought the support of weak states such as Switzerland. Against stronger nations he often used force, even to settle matters of diplomatic protocol. When the Pope failed to apologize promptly enough for an affront to the French ambassador in Rome, Louis dispatched an army toward Italy. The Pope was able to call Louis off only by sending his own nephew, Cardinal Chigi, to France with a full apology, and by agreeing to raise a monument commemorating the apology.

GRANTING AN AUDIENCE (left), Louis receives Cardinal Chigi at the country palace at Fontainebleau. According to one courtier, the King loved inviting cardinals there because he admired the effect of their scarlet robes against the lush green foliage of the gardens.

RENEWING A TREATY, a splendidly wigged Louis arranges with Swiss ambassadors to lend them money and to hire up to 16,000 Swiss soldiers. By granting such favors Louis was able to keep Switzerland neutral in the warfare between France and Austria.

IN PURSUIT OF PLEASURE

Louis believed that it was a king's duty to pursue royal pleasure as relentlessly as he pursued royal business. No matter how worried or exhausted he might be, he went hunting or played tennis every day, and at night gave dances and plays.

For his courtiers these events were often more like torture than pleasure. A lady invited to Versailles for the evening had to arrive at six, in full court dress, and might not leave until eight the following morning. During those 14 hours she might attend a comedy, a ballet and a ball, interspersed with two suppers and perhaps some roulette or cards. Through all of this, she had to observe the most rigid etiquette. One duchess, who broke the rules by sitting down at the gaming table when she was not playing, was never received at court again.

RIDING TO HOUNDS, *Louis leads a band of nobles through the hills near Fontainebleau. Louis loved hunting so much that he kept no less than 1,000 dogs kenneled at Versailles. As an old man, unable to sit a horse, he hunted deer from a coach.*

ATTENDING A BALLET *at the Louvre, Louis and his royal court observe a performance of "Psyché," composed for the King. Louis himself often took a part in such court theatricals. Appropriately, one of the "Sun King's" first roles was as the Sun.*

A CONNOISSEUR OF CRAFTS, *a plumed and red-brocaded Louis inspects vases, tapestries and carpets displayed by artisans at the Paris Gobelins factory.*

A BUILDER OF VISIONS, *Louis approves the roll of plans for the Invalides, shown above in a glimpse into the future, already under construction.*

ROYAL PATRON OF THE ARTS

The King's determination to patronize the arts raised France during his reign to its cultural apogee. One of his first acts was to purchase and place under state control the Gobelins, a factory in Paris that produced exquisite handicrafts. From its workshops poured forth tapestries, silver and furniture that soon filled the royal residences.

Louis was also the first French King who consistently encouraged writers. He granted an annual allowance to such authors as the famed playwright of comedies, Molière, and the tragic dramatist Racine. He also supported a court composer, Jean Baptiste Lully, who conducted with a baton so long that one day he punctured his foot with it, and died of the resulting infection.

As a builder, Louis was indefatigable. In Paris he rebuilt the Louvre, erected a huge home for disabled veterans, the Invalides, and approved the construction of two beautiful squares, the Place des Victoires and the Place Vendôme. His masterpiece, however, lay outside the city at Versailles, where he built a palace so expensive that he destroyed many of the bills for it, to keep his critical ministers from discovering exactly how much it cost.

THE HEIR TO
HEROES AND GODS

During the 17th Century in France, cultivated Frenchmen regarded ancient Greece and Rome as the high points in history—equaled only by the reign of Louis XIV. Artists flattered Louis by reinforcing this comparison. In the tapestry at right, Alexander the Great's triumphal entry into a defeated city portrays the ancient hero as looking vaguely like the French King, who was supposed to resemble Alexander in military prowess.

From flattering Louis himself, his idolators went on to praise the nation he ruled. In 1687 a poem, "The Century of Louis the Great," compared Louis' France to Classical Greece—to Greece's disadvantage. In the ensuing controversy, Descartes was called a greater philosopher than Plato, Racine a more profound dramatist than Sophocles.

Louis underlined all of these Classical references with a few of his own. He once led a parade through Paris dressed as a Roman Emperor, and he called the throne room at Versailles the "Salon of Apollo."

4
TUMULT IN THE ARTS

On the last day of May, 1665, a royal coach drawn by six horses and bearing a royal steward set out from Paris to meet a distinguished visitor and conduct him to the King. The visitor was Gianlorenzo Bernini, the century's greatest sculptor and one of its most gifted architects. Invited by Louis XIV to plan the rebuilding of the Louvre, then the residence of the Kings of France, Bernini eagerly accepted. He was, he said, delighted "to design for a king of France, a modern king [*un roi d'aujourd'-hui*], buildings grander and more magnificent than the palaces of the emperors and the popes."

Coming from an artist of Bernini's accomplishments, this held immense promise. He was already famous for the glorious colonnade in St. Peter's Square in Rome—the curving, embracing arms that draw the faithful into the church—and he had conceived two other masterpieces for the church itself. One was the bronze *baldacchino*, or canopy, rising on four huge twisted columns over St. Peter's tomb. The other, just reaching completion, was the dazzling shrine of marble, bronze and stained glass enclosing St. Peter's chair.

France was ravished by the thought that the greatest artist of the age was now about to devote his talents to the glorification of its King. From the moment Bernini crossed the French border, his journey became a kind of triumphal progress. Artists and leading citizens of every town he passed through turned out to pay him tribute. His arrival in Paris, on June 2, 1665, was an occasion for the most intense excitement in courtly and artistic circles.

And yet, less than five months later, Bernini left Paris in disgust. Political intrigue, national pride and differences in taste led to the rejection of his plans for the Louvre. But the abortive collaboration between architect and monarch did produce one major result. During his residence in Paris, Bernini carved a marble bust of Louis that was to become one of the century's most important works of art—partly because of its artistic qualities, partly because of the circumstances under which it was created. Many critics have singled it out as a supreme expression of Baroque art, a perfect wedding of subject and style, a work that captures the essence of the age. Strength, arrogance and a kind of restless dynamism are expressed with enormous effective-

A STUDY IN EMOTION, *this sculptural detail by the master Gianlorenzo Bernini shows St. Athanasius lost in ecstatic reverence before the Chair of St. Peter in St. Peter's Cathedral in Rome. Like other Baroque artists, Bernini strove to arouse deep religious sentiments in viewers of his work.*

ness in the pose of the head, the glance of the eyes, the swirl of the draperies. The work projects precisely what Bernini intended it to project: this is what a king is; this is what majesty means.

Happily, every step in Bernini's creation of this masterpiece is a matter of record. Chantelou, the royal steward who served as his interpreter and guide, kept a journal that is rich not only in fascinating details about Bernini's thoughts and actions, but also about the character of Baroque art—what it was attempting to do, the means it used to do it. On June 11, according to Chantelou—scarcely more than a week after he arrived in Paris—Bernini wanted to know if the rumor was true that the King wanted him to do a portrait bust. When he learned that it was, he admitted that he had already ordered the clay for the preliminary models. On June 21, a day after the bust was officially commissioned, Bernini set out to find a suitable block of marble. He finally selected three, each of which he tested carefully until he found one that satisfied him.

For the next three weeks Bernini worked alternately at two preliminary tasks. One was the modeling of a clay bust, a task that he approached with no particular regard for Louis' exact features. Bernini's concern, at this point, was not to capture the look of Louis, but the look of the greatest monarch on earth—an ideal, an abstraction. Simultaneously, but quite separately, Bernini undertook, as he put it, "to steep myself in, and imbue myself with, the King's features." He watched Louis playing tennis, Louis presiding at meetings of his council, Louis riding to hounds—and made innumerable rapid sketches of his subject in action. This preoccupation with motion was Bernini's method for discovering the individuality of each of his subjects. "If a man stands still and immobile," he once said, "he is never as much like himself as when he moves about; his movements reveal all those personal qualities that are his and his alone."

On the 14th of July, Bernini put aside his sketches and his clay models, and attacked his chosen block of marble. With consummate daring, he carved simply from memory. "I don't want to copy myself," he declared. The bust took 40 days to complete, and on only 13 of them was the King present for a sitting. On October 5, Bernini marked the position of the eyes with chalk, carved them, and pronounced the work finished. He had meant it to sit on a special, allegorical pedestal, designed to express the greatness of his subject: a globe on which would be emblazoned the words, "too small a base." The pedestal was never made, and never needed; the sculpture conveyed the message quite well enough.

Great works of art can never be finally explained except in terms of the genius who creates them. Nevertheless, Bernini's bust of Louis XIV perfectly sums up the intention of 17th Century art. Whatever the artist's country of origin or his artistic medium, his aim was to capture in some enduring form —in stone, in paint, in words—a sense of motion and immediacy. In doing so, he created a new kind of artistic order, a vital new style: the Baroque.

The word Baroque was first applied to 17th Century art by later generations, and it was used as a term of contempt. To the cool, controlled rationalists of the 18th Century, the art of their predecessors seemed to violate every rule of decorum and every canon of good taste. They chose to describe it with a word that may have come from the Portuguese *barroco*, a large and irregularly shaped pearl, or from the Latin *baroco*, a term used by medieval scholars to describe a particularly intricate and difficult bit of reasoning in the construction of a system of logic. In either case, the point was clear: Baroque was somehow grotesque and overly elaborate.

This scornful dismissal of the art of the Baroque persisted until the 20th Century, when suddenly its great strengths were rediscovered. Like their contemporaries in other fields—philosophy, science, pol-

A PORTRAIT OF POWER, *Bernini's bust of Louis XIV is partly a likeness of the King, partly an abstract study of the authority and arrogance of absolute monarchy.*

itics—the artists of the 17th Century were confronted with the ruins of an old order, and the challenge of replacing it. Specifically, the harmony and clarity of Renaissance art had been shattered by a vigorous but short-lived movement known as Mannerism. The Mannerists, having mastered all the problems of technique and style set by Renaissance art, grew bored and began to break the rules. As the name implies, their work soon degenerated into a mannered, affected style incapable of further development. The Baroque, which followed it, was more successful. Like all great artistic styles, it grasped and expressed the spirit of its age—the doubts and conflicts, the excitement and pride. It is an art full of vitality and emotion. Developed first in Italy, and within a very specific frame of reference, Baroque went on to become the dominant artistic force of Europe, modified in form in different localities but essentially the same in spirit.

The first Baroque art was associated with the Counter Reformation. The Catholic Church, in its attempt to revitalize itself and stem the tide of Prot-

estantism, encouraged a religious art that served these ends. The decorations of Baroque churches were intended, in the words of the 34th Psalm, to "magnify the Lord . . . and . . . exalt His name," and in so doing intensify the worshipers' piety and devotion. This proselytizing origin helps to explain one of the main features of all Baroque art, its emphasis on communication. Every typical work of this period—architectural or sculptural, literary or musical—strives above all else to create an effect upon its audience, to involve it, to stir it. No other style of art has ever been quite so spectator-oriented.

The means to this end is sometimes sheer size, as in the overwhelming scale of Versailles. Sometimes it is the richness and sumptuous variety of the materials, as in Bernini's chair of St. Peter. More often, however, the means are not so easy to identify, being more subtle and complex. The interior of a Baroque church, for instance, is composed of many elements, put together with painstaking care and elaborate ingenuity. The ceiling is often a blend of architecture, sculpture and painting, miraculously combined to draw the worshiper into an apparently infinite distance. Statues wrapped in swirling marble draperies are illuminated by an unearthly light coming from some unseen source. Twisted columns convey a sense of power and motion, tension and restlessness. Amid the convoluted forms, the gilded sunbursts and broken arches, there is no place for the eye to come to rest. The whole effect is one of intense emotion and incredible grandeur. The Baroque church was an arena within which a militant Catholicism struggled for the souls of men.

By the middle of the century, the Baroque had widened its social base and broadened its artistic range. It had become the dominant style of royal courts and even, to some extent, of the Protestant, middle-class Netherlands. The same feelings of assertiveness (and perhaps of underlying insecurity) that had prompted the Church to adopt the new

Lady with a Lute
Jan Vermeer

Syndics of the Cloth Drapers' Guild
Rembrandt van Rijn

The Night Watch
Rembrandt van Rijn

Lady with a Fan
Rembrandt van Rijn

Saul and David
Rembrandt van Rijn

The Merry Lute Player
Frans Hals

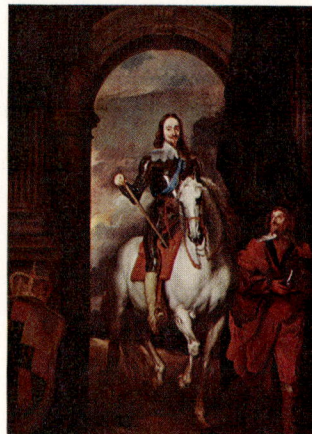

Charles I of England
Anthony van Dyck

Philip IV of Spain
Diego Velasquez

Louis XIV
Hyacinthe Rigaud

Andromeda Liberated by Perseus
Peter Paul Rubens

Detail *Fountain of the Four Rivers*
Gianlorenzo Bernini

BAROQUE ARTISTS *were deeply concerned with the reality of human existence, but each saw it in his own way. For Vermeer reality lay in luminous detail; for Rembrandt, in the shadowed drama of personalities. Frans Hals found it in the vigorous faces of burghers and peasants, Rubens in the voluptuous contours of the human body. Even the aloof aristocrats painted by Van Dyck, Velasquez and Rigaud are real people and Bernini's marble gods seem made of living flesh.*

style now led princes and wealthy merchants to turn it to secular purposes. Louis XIV saw a political usefulness in buildings "grander and more magnificent than the palaces of the emperors and the popes." Solid Dutch burghers gained a reassuring sense of their own heroism from Rembrandt's intensely dramatic painting of an outing of their shooting company—the familiar *Night Watch*. At the same time, what had begun strictly as a style of architecture now became a more general artistic order, embracing even the nonvisual arts of literature and music. But the overriding purpose remained the same—to overwhelm the senses, to appeal directly to the emotions, although the techniques for doing this were necessarily different in the different arts.

In their constant attempt to break down the barrier between the work of art and the audience, Baroque artists used every imaginable device. Painters, for example, lit their figures dramatically and placed them against dark and impenetrable backgrounds. Their subjects look directly at the viewer or, even more typically, at some point outside the canvas, some object or event in the viewer's world. Often the painting includes an artificial "frame," and the figure is portrayed in the act of moving through it, as though into the outside world. Anthony van Dyck's *Charles I*, for example, rides through a magnificent triumphal arch directly toward the viewer. Rembrandt's *Lady with a Fan* rests her hand against a frame painted into the picture, with her thumb overlapping the edge. The impression is one of startling immediacy.

The same is true of Baroque sculpture. Bernini's great bust of Louis XIV, although shaped to conform to an idealized vision of majesty and grandeur, is nevertheless vital and alive, capturing forever a transitory moment: Louis is about to speak. An even better example is Bernini's *David* in the act of slaying Goliath. The motion of the youthful challenger's body and the intensity of his gaze so powerfully suggest Goliath's presence that the actual focus of the work seems to be outside the statue, in the vicinity of the viewer. The boundary between the work of art and the real world has been dissolved.

Baroque art also broke down the traditional distinctions between the various branches of art. Architecture and sculpture merged into one another so indistinguishably that it was impossible to say where one ended and the other began. Baroque sculptors strove to achieve effects with light and color that had once been the special province of painters, while painters delighted in ornamenting architecture with deceptively real paintings of architectural ornaments and details. Poets took to building up words into elaborate pictures, and musicians piled one musical effect upon another in a manner that was truly architectural. In their constant striving for more and more dramatic and startling effects, Baroque artists pushed every technique to its outermost limits. In sheer virtuosity, in utter mastery of the means at hand, they have never been surpassed.

This is not to say that the sum total of Baroque is sensationalism. Although some of its more flamboyant examples do approach the bombastic, there is more to it than that. Baroque, at its best, uses its virtuoso skills to express the deep emotions, the profound hopes and fears of its time. Its special genius, in fact, was precisely this ability to convey the extremes of human emotion. It was a style admirably suited to the task of representing icy hatred and burning love, overweening arrogance and abject terror, soaring ambition and utter humility. To an age of great tension and doubt, and of equally great vitality, it offered the ideal medium for expressing the essential drama of life.

The work that has been called the only great epic poem in the English language is a perfect example of the Baroque spirit in action. John Milton's *Paradise Lost* is a retelling of the familiar story of Adam and Eve and their fall from Grace, but in his hands it is no longer the simple tale told in one chapter of *Genesis*. Milton has expanded it literally and figuratively into a huge cosmic drama of the clash between God and Satan. The poet's devout Protestantism cannot be questioned; nevertheless, it is quite clear that the figure of Satan inspires his most glorious verse. To Milton, the fascination of Satan obviously lay in his enormous power and towering ambition. Milton makes him the true embodiment of Baroque majesty:

> High on a Throne of Royal State, which far
> Outshon the wealth of Ormus and of Ind,
> Or where the gorgeous East with richest hand
> Showrs on her Kings Barbaric Pearl and Gold,
> Satan exalted sat, by merit rais'd
> To that bad eminence; and from despair
> Thus high uplifted beyond hope, aspires
> Beyond thus high, insatiate to pursue
> Vain Warr with Heav'n.

The language Milton used to describe Satan's portentous council of war against God, a council held in his royal palace of Pandemonium, is the verbal counterpart of the visual effects created by Baroque sculpture and painting. Grotesque names, bizarre images and the most vivid and horrifying details pile up in dizzying succession. Their meaning is less important than the effect they create; their result is less a description than a kind of incantation—Milton is using language to evoke emotions of awe and to weave a magic spell:

> First, Molock horrid King besmear'd with blood
> Of human sacrifice, and parents tears. . . .
> Next Chemos, th' obscene dread of Moabs Sons,
> From Aroer to Nebo, and the wild
> Of Southmost Abarim; in Hesebon
> And Horonaim, Seons Realm, beyond
> The flowry Dale of Sibma clad with Vines,
> And Eleale to th' Asphaltick Pool. . . .

If Bernini's bust of Louis stands for all time as the very image of the King, so Milton's Satan is the archetype of the Rebel:

> . . . Peace is despaird;
> For who can think Submission? Warr then, Warr
> Open or understood must be resolv'd.
> He spake: and to confirm his words, out-flew
> Millions of flaming swords, drawn from the thighs
> Of mighty Cherubim; the sudden blaze
> Far round illumin'd hell: highly they rag'd
> Against the Highest, and fierce with grasped Arms
> Clash'ed on their sounding shields the din of war,
> Hurling defiance toward the Vault of Heav'n.

Like much of the religious art of Bernini, Milton's *Paradise Lost* illuminates a cataclysmic subject, and uses the Baroque style in a manner suited to that purpose. It is drama of a particular kind—but it is not the only kind. One of the greatest painters of the Baroque era, Rembrandt van Rijn, also used the devices of Baroque style to dramatize, but it is a drama devoted to a very different end. The posing of his figures, the complexity of their relationships in space, the somber richness of his colors and vivid contrasts of light and shadow all add up to a powerful impression of emotion and immediacy. But the drama that Rembrandt chose to portray was less obvious and more internal, less concerned with dramatic events than with the drama of personality—the thoughts and feelings of individual human beings. As much as any artist who ever lived, Rembrandt achieved what one contemporary described as the goal of all artists: "to enter into the passion of their subject."

Rembrandt's preoccupation with the inner life is clearly reflected in his choice of subjects. Many of his most powerful and striking portraits are of people with no worldly importance, the anonymous, ordinary people of Amsterdam. Even when he chose to depict kings, as he did sometimes in his religious paintings, his focus was on their human qualities rather than their trappings of office. The King Saul of his *Saul and David* wears the raiment of a king, but his face is the face of a man torn by conflicting feelings; David's music soothes him but David is nevertheless his political rival.

Only in the Netherlands were artists of the Baroque period so dominated by the desire to show the ordinariness of men and life. The robust portraits of Frans Hals and the luminous interiors of Jan Vermeer, like Rembrandt's intensely human Dutch burghers, are a distinctly unmonarchial variant of the Baroque, conceived by a people who had only in that century freed themselves from Spanish rule to set up their own government by an aristocracy of merchants. Elsewhere in Europe, and more typical of the age, men like the Flemish painter Anthony van Dyck and the French painter Hyacinthe Rigaud devoted their lives and skills to the glorification of their royal and noble patrons.

Unquestionably the two greatest of these court painters were the exuberant Peter Paul Rubens and the cool and elegant Diego Rodriguez de Silva y Velasquez. Rubens used slashing diagonals and writhing S-shapes as a basis for his compositions, and gloried in painting sumptuous silks and brocades and radiant flesh tones. The vast canvases that he and his many assistants turned out by the hundreds are typical of the Baroque at its most voluptuous and energetic. By contrast, the paintings of Velasquez are severe and formal. His portraits of the Spanish royal family are marvels of technical refinement: tiny princesses pose gravely in enormous, stiff court dresses; Philip IV sits haughty and aloof, astride his prancing thoroughbred. Yet miraculously, Velasquez penetrates the gravity and the regal bearing to discover the child who is the princess and the man who is the king. Outward appearances and inner reality are revealed simultaneously, and in each of his paintings the dramatic contrast between the two is the ultimate focus of attention.

When a painter as restrained and refined as Velasquez was attracted to the conflict and drama in his subjects, it is small wonder that the most dramatic of arts, the theater, exploded into lavish spectacles. In stage design, architects and sculptors, freed of the necessity to be practical, indulged their imaginations to the full, concocting Baroque fantasies in wood and plaster, canvas and paint that made even Versailles and St. Peter's pale by comparison. Despite their limited technical knowledge, they staged incredible effects of light, sound and movement. Fountains plashed, thunder rolled, and gods and goddesses descended from on high, riding painted clouds. One of the French court's favorite designers, Giacomo Torelli, produced stage tricks so clever that he reputedly had fled Venice to escape audiences who accused him of being in league with the devil.

The works that were performed in these glorious settings ranged from humble Punch and Judy shows —one of the enduring minor creations of the Baroque age—to opera, the one theatrical form that in many ways sums up the artistic life of the century. "Without opera," the French author Romain Rolland has written, "we should scarcely be acquainted with half the artistic mind of the 17th Century, for we should see only the intellectual side of it. Through opera, we best reach the depths of the sensuality of that time—its voluptuous imagination, its sentimental materialism. . . ."

Like almost every other form of Baroque art, opera originated in Italy. Its antecedents were the masque, a kind of musical masquerade, and the liturgical drama called *sacre rappresentazioni*, both of which combined words and music. But opera, unlike either of them, attempted to provide more than just a musical accompaniment to the words. It sought to intensify their meaning, to create in effect a musical poetry that matched the verbal poetry. The first published opera was *Eurydice*, performed in Florence in 1600 on the occasion of the marriage of Henry IV of France to Marie de' Medici. Its composer was Jacopo Peri, one of a group of musical antiquarians who thought that their art form—which they called *dramma per musica*—was probably similar to the musical dramas of the ancient Greeks.

"It seemed to me," wrote Peri in the preface to his opera, "that the ancient Greeks and Romans . . . must have made use of a sort of music which, while surpassing the sounds of ordinary speech, fell so far short of the melody of singing as to assume the shape of something intermediate between the two." This musical imitation of speech was also Peri's goal, although he admitted that "doubtless no one ever yet spoke in singing." He also recognized that the sounds of Greek and Italian were not the same, and adapted his musical composition to Italian speech: "In our speech, some sounds are intoned in such a way that harmony can be based upon them."

Harmony, in fact, was what gave opera its distinctive character, for it added emotion and feeling to the *dramma per musica*. The conventional musical form of Peri's day was polyphony, an intertwining of many musical voices, each singing its own distinct melody. The new music of Peri and his friends contained only one melody; all the other voices supported it, and the nature of this harmonic support gave the melody mood and color. For the abstract beauty of polyphonic sound, the new music substituted emotional appeal; it was music that expressed sadness or joy, tranquillity or anguish. Understandably, Baroque audiences loved it. "There was no one in the audience who was not greatly moved," wrote one contemporary reporter of a performance of Claudio Monteverdi's *Ariadne* in 1608. "None of the ladies present, at the singing of the beautiful 'Lament,' could withhold their tears of sympathy, so filled with vehement passion was the music, and so movingly was it sung."

It was the genius of Monteverdi that gave opera a life of its own. Turning loose a torrent of musical ideas upon the careful reconstructions of Peri and his friends, he overwhelmed his audiences with new melodies, new harmonies and unprecedentedly rich combinations of orchestral sound. Opera became phenomenally successful. By 1637 Venice had an auditorium just for opera—the first opera house in the world; by 1700, 700 operas had been composed in Italy alone. Many of these works, and more important, the operatic form itself, were rapidly exported to the rest of Europe. Long before the middle of the century, Italian opera was being presented in Dresden, Prague and Vienna, and by the end of the century it had reached Poland.

Nowhere, however, was opera given more elaborate productions than in France. Jean Baptiste Lully, who composed some 16 operas for Louis XIV, was the virtual musical dictator of the French court. Lully, born Giovanni Battista Lulli, came to his position of eminence by way of the kitchen—he was a scullery assistant in the retinue of Madame de Montpensier, the King's cousin. Naturally gifted at music and dancing, he soon managed to advance himself to the position of composer of the royal ballets that were one of the feature entertainments of court life. When he moved from ballet to opera, he shrewdly incorporated the pageantry of the old medium into the new. French opera, as Lully wrote it, included grandiose overtures, elaborate choral and instrumental effects and interludes of ballet. It was, in spirit and substance, the quintessential expression of Baroque art. Like the Baroque church, which it resembled, opera overwhelmed its audiences with sensory experiences and sought to create out of many arts a single artistic unity. It was truly a child of its century.

CLASPING A ROSARY, *the hands of a worshiper express the intense piety Bernini felt late in life when he carved them for a figure in a family chapel.*

TITAN OF THE BAROQUE

Few sculptors in history have been more skilled, more productive or more representative of their age than Gianlorenzo Bernini, the genius of Italian Baroque art. Bernini carved his first statue, a classical tableau of the infant god Zeus, when he was 17 or younger, and his last, a figure of Christ, when he was 81. In the six decades between, he not only helped to revolutionize sculpture but also became one of the most sought-after architects in Rome, filling the city with spectacular churches, piazzas and palaces for a succession of cardinals and popes.

The style that Bernini helped to originate cast off conventional restraints. Exuberant, theatrical, yet often intensely personal, it attempted to destroy the boundaries between art and life; under Bernini's own masterful chisel, gripping hands often seemed about to move and marble tears to flow. So convincing did his sculpture become that a Roman cardinal once pointed at a man who had just finished posing for Bernini and said, "This is the portrait of Monsignor Montoya." Then, turning to Bernini's bust, the cardinal added, "*This* is Montoya."

FLEETING MOMENTS FROM MYTHOLOGY

Baroque sculpture often sought to tell a whole story by showing just its climactic moment, and this characteristic strongly marked much of Bernini's most important work. Many Renaissance artists before him had illustrated Greek myths, but none showed more dramatically the instant when Daphne's hands sprouted into leaves *(below)* or the moment when Proserpina was carried screaming through the gates of hell *(right)*. The impact of such statues reflected the viewpoint of the leading Italian poet of the day, Giambattista Marino. The artist's goal, he said, was to "astonish the crowd."

A RAPID METAMORPHOSIS *occurs as Daphne is changed by a river god into a tree and is saved from the embraces of the pursuing Apollo. Bernini regarded her flowing hair as one of his highest technical achievements.*

STRIVING FOR FREEDOM, *Proserpina writhes in the arms of Pluto, Lord of the Underworld, while his dog snaps at her heels. The captor's fingers pressing into her flesh reveal Bernini's superlative command of stone.*

THE TECHNIQUES OF REALISM

Bernini perfected, and taught other Baroque artists, innumerable ways of creating the illusion of reality. Not only was he a master at reproducing the human form, but he captured the emotions of his subjects as well. While working on his David *(left)*, he repeatedly scrutinized his own face in a mirror to get the expression of grim purpose exactly right. When he depicted Daniel, he concentrated not only on the main figure with anatomical accuracy, but also on the lion as a realistic and docile pet *(below)*. Once, it is said, he was so carried away by his passion for verisimilitude that, when carving a figure of a saint martyred by burning, he put his own leg into a fire in order to study the agony on his face.

A DETERMINED WARRIOR, *David prepares to hurl his stone at Goliath. Although many sculptors had shown David before or after his encounter, Bernini was the first artist to picture the actual moment of conflict.*

A FRIENDLY LION, *miraculously pacified by God's will, licks the foot of the Old Testament hero Daniel. The texture of the lion's head, carefully chiseled to suggest fur, contrasts sharply with the man's smooth leg.*

A HEROIC PORTRAIT
IN STONE

Much of Baroque sculpture was meant to be seen from a single viewpoint, and for this reason was often set against a wall or in a niche. When Bernini conceived a monument like his portrait of Constantine, the first Christian Emperor of Rome, he knew in advance where it would be placed and tried to take advantage of the architectural setting.

The Constantine was destined for a niche in the Vatican where it would be bathed by daylight pouring in through a high, unseen window. Bernini used this beam of natural light as one of the focal points of the composition: the vision of the Cross in the sky that Constantine saw in 312 A.D. and that so overwhelmed him he became a Christian.

By placing the statue against a wall, Bernini, like a painter, was also able to create a background for the figure—in this case a wind-swept stucco curtain that echoes and emphasizes the silhouette of the Roman ruler and his horse. Through such a controlled handling of the sculpture's environment, Bernini attempted to show not only how the scene might have looked to an observer, but also how it felt to be a man suddenly transfixed by Divine light.

THE ECSTASY OF ST. TERESA

Bernini's most famous religious sculpture dramatizes the mystical experience of a 16th Century Spanish nun. Designated for a small Carmelite church in Rome, it shows a beatifically smiling angel piercing the heart of the swooning St. Teresa with the arrow of Divine Love. The scene was vividly described by the saint herself: "In his hands I saw a great golden spear, and at the iron tip there appeared to be a point of

fire. This he plunged into my heart . . . and left me utterly consumed by the great love of God."

The Ecstasy of St. Teresa represented a new kind of religious art that Baroque sculptors and painters were creating for the Catholic Church. "The Church wants to inflame the souls of her children," a cardinal had written in 1594, and artists tried to involve the masses in the mystical experiences of their faith. To do it they used all the technical devices at their command. Bernini vividly re-created holy experiences such as that of St. Teresa; other artists attempted to achieve the illusion that figures were actually moving out over an altar into the congregation, or that the roof of the church had been torn asunder to reveal a flood of angels. Bernini himself created such an illusion of Heaven for St. Peter's in Rome *(overleaf)*.

A HEAVENLY HOST *of angels and cherubs swirls about the inside of St. Peter's in Rome. At the center of this composition the sculptor elaborately encased*

in bronze the wooden chair that, according to tradition, had belonged to Peter. Above the chair glows a stained-glass representation of the Holy Dove.

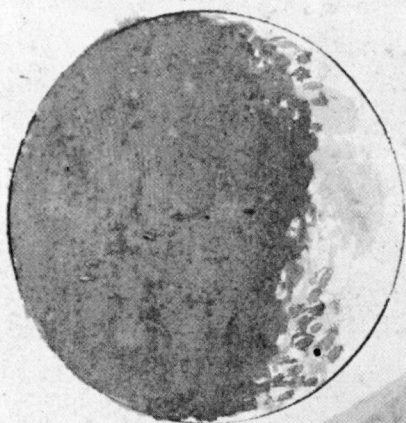

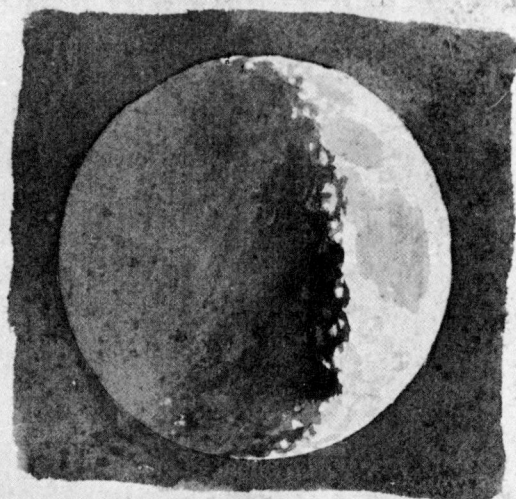

5

A RECONSTRUCTED UNIVERSE

The soaring ambition of the Baroque age reached literally into the heavens, to find a new order in the planets and stars and reshape man's view of the universe. The search for order was not itself new: men had always looked for patterns and regularities in nature's ceaseless motion, and had tried to fit them into a coherent system. But the greatest advance in this search took place in the 17th Century, and it revolutionized science.

The immediate consequences of the revolution were enormous. Man's knowledge of nature was vastly increased and so was his ability to control natural forces. But there was another consequence, even more significant. The techniques and attitudes of the new science were soon to be applied to non-scientific matters, to beliefs and values that had been built up over centuries of patient effort. The result was an intellectual and spiritual crisis that shook the foundations of Western society and ushered in the modern world.

The first and most important battleground of the revolution was the science of astronomy. Traditionally, the heavens were thought to operate according to a system worked out by the Alexandrian astronomer Ptolemy in the Second Century. Ptolemy based his construction upon the ideas of the ancient Greeks. His universe was made up of a number of concentric spheres, at the center of which was the earth, a sphere composed of solid matter. The spheres that surrounded the earth, however, were made of a mysterious crystal-clear substance of great purity.

These crystalline spheres all revolved around the earth, and within each sphere was embedded one or more luminous orbs, or heavenly bodies, that moved with it. The sphere nearest the earth contained the moon. Beyond that were the spheres that contained Mercury and Venus, followed by the sphere that held the sun. Beyond that were three distant spheres, containing the remote planets, and a fourth sphere, which contained the fixed stars. In the daytime the existence of these spheres was revealed by the blueness of the sky, caused by layer upon layer of heavenly substance. At night it was revealed by the movement of the stars and planets, set into them like jewels.

In many ways this must have been a most satisfying view of the universe. It offered men the comforting knowledge that the earth was the center around which all else revolved. Then, too, there was a certain rightness in the idea of a heaven made of some pure, ethereal substance, rather than the grosser stuff of which the earth was made. It must also have seemed appropriate to have a heavenly architecture based on the circle, most perfect of shapes. And finally, of course, this notion of the universe fitted reasonably well with what men could observe with their own eyes.

The fatal weakness in Ptolemy's universe lay in the "reasonably well." By the middle of the 15th Century, Ptolemy's successors had found a number of small errors in his system—discrepancies between what he predicted would happen and what actually seemed to be happening. In order to save the essential features of his universe, they began to introduce minor revisions into it. These came with some frequency, and, as they accumulated, the beautiful simplicity of Ptolemy's original scheme became submerged in a welter of small details. John Milton, in the Eighth Book of *Paradise Lost*, describes the process well:

> *. . . when they come to model Heav'n,*
> *And calculate the Starr; how they will wield*
> *The mightie frame; how build, unbuild, contrive*
> *To save appearances; how gird the Sphear*
> *With Centric and Eccentric scribl'd o'er,*
> *Cycle and Epicycle, Orb in Orb.*

Although the system, with the necessary adjustments, continued to account for everything man saw in the heavens, one Polish astronomer found its complexity offensive. Nicholas Copernicus, a firm believer in the simplicity and economy of nature, began to suspect that there was something fundamentally wrong with a system that required so many "cycles" and "epicycles" to come out even.

He thought about the problem for years, and finally discovered a way to save the elegant simplicity of Ptolemy's original: Copernicus made the sun, rather than the earth, the center of the universe.

Copernicus' book, *On the Revolutions of the Heavenly Bodies*, published in 1543, was an intellectual event of epochal proportions. The theological and psychological consequences of removing the earth from its position at the center of creation were enormous. And yet, in terms of the development of science, Copernicus was essentially a man of the past. By a mighty effort of the imagination he had succeeded in salvaging the traditional view of the universe: his heavenly bodies continued to move in perfect circles at a uniform rate of speed. All that had changed was the position of the two chief components. Although his work became the starting point for nearly all later astronomers, the true revolution in astronomy did not occur until the century after Copernicus' death.

The new astronomy had two essential features: vastly improved methods of observation and far more sophisticated mathematics. In fact, the dazzling success of virtually all the sciences in the 17th Century sprang from this same combination. Just as Bernini, in carving his bust of Louis XIV, observed Louis in action, and combined what he saw with what he thought a king should be, so the great scientists of the 17th Century looked closely at the world of reality and combined what they saw with mathematical logic. What emerged was scientific truth of a wholly new order. The process is clearly revealed in the strange collaboration of two astronomers. One was a Danish nobleman, Tycho Brahe; the other was a German mystic, Johannes Kepler. Their joint careers straddled the 16th and the 17th Centuries.

Tycho Brahe's lifelong passion for astronomy began when he was 14 years old. Observing that an eclipse of the sun had occurred at precisely the

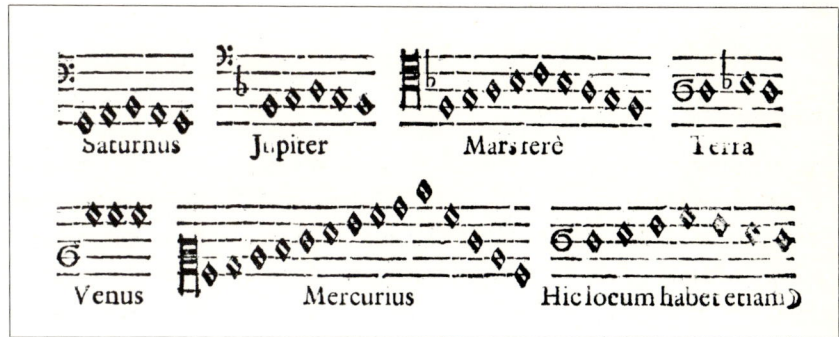

HEAVENLY HARMONIES, *worked out by the astronomer Johannes Kepler, assigned to each of the known planets a musical theme. The faster a planet orbited the sun, the higher its tune—Mars's melody has five different notes; Mercury's, ten. The notation in Latin at lower right reads: "Here is the moon's position."*

moment predicted for it by astronomers, he decided that there was "something divine" about such a science. Although he dutifully studied law and philosophy to please his family, at the same time he was secretly studying the heavens, a pursuit that was soon to make him famous. In 1576 King Frederick II of Denmark, impressed by Tycho's discovery of what seemed to be a "new" star in the constellation of Cassiopeia (it was actually a nova, a dim star that had suddenly become bright), built him a magnificent observatory at Uraniborg. The telescope had not yet been invented, but Uraniborg had "observing apartments," a shop for making instruments, a library and a printing office—all within a castle surrounded by extensive gardens.

From 1576 to his death in 1601, Tycho devoted himself with great singleness of purpose to the monumental task of plotting and describing the motions of every visible body in the heavens. He had a number of instruments, mostly of his own design, that allowed him to do this with unprecedented accuracy—and he approached his work with a remarkably open mind. Most men of his day, believing that the planets moved in perfect circles, felt that it was only necessary to observe them in a few positions in order to calculate their courses. Tycho, however, undertook to follow the course of each planet continuously, night after night, throughout its entire cycle. His observations, noted down in a mass of data, led to the later discovery that the orbits of the planets were elliptical.

In 1588 the Danish King who had been Tycho's patron died, and his successor was not as generous, nor as interested in astronomy. In 1598 Tycho left Denmark for Prague, to become the protégé of Rudolph II, the Holy Roman Emperor. There, in 1600, he was joined in his new observatory by a young assistant, Johannes Kepler. It was Kepler, an eccentric mathematical genius, who fell heir to the product of Tycho's years of patient work, and who shaped his findings into the first modern system of astronomy.

Few great men have exhibited a stranger combination of talent and stubborn wrong-headedness than Johannes Kepler. He was at once a skilled mathematician and a passionate mystic, a distinguished astronomer and an astrologer of popular acclaim. His most imposing discoveries were by-products of his determined search for a cosmic will-o'-the-wisp. Kepler believed with an almost religious fervor in a mystical, mathematical harmony that pervaded the entire universe. He was certain that the position and movement of the planets, if properly understood, held the key to this harmony. With Tycho Brahe's voluminous observations as his raw material, and by using a process of trial and error, Kepler tried for years to crack what he thought of, in effect, as an immensely complex code.

At one time Kepler toyed with the notion that the distances between the six known planets corresponded in some unknown way with the five notes of the ancient Greek musical scale. He was especially fond of this theory because it seemed to bear out the ancient concept of the "music of the spheres." Later, Kepler thought he had found the key to his harmonic universe in a series of occult relationships. He discovered that the space between the plotted courses of any two planets could be filled by one of the classic "Platonic bodies"—the five equal-sided, equal-angled geometrical figures, of which the four-sided pyramid is the simplest and the 20-sided icosahedron is the most complex (the others are the cube, the eight-sided octahedron and the 12-sided dodecahedron). Unfortunately, however, he based this discovery on a mathematical error, and ultimately had to discard it.

Despite his preoccupation with "heavenly harmonies," Kepler's work was of immense significance to modern astronomy. It was Kepler who discovered the three laws of planetary motion that sealed the fate of the old astronomy and opened the way for the new one. The first of these laws, stating that the planets move around the sun not in circles but in ellipses, shattered the idea of "perfect motion." The second law, hardly less revolutionary, stated that the planets do not move around the sun with unvarying velocity, but move more rapidly when their orbits bring them nearer the sun. The third law, as if to vindicate Kepler's belief in a heavenly pattern, held that there is an unvarying mathematical relationship between the distance of the planet from the sun and the time it takes that planet to revolve around the sun. To put it in the elegant economy of mathematics: the square of the time is proportional to the cube of the distance.

The implications of Kepler's three laws were staggering. They demonstrated that the concrete world of matter and the abstract world of mathematics were completely compatible. Out of Tycho Brahe's talent for observation and Kepler's talent for calculation, modern science was born. Soon mankind was to learn what could be achieved when the two talents were united in the person of a single man of surpassing genius.

Galileo Galilei was born in Pisa in 1564, on the very day of the death of Michelangelo, the painter whose work epitomizes the Renaissance. He died in 1642, the same year that saw the birth of Isaac Newton, the scientist whose work was the touchstone of the Enlightenment. The symbolism was singularly appropriate. Galileo's career spanned the first stirrings of modern science and its full flowering.

Galileo was the son of a distinguished musical scholar, Vincenzio Galilei, who intended his son to be a doctor and sent him to study medicine at the University of Pisa. But Galileo had other ideas. Sitting one day in the Cathedral at Pisa, in 1583, he became interested in watching a lamp swinging back and forth at the end of a chain. As he watched, he noticed that no matter how far the lamp swung, each swing seemed to take exactly the same length of time. Fascinated, Galileo went home and began to experiment with pendulums of all sorts, timing their arcs as best he could with the primitive equipment available to him. He discovered that his first impression had indeed been correct: the rhythm of a pendulum is absolutely regular no matter how great its arc. Using this bit of information, he designed a little device with an adjustable pendulum, called a pulsilogium, for doctors to use in taking patients' pulses—out of which in due course came the modern pendulum clock.

Galileo's first discovery reveals many of the gifts that made him such a formidable scientist. Men had always been looking at pendulums of one sort or another, but no one before had ever bothered to notice how they behaved. Galileo not only noticed, but also converted the swinging object's behavior into a generalized rule—and then proved the rule by experiment. Finally, having proved it, he turned his discovery to practical use.

This combination of observation, generalization and application was one side of Galileo's remarkable scientific equipment. The other, and complementary, side was mathematical skill. In the same year that he discovered the law of the pendulum, Galileo was introduced to mathematics by a scholar named Ostilio Ricci. His first glimpse of the subject so enchanted him that he insisted upon becoming Ricci's pupil and his father reluctantly agreed—on the condition that his new lessons were not to interfere with his medical studies. The condition was quite useless. Galileo was soon devoting all his time to mathematics, and in six years had advanced from novice to master. In 1589, at the age of 25, he received an appointment to teach the subject at the University of Pisa.

Unlike Kepler, whose interest in mathematics was abstract and mystical, Galileo looked upon it as a tool to be used in the solution of practical problems—the understanding of the forces of nature. It was, in fact, the most powerful tool that could be imagined. "Philosophy," he wrote (and by "philosophy" he meant science), "is written in this grand book—I mean the universe—which stands continually open to our gaze, but it cannot be understood unless one first learns to comprehend the language and interpret the characters in which it is written. It is written in the language of mathematics, and its characters are triangles, circles, and other geometrical figures, without which it is humanly impossible to understand a single word of it."

In 1592, Galileo left the University of Pisa for the University of Padua, where he remained for 18 years—the happiest years, he was later to say, of his life. Surrounded by friendly colleagues, enjoying at least a modicum of financial security, he plunged into the study of dynamics and astronomy, the two fields which brought him fame—and the unwelcome censures of the Church.

In Padua, following his usual practical bent, Galileo opened a small shop for the design and manufacture of scientific instruments. Among its products were the first crude thermometer, a hollow bulb and tube inverted in water, and a device called "the geometric and military compass," a calibrated gadget for performing mathematical operations. But by far the most important instrument to come out of this shop was Galileo's telescope. A few years before, sometime between 1604 and 1608, Dutch spectacle makers had discovered the trick of putting various lenses together to increase the range of man's vision. But no one had seen a practical use for the discovery until 1609, when word of it reached Galileo.

The same powers of imagination that he had directed upon the swinging lamp now went to work on the magnifying lenses. On August 11, 1609, with considerable fanfare, Galileo presented a model of the world's first astronomical telescope to Padua's rulers, the officials of the Republic of Venice. With it went a letter explaining how useful the instrument would be in time of war, since ships could be seen "two hours before they were seen with the naked eye, steering full-sail into the harbor." The Venetian senate, in gratitude, doubled Galileo's salary at the university and made him a lifetime professor.

Galileo, excited by his first telescopic observations, immediately began to make new and improved versions of his instrument. With these, he set out upon a systematic study of the heavens, and made a series of astonishing and portentous discoveries. On March 12, 1610, he published his first account of them in a little book appropriately entitled *The Starry Messenger*. The *Messenger* announced, among other things, that the Milky Way was a mass of untold thousands of stars, that the planet Jupiter had four satellites (which the opportunistic Galileo, always a little short of cash, tactfully named the "Medicean planets" in the hope of gaining some financial reward from the Medici, the ruling family of Tuscany).

Other discoveries followed, and they all seemed to lead to two inexorable conclusions. One was that Copernicus had been correct in claiming that the planets revolve around the sun. The other was that tradition was mistaken in arguing that there was a difference in the composition of the earth and that of the so-called heavenly bodies. Soon Galileo had formulated the crucial idea that nature was uniform, that all of creation operated in accordance with the same physical laws. If this was so, all of Galileo's discoveries about the behavior of bodies on earth were just as relevant to the behavior of bodies in the heavens. The laws of motion that grew out of such experiments as rolling balls down inclined planes or dropping weights out of towers might be applied with equal accuracy to the motion of the planets. Galileo had found the key that was eventually to unlock the riddle of the universe.

Not surprisingly, his discoveries were not universally welcomed. Defenders of traditional order, particularly theologians—Catholics and Protestants alike—were frightened and angered by Galileo's claims to have actually *seen* many of the things surmised by Copernicus and Kepler. At stake was not simply the truth or falsity of a few astronomical theories, but something much larger. The traditional world order was a carefully interwoven system of thought and belief, so intricately put together that it could only stand or fall as a whole. This magnificent structure, embracing religion, philosophy and science, was now threatened with destruction by one of its parts.

The first counterattack was aimed quite logically at the telescope itself. Was there any reason, Galileo's enemies asked, to suppose that what a man saw through a telescope actually existed?

Might he not be fooled by some optical trick, or by some imperfection in the glass of which the lenses were made? Might not a man just as well look into a kaleidoscope and announce that all the world was a brightly colored chaos?

In one sense, the points were well taken. Galileo himself did not know how the telescope worked; he did not understand the laws of optics. But he had checked the telescope's accuracy by looking through it at distant objects on earth, and then examining those objects close-up. And he was stung by the criticisms. "Nor can it be doubted," he wrote in May 1611, "that I, over a period of two years now, have tested my instrument (or rather dozens of my instruments) by hundreds and thousands of experiments involving thousands and thousands of objects, near and far, large and small, bright and dark; hence I do not see how it can enter the mind of anyone that I have simple-mindedly remained deceived by my observations."

Furthermore, Galileo's observations were soon being substantiated by other astronomers throughout Europe, who were observing through their own telescopes precisely the same things. In 1611 the great Kepler added the weight of his authority: "To you indeed, gentle reader," he wrote in his *Narrative of Personal Observations of the Four Wandering Satellites of Jupiter*, "by this sharing, such as it is, of some scanty and hasty observations with the public, I recommend that either you follow my faith and that of my testimonies, all doubts laid aside, and henceforth know the naked truth; or look forth from a good instrument, which in the present matters brings down to you an eyewitness." Against the weight of such testaments, the arguments of the skeptics became increasingly ineffective.

The second attack against Galileo's findings was more ingenious. It consisted in introducing into the heavens objects that, by definition, could not be seen by the telescope or indeed any other means. Galileo had seen the mountains of the moon, contradicting the traditional belief that the moon was a perfect sphere. Well and good, said a German Jesuit, Father Christopher Clavius, perhaps Galileo's mountains did exist—but they must be covered with some transparent crystalline substance whose outer surface formed a perfect sphere. Father Clavius' theory gallantly tried to reconcile the old belief with the new, and it was of course incontrovertible. Short of actually traveling to the moon, there was no way to contradict it. Galileo gave the only answer possible: "Really, this is a beautiful flight of the imagination. . . . The only thing lacking in it is that it is neither demonstrated nor demonstrable." Furthermore, he added, if he had to admit the existence of the crystalline substance, he would simply claim that it covered the moon in mountains and valleys 10 times higher and deeper than those he had actually seen.

The third, and by far most sinister attack upon Galileo was backed not only by hypothetical arguments but also by the ecclesiastical authority of the Roman Catholic Church. To this was added, in spirit at least, the support of Protestant theologians, who were equally unsympathetic to Galileo's ideas. On February 24, 1616, the Congregation of the Holy Office, the Church's official agency for rooting out heresies, began its assault by condemning the Copernican ideas upon which Galileo based his work. The ideas, it unanimously proclaimed, were "absurd in philosophy, and formally heretical, because expressly contrary to Holy Scripture." Two days later, on explicit instructions from Pope Paul V, Galileo was summoned before the leading Catholic theologian of the century, Robert Cardinal Bellarmine, and informed of the decision of the Holy Office. Bellarmine admonished Galileo to abandon the condemned ideas, and Galileo promised to do so—influenced, no doubt, by the well-

known fact that the Holy Office, better known as the Inquisition, was empowered to use torture and impose the most severe penalties upon those found guilty of heresy.

For years after this warning, Galileo remained silent. He continued to pursue his astronomical studies but, with the exception of one short, relatively unimpressive treatise, did not publish the results. When he finally broke his silence, in 1632, it was to present to the world the greatest of his astronomical writings, the *Dialogue on the Two Chief Systems of the World.* The very form of the book was a challenge to the Church's authority. Instead of being an abstruse monograph, written in Latin and addressed to fellow scholars, it was a lively dialogue written in Italian and intended for the educated public. Ostensibly it was an objective analysis of the contradictory systems of Ptolemy and Copernicus. In fact, Galileo rather gave away the case for even-handed objectivity by naming the spokesman for Ptolemy's position "Simplicio," i.e., simpleton. The *Dialogue* was the most thorough and effective defense of the Copernican system that had ever been written—and the Church was not long in replying.

On September 25, 1632, seven months after the *Dialogue* had been published, Galileo was ordered to appear in Rome for trial as a heretic before the Commissary General of the Holy Office. He tried desperately to avoid the trial, but succeeded only in postponing it. In February of the following year, he arrived in Rome, only to be kept waiting for three months. Finally, between April 12 and June 21 he was repeatedly interrogated by the Holy Office—although apparently never tortured. On June 22 he was taken to the great hall of the Dominican convent of Santa Maria Sopra Minerva (a Christian church built upon the site of a temple to the Roman goddess of wisdom) and there sentenced before the Congregation of the Holy Office.

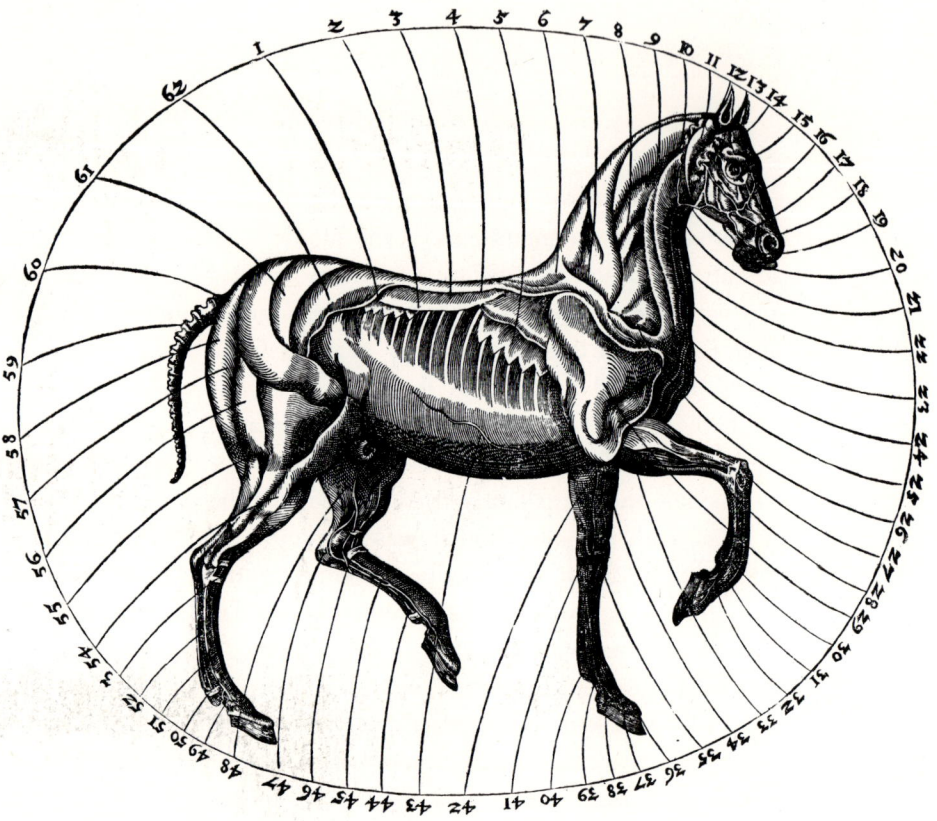

EQUINE ANATOMY, *drawn for an early 17th Century manual on horsemanship, bares 62 bones, muscles and veins as an aid to grooms in the care of sick or injured horses. The study of anatomy, both animal and human, made great progress in this century.*

The *Dialogue* was ordered suppressed and its author, "vehemently suspected of heresy," imprisoned. After being sentenced, Galileo was compelled to kneel and recant:

"I, Galileo, son of the late Vincenzio Galilei of Florence, my age being seventy years, . . . do swear that I have always believed, do now believe, and with God's aid shall believe hereafter all that which is taught and preached by the Holy Catholic and Apostolic Church. But because, after I had received a precept which was lawfully given to me that I must wholly forsake the false opinion that the sun is the center of the world and moves not, and that the earth is not the center of the world and moves, and that I might not hold, defend, or teach the said false doctrine in any manner . . . I wrote and published a book in which the said condemned doctrine was treated, and gave very effective reasons in favor of it without suggesting any solution, I am by this Holy Office judged vehemently suspect of heresy; that is, of having held and believed that the sun is the center of the world and immovable, and that the earth is not its center and moves; Therefore . . . I do abjure, damn, and detest the said errors and heresies . . . and I do swear for the future that I shall never again speak or assert, orally or in writing, such things as might bring me under similar suspicion. . . ."

Legend says that after this abject recitation, Galileo rose from his knees, stamped his foot upon the earth that "moved not" and muttered to himself, "Eppur si muove!"—"And yet, it does move!" Whether or not Galileo actually spoke them, the words were an apt commentary on the futility of attempting to stop the new science by the sheer weight of authority. The hard facts of nature and the exuberant intellectual climate of the day doomed any such enterprise to failure. In fact, not even Galileo himself kept silent. In the last years of his life, despite being confined by house arrest, he produced the most influential of all his books, *Discourses on Two New Sciences*, in which, skirting the controversial issue of astronomy, he set down the result of his studies of motion and the structure of matter.

However harsh Galileo's punishment, other men all over Europe were prepared to carry on the great work to which he had devoted his life. In fact, right from the beginning the new science had been remarkably international. Galileo's discoveries had rested upon those of a Pole, a Dane and a German. Now, as the century progressed, the flow of information increased. Virtually every country in Europe was producing scientists of talent, and the work of each one was being strengthened by communication among them all. A true community of scientists had come into existence, too powerful to be resisted by any traditional institution.

While Galileo, in Italy, was revolutionizing astronomy with his observations, in England, Francis Bacon, although not himself an important scientist, was vigorously publicizing the scientific method. Bacon's two chief books, the *Advancement of Learning* and the *Novum Organum*, preached the virtue of "long and close intercourse with experiments and particulars," and warned against hasty theories and facile generalizations. His emphasis upon sticking close to the concrete results of experiment came to be called empiricism. Unhappily, Bacon himself became a martyr to his own scientific curiosity. Driving in the country one winter day in 1626, he stopped his carriage to gather some snow, with which he proposed to stuff a chicken to see if it would keep the bird from spoiling. In the process he caught a chill, and died.

Bacon's ideas became the dominant force in English science, influencing, among others, Robert Boyle, the author of Boyle's Law and the father of modern chemistry. Boyle was so ardent a champion of empiricism that he refused for many years to read *Novum Organum*, fearing that he might prefer to accept Bacon's conclusions about heat and cold instead of discovering his own. In his most famous book, the *Sceptical Chymist*, Boyle observed contemptuously, "It has long seemed to me . . . [that not] the least impediment . . . [to] the real advancement of true natural philosophy [is] that men have been so forward to write systems of it." His own conclusions about the behavior of gases, from which he formulated his famous Law, were the result of patient observation and experiment.

Even when applied to living things, the methods of the new science were rewarding.

One of the classic examples of early biological inquiry is William Harvey's discovery of the circulation of the blood. Harvey was an English doctor, physician to two English Kings, James I and Charles I. His discovery helped to clarify what had been, before his time, a hopeless jumble of information about the nature and behavior of blood. According to the most popular theory of the day, blood was continuously manufactured in the liver for delivery to the heart, which pumped it out to be absorbed by all parts of the body. During its passage through the heart, the blood was thought to mix with "vital spirits" from the air. These "vital spirits" supposedly moved from the lungs to the heart through the same passage at the same time that the blood moved from the heart to the lungs. In other words, the two somehow passed each other, moving in opposite directions.

With a few simple calculations, Harvey proved that this theory was absurd. The heart ventricle, with a capacity of two ounces and a beat of 72 strokes a minute, pumped in one hour 8,640 ounces of blood—or 540 pounds. If all this blood was being newly manufactured, it meant that a man's body was creating and absorbing in one hour something like three times its total weight. This was so obviously ridiculous that Harvey felt sure there was another explanation. In 1628 he made a dramatic announcement: "When I surveyed my mass of evidence, whether derived from vivisections, and my various reflections on them, or from the ventricles of the heart . . . . I began to think whether there might not be *a motion, as it were, in a circle.* Now this I afterwards found to be true."

Harvey's faith in the scientific method, in the irresistible logic of his observations and measurements, was as strong as other men's faith in religion. He believed that the blood must pass from the arteries to the veins, even though he could not explain how such a passage occurred. Four years after his death in 1657 his hypothesis was confirmed by the discovery of the capillaries, the tiny passageways that complete the circuit. Marcello Malpighi, who made the discovery, did so with a microscope—the other great technical invention of the age. Thus the sciences moved forward together to perfect man's knowledge.

As with Galileo, however, it remained for a single man of genius to pull together all the strands of the new science, and from them create a new theory of the universe. "I do not know what I may appear to the world," said Isaac Newton shortly before he died, "but to myself I seem to have been only like a boy playing on the seashore, and diverting myself in now and then finding a smoother pebble or a prettier shell than ordinary, while the great ocean of truth lay all undiscovered before me." In fact, it was Newton who did more than any other man to explore that ocean of truth. Putting together experimentation, mathematical skill and theoretical boldness, Newton found the missing link that tied together the parts of the physical world into an ordered whole: the Law of Universal Gravitation.

Newton's experiments in optics and his invention of the calculus were scientific contributions of the highest order, but it was his formulation of the law of gravity that truly ushered in the age of modern science. Building upon the discoveries of his predecessors, Newton went beyond mere description of the order of the heavens to lay down, in precise mathematical terms, the explanation of why the earth and planets are where they are, and why they move as they do. The law of gravity accounts for everything from the falling of an apple to the earth to the revolution of the planets in the heavens.

From Newton's all-embracing synthesis sprang a new era of intellectual history, the Enlightenment. Men began to sense a new kind of coherence in the universe, one built upon reason rather than religion and open to discovery through the human intelligence. If ancient errors could be discarded, if the weight of traditional authority could be removed, men might be able to find the answers to questions that had plagued them all through history. In England, Thomas Hobbes, in his *Leviathan,* had already tried to prove by scientific means that men should obey their rulers, thus permitting kings to reign without recourse to the doctrine of divine right. In the Netherlands, Baruch Spinoza had written *Ethics Demonstrated in the Geometric Manner,* in which he considered "human actions and desires in exactly the same manner as though I were concerned with lines, planes and solids." Science was being applied not just to the study of nature, but to the study of human societies.

But the results of all this in practical terms were still a century away. Human society, in the 17th Century, was ordered not by logic but by the dictates of kings. When Louis XIV put his seal upon what was right or wrong in the cultural life of France, he did so not out of any concern to improve human society but for one simple reason: to glorify the Sun King.

Combining the cosmological discoveries of his era with the obvious fact that things fall down, this Cambridge astronomy professor developed a scientific theory that shook his world. Closely reasoned and expressed in clear-cut formulas, his theory of gravitation, based on his laws of moving bodies, was a classic example of the scientific method. One of Newton's geometric figures (below) shows in essence how the gravitational attractions of the sun (Q) and the earth (S) act together to maintain the moon (P) in its orbit. Newton also demonstrated the many-colored nature of white light, devised the reflecting telescope, and invented a form of calculus so offhandedly that he neglected to publish this basic mathematical tool for years. At 56 he took up a new career as Master of the Mint, where he reformed Britain's coinage system.

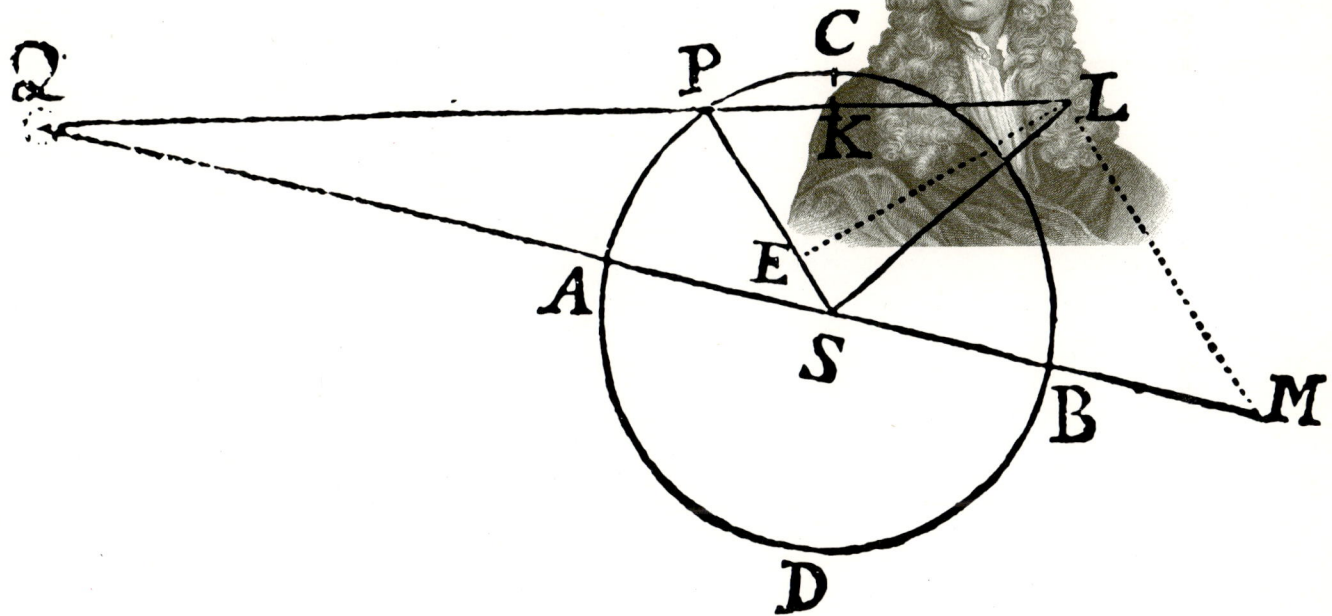

THE NEW SCIENTISTS

In the 17th Century men of many talents were scrutinizing the material world with new instruments and probing minds. Microscopists like Leeuwenhoek and Malpighi peered for the first time at life's tiny organisms; astronomers like Hevelius and Halley penetrated far into the vastness of the sky. In the course of their observations, the new scientists—or "virtuosos" as some of them called themselves—discovered basic laws of physics, optics, geology, astronomy and biology. Their pragmatic, experimental attitude toward nature, their methods and their achievements—culminating in Newton's brilliant exposition of universal gravitation—were to dominate Western scientific thinking for the next 200 years.

ANTON VAN LEEUWENHOEK, 1632-1723

An untutored shopkeeper of Delft, the Dutchman Leeuwenhoek awed his contemporaries by the discoveries he made with his skillfully crafted microscopes. He investigated everything from the open cells that carry sap through trees (below, right) to his own saliva, in which he discovered bacteria. He was a prized correspondent of England's Royal Society, and among the things he first saw and described were red blood corpuscles, spermatozoa and protozoa. His simple microscopes, only 2 inches high, were all basically the same (below): a single, tiny lens set between two metal plates, with an adjustable specimen mount. The wonder was in the lenses—Leeuwenhoek ground them himself—and in the beholder's remarkable eyes and mind; though he left many microscopes, no one else ever saw such fine detail through them—and few other men would risk blindness as he did to watch gunpowder explode an inch or two away.

ROBERT HOOKE, 1635-1703

A mechanical genius, and the Royal Society's Curator of Experiments for 41 years, Robert Hooke made many improvements in the instruments of his time. The ingenious device shown in his own engraving at left, above, concentrated light on the viewing area of his double-lensed microscopes, one of which is shown in the photograph. The lamplight shone through a water-filled globe and was focused onto the specimen by a convex lens.

For his classic "Micrographia," published in 1665, Hooke magnified and engraved many specimens, including the eye of a fly (enlargement, left), which shows the reflection of two windows of Hooke's study in each tiny lens. The exquisite standards set by this volume —Hooke was trained by the portraitist Peter Lely—were unsurpassed in illustrations of the infinitely small until the advent of photography. It was the first treatise to apply the word "cell" to natural tissue and the first to give a correct definition of combustion.

Hooke also invented the wheel barometer, the simple string telephone, the diaphragm lens shutter and the universal joint, and enunciated the law of elasticity named after him. As an active surveyor and architect, he worked with Christopher Wren to rebuild London after the Great Fire, and designed such buildings as the College of Physicians and Bedlam Hospital.

BLAISE PASCAL, 1623-1662

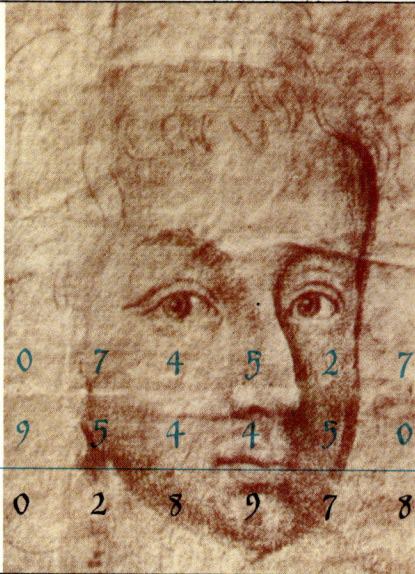

Philosopher, mathematician, physicist, mechanic, the Frenchman Pascal shone in many fields during his short life. When he was only 19, he devised the calculating machine below to avoid the drudgery of bookkeeping for his tax-collector father. The figures are entered by turning the telephonelike dials; connecting gears transmit diminishing fractional turns to the next wheel at the left, and rotate spools giving the results at the top.

```
  3 0 7 4 5 2 7 6
+ 3 9 5 4 4 5 0 8
─────────────────
  7 0 2 8 9 7 8 4
```

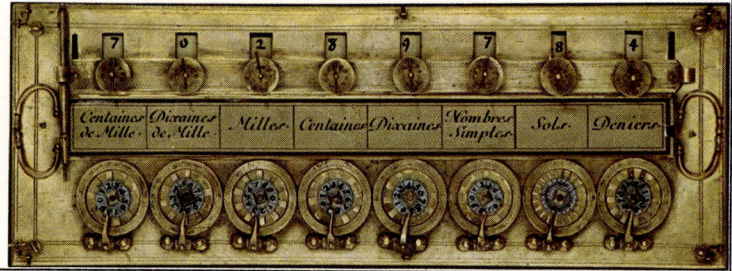

OTTO VON GUERICKE, 1602-1686

Another inspired amateur, and mayor of his native Magdeburg for 35 years, von Guericke used an air pump and two bronze hemispheres (below) to illustrate atmospheric pressure. In a dramatic demonstration before the Imperial Diet at Regensburg in 1654, von Guericke fitted his hemispheres tightly together, pumped as much air as he could out of them and hitched an eight-horse team to each side. Though the teams pulled their hardest, atmospheric pressure held the globe together; when the valve was opened, the two halves fell apart. Von Guericke also investigated electricity, and in 1660 made the first rotating generator.

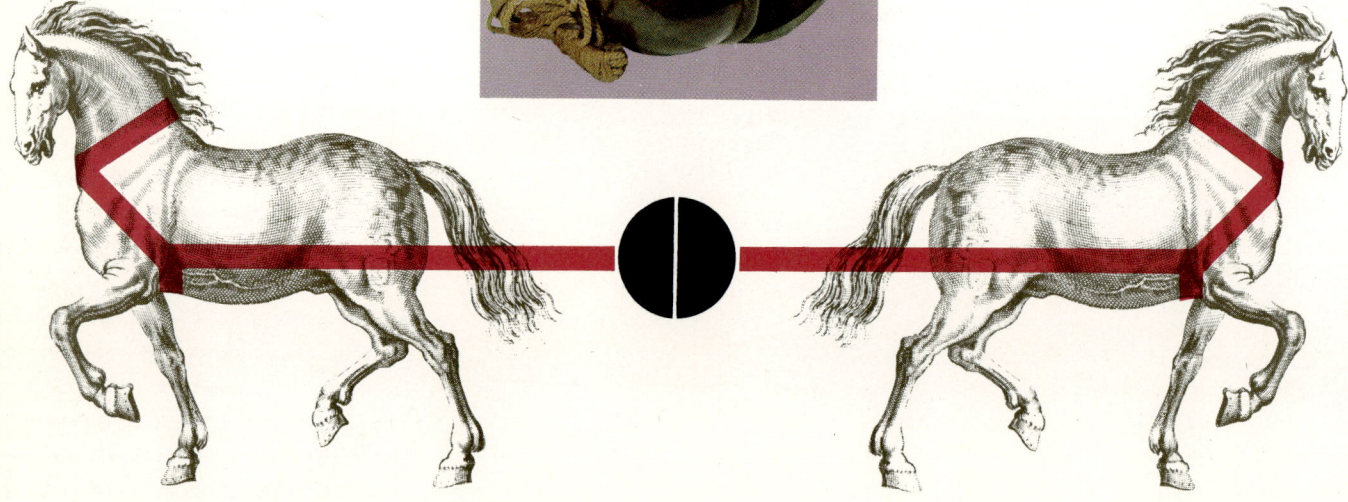

This Dutch astronomer and mathematician, who discovered Saturn's rings, published his first designs for precise pendulum clocks (below) in 1658. Dissatisfied with their accuracy, he continued experimenting and the following year demonstrated—with the instrument shown at bottom right—that the circular arc of the pendulum's swing should be controlled by curved stops, seen at the top of his device. To achieve this, he placed "cheeks" near the pendulum's pivot point, as can be seen on the back of the clock pictured at right.

TAB. I.

NICOLAUS STENO, 1638-1687

While practicing medicine in Florence in 1669, a widely traveled Danish physician and theologian named Niels Stensen—better known by the Latinized name above—founded a new science: geology. He described the formation of sedimentary rock and recognized the origin of fossils. In the colored diagram below, the primary rock layers shade upward from reddish brown for the earliest to yellow for the most recent; they are overlain by a later, secondary series whose time sequence is indicated in tones of purple to light blue. Steno—whose numbered diagrams start with the newest formation and work back to the earliest—showed the original layers of sediment (figure 25) hollowed out by underground waters (24) and finally collapsing (23), a common occurrence in limestone country like Tuscany. Figure 22 shows new deposits building up in the resulting basin, and figures 21 and 20 repeat the events shown in 24 and 23.

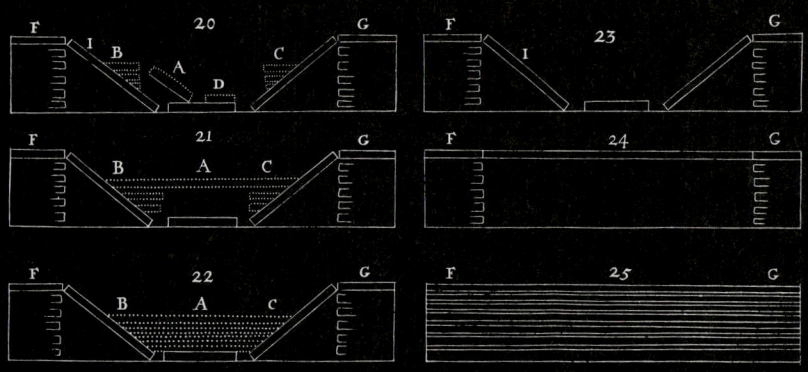

Renowned as the discoverer of capillary circulation in the lungs and the founder of microscopic anatomy, Malpighi, an Italian physician and professor of anatomy, also turned his microscope on the world of plants. In his botanical investigations, he proved that a tree's age can be determined by counting the rings in a cross section of its trunk (top) and he was the first to see other details of plant structure, such as the network (E, F and G in the engraving below the tree rings) that surrounds the long vertical fibers of the wood.

Following Harvey's discovery of the heart's role in blood circulation, Malpighi completed the cycle by discovering the capillary vessels that connect the arteries to the veins. His meticulous engraving (bottom) of the network of blood vessels in a frog's lungs, illustrating his observations, was published in 1660. He also studied secreting glands, and discovered the Malpighian, or generative, layer of the skin.

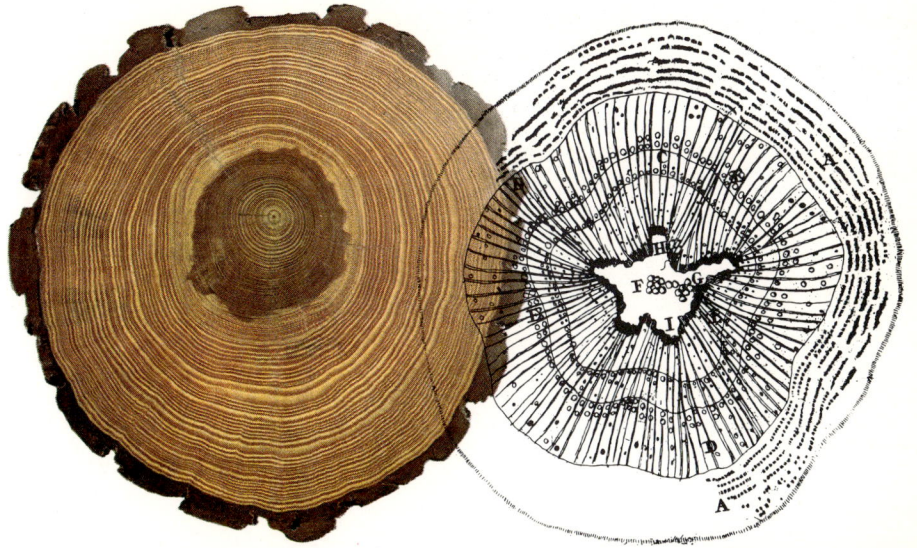

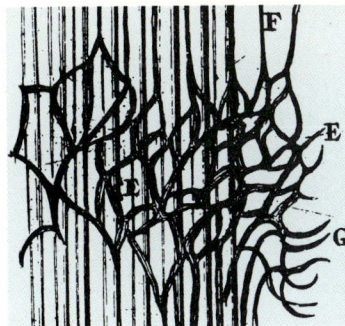

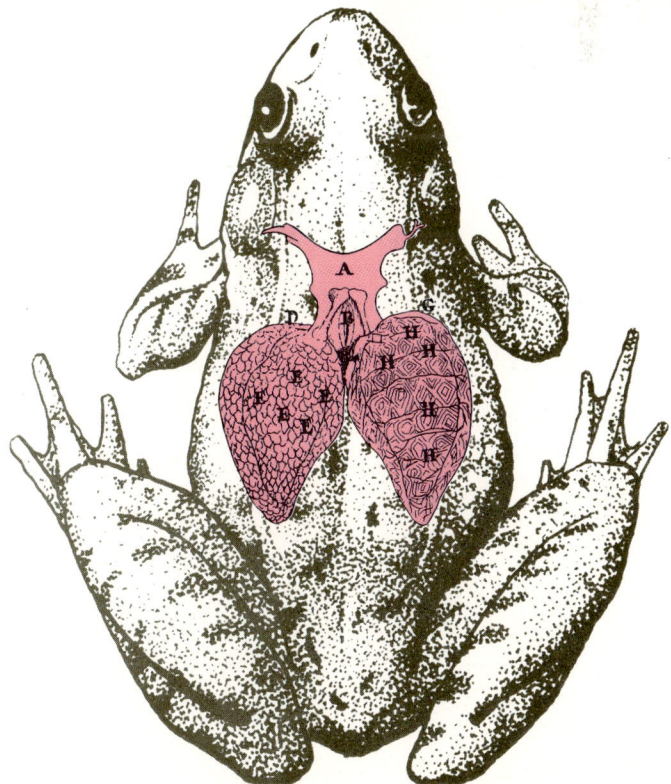

A wealthy amateur astronomer of Danzig, Hevelius designed and built the most elaborate observatory in all Europe (below), on the roof of his palatial home. Long, open, many-lensed telescopes were assembled in the attic and raised through slots uncovered in the roof; here they were rigged to a tower to be moved as desired by pulleys and rotating arms that were controlled by the intricate mechanism shown in the four small diagrams. As a result of his observations, Hevelius in 1647 published "Selenographia," a study of the moon, from which the two engravings at right are reproduced. The upper diagram shows the various phases of the moon—the sunlit portions visible as it moves around the earth. Below this diagram is a finely detailed topographical map of the waxing crescent moon, one of the many that Hevelius recorded with great accuracy and exquisitely engraved himself.

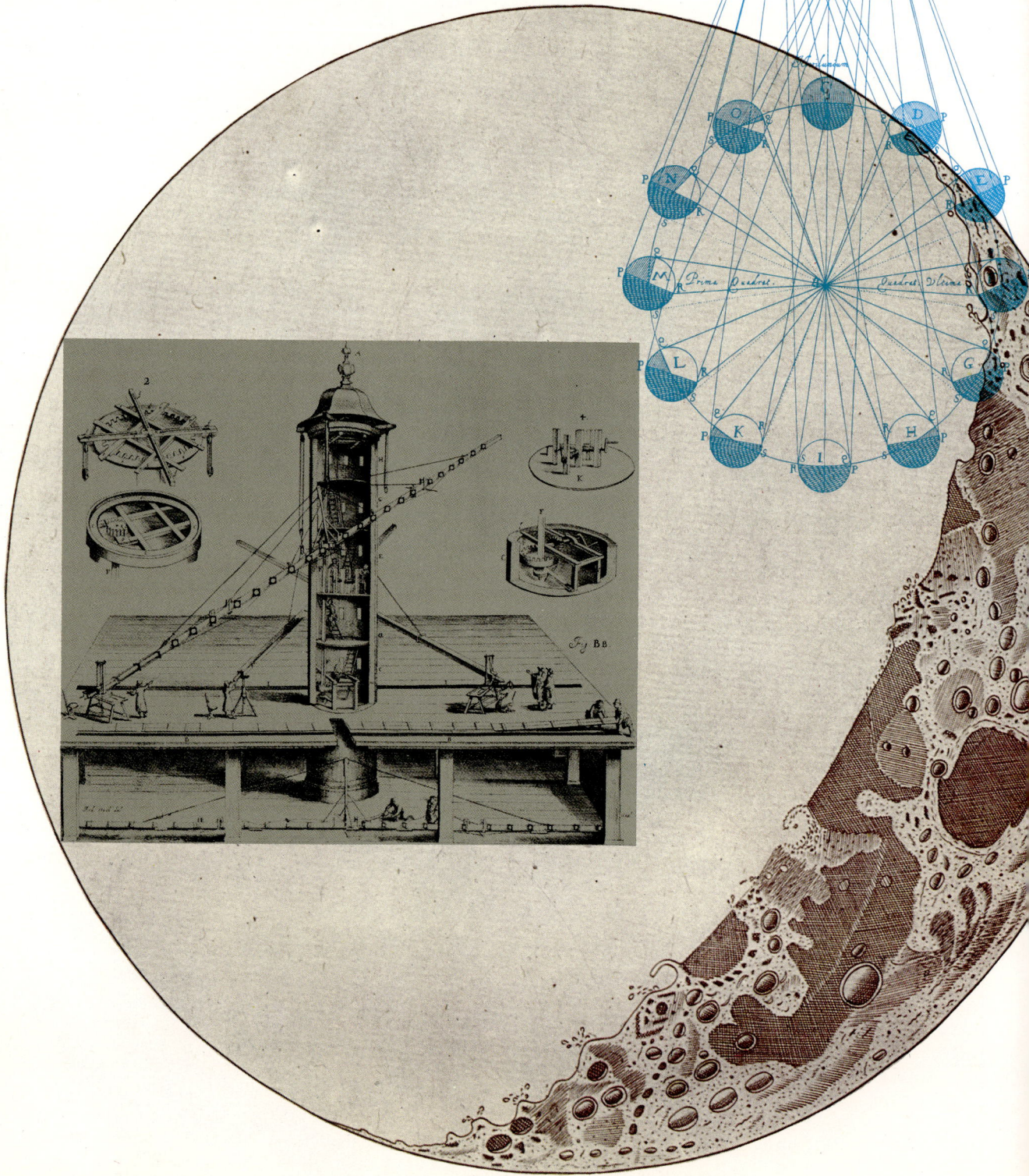

EDMUND HALLEY, 1656-1742

The British astronomer and meteorologist Halley is best known because he accurately predicted the return of the great comet of 1682 that now bears his name. He foretold not only that it would come back in 1758, but also that it would appear in the sector of the sky assigned to the zodiacal sign Aquarius, the Water Bearer (below, right). His prediction, which astounded his contemporaries, was based on his periodic table of comets (superimposed on his portrait below).

Halley charted some 350 stars of the southern skies, collected meteorological data which he included in the first map of the trade winds, and published the first magnetic chart. A modest man, Halley felt that his most important contribution was none of these, but the fact that he had persuaded his idol and mentor, Isaac Newton, to publish his work on motion and gravitation, which Halley also financed.

6

PATTERNS OF REASON

The 17th Century's search for order found its supreme fulfillment in the France of Louis XIV. In one of those mysterious moments in history when all of man's endeavors seem to come together to create a new style of life, the separate elements of French culture merged under Louis to create what Frenchmen still call *Le Grand Siècle*, The Great Century. The arts, the sciences, philosophy and manners—each contributed to the synthesis and each was transformed by it; the whole was somehow greater than the sum of its parts. The Great Century stands, with Periclean Athens and Elizabethan England, as one of the high points in Western civilization.

The setting for this new style was provided by Louis' absolute monarchy, and the Sun King was its symbol and guiding spirit. But the intellectual force that gave it unity and coherence came from the philosophy of one of the most influential thinkers of all time: René Descartes.

Cartesian thought was perfectly suited to the needs and temper of the times. Boldly, and with a considerable degree of arrogance, Descartes proposed to sweep away the whole of traditional learning and opinion. In its place would be erected a new system of knowledge, founded upon the techniques of the new science. It would embrace every aspect of reality and leave no room for doubt or confusion; truth alone would prevail and men would be governed by reason. Just as science was bringing order to the physical world, so Descartes proposed to bring order to thought itself. The result was nothing less than a revolution in the intellectual life of Western man.

For all this stress upon order and clarity, Descartes' own life was a mass of contradictions. The father of modern philosophy fits none of the stereotypes of what a philosopher is or how he should behave. Instead of burying himself in books, he spent much of his youth wandering around Europe. He served briefly in the army of Protestant Netherlands and then, after the outbreak of the Thirty Years' War, joined the Catholic army of Maximilian of Bavaria. In 1628 he shifted again, this time to the royal army of France, where he became a master of horsemanship and fencing—and is said to have fought a duel over a woman.

A GEOMETRICAL LANDSCAPE, *this French engraver's plan for an ornate garden reflects the 17th Century's craze for symmetry and order. Schemes almost as fanciful were used to design Louis XIV's elegant gardens at Versailles.*

Despite all this youthful activity, Descartes was essentially a lazy man. He read as little as possible and preferred to do his thinking while lying in bed. In a letter to Princess Elizabeth, daughter of the ill-fated Elector Palatine, he wrote that his guiding principle, "which I have always observed in my studies, and which I believe has helped me most to gain what knowledge I have, has been never to spend beyond a few hours daily in thoughts which occupy the imagination, and very few hours yearly in those which occupy the understanding, and to give all the rest of my time to the relaxation of the senses and the repose of the mind."

In search of this relaxation and repose, in 1628, when he was 32 years old, Descartes left France for the Netherlands—where the conditions of life were less distracting. "I sleep here 10 hours every night," he wrote from Amsterdam, "and no care ever shortens my slumber. . . . I take my walk every day through the confusion of a great multitude with as much freedom and quiet as you could find on your rural avenues." But the privacy did not last; during his 20 years in the Netherlands, Descartes lived in no fewer than 24 houses in 13 cities. Wherever he went, his friends seemed to find him and disturb his meditations by routing him out of bed as early as 11 o'clock in the morning. Worse was to follow.

In 1645, Queen Christina of Sweden, the brilliant and headstrong daughter of Gustavus Adolphus, heard about the eminent philosopher through the French ambassador to her court, and was determined to lure him to Stockholm. (Christina, not yet 20, was to shock all Europe a decade later by becoming a Catholic, renouncing her throne, and taking up residence in Rome.) The young Queen and the eminent philosopher exchanged letters and treatises on such things as love and passion, and before long, Christina issued her invitation. Descartes hesitated. Now 53, and secure in his own way of life, he had no intention of giving up his hard-won comfort and solitude. But he reckoned without Christina's strong will. The invitation was urgently repeated, seconded by the French ambassador. Finally, in September 1649, a Swedish warship appeared in the harbor of Amsterdam to carry home the prize. Unable to withstand the pressure, Descartes succumbed.

Winter in Stockholm is fairly bleak even in the best of circumstances. For Descartes, who loved warmth—and who was to puzzle posterity by announcing that he had made his most important philosophical discovery while sitting "in a stove" —it was a disaster. No sooner had he settled down to pursue his work than the young Queen announced that she wished to be tutored in philosophy. The only hour she could spare for the purpose was 5 o'clock in the morning. Bidding goodbye to the days of luxurious meditation in a warm bed, Descartes rose, instead, in the icy blackness of predawn and made his way through the snow to the royal palace. It was more than he could bear. Within five months of his arrival in Stockholm, Descartes was dead of pneumonia.

This grotesque end cut short a life of extraordinary intellectual achievement. Despite his notorious indolence—which may have been as much a pose as a reality—Descartes was one of the world's greatest mathematicians, as well as a serious student of physics, optics and physiology. No discovery of the 17th Century did more to confirm men's belief in the ultimate unity of the natural world and the abstract world of mathematics than Descartes' invention of what came to be known as coordinate geometry. With coordinates—numerical points of reference—it was possible to plot an algebraic equation as a curve on a graph, and conversely to translate a curve into an algebraic equation. Physical reality, in other words, could be reduced to a mathematical abstraction.

Descartes himself proceeded to regard everything in nature, with the exception of man's mind, as a mechanism. He proposed to strip the physical world down to its bare essentials: matter (which, to him, was anything that had "extension" in space) and motion. "Give me extension and motion," he boasted, "and I will construct the universe." It was a cold, formal universe, a geometrical universe in which nothing was permitted to happen by chance. Only human thought was free, because only the mind, or soul, was not governed by physical laws. Descartes' own system of logic should have led him to conclude, therefore, that the mind had no material existence. But he could not go this far. Instead, he decided that the mind must have an existence of sorts—that it was connected in some mysterious way with the pineal gland, a small organ at the base of the brain that in Descartes' day was thought to exist in man alone, and must therefore be the seat of reason.

It is typical of Descartes, the least scholarly of philosophers, that his most profound ideas should be presented in the form of a brief, gracefully written essay. The "Discourse on Method," published in 1637, is a kind of informal intellectual autobiography. In it, Descartes describes how he arrived at the method of reasoning that is still associated with his name. He begins by observing, rather slyly, that reason, or good sense, must be the most evenly distributed of all human gifts, since no man complains of having too little. This being so, the differences in men's intellectual attainments must result from the *way* they think rather than from any difference in their natural endowment. "My present design," he says modestly, "is not to teach the method which each ought to follow for the right conduct of his reason, but simply to describe the way in which I have endeavored to conduct my own."

First, he explains his dissatisfaction with everything he had learned from books and scholars.

Then he goes back to the momentous day in 1619 when he discovered the fundamental principle of his own method. "I was then in Germany," he writes, "attracted thither by the wars in that country, which have not yet been brought to an end; and as I was returning to the army from the coronation of the Emperor, the coming of winter forced me to stop in a place where, as I found no society to interest me, and was also fortunately undisturbed by any cares or passions, I remained the whole day in a stove, with ample opportunity to devote all my attention to my own thoughts."

The thoughts that occupied his attention in the stove—which may have been simply a heated room —centered on the question of what man knows, and how he knows it. Is there, Descartes pondered, anything of which man can be absolutely certain? If one systematically doubted everything, would there be one thing that survived all doubt? Meditating upon these questions, Descartes was led to conclude that all the conventional sources of man's knowledge were unreliable. The writings of ancient scholars, traditionally the fount of wisdom, obviously contradicted one another at every turn. The evidence of the senses was equally deceptive —witness such things as dreams, optical illusions and hallucinations. Even reason was far from infallible, as any man who had ever made an error in arithmetic knew.

Having doubted everything, Descartes was left with one thing that he could not doubt: his own existence. "While I wanted to think everything false," he writes, in the most famous passage in modern philosophy, "it was absolutely necessary that I, who was thinking thus, must be something. . . . *I think, therefore I am.*" So solid and certain was this knowledge, Descartes continued, that "I judged that I could accept it without scruple as the first principle of the philosophy I sought."

Upon this single unassailable premise Descartes

constructed his entire philosophical system. Resolving to accept nothing as true except "what was presented to my mind, so clearly and distinctly as to exclude all grounds for doubt," he found that by reason alone he could rebuild the structure of knowledge. As one clear and distinct idea succeeded another, gradually the whole universe and all its parts took shape in his mind. It was a universe of truly mathematical order, without conflict, without mystery. In place of the traditional Christian idea of a God known through love, Descartes proved God's existence through cold and perfect reason. "When I returned to my idea of a perfect Being . . . I discovered that existence was included in that idea in the same way that the idea of a triangle contains the equality of its angles to two right angles, or that the idea of a sphere includes the equidistance of all its parts from its center. Perhaps, in

fact, the existence of a perfect Being is even more evident. Consequently, it is at least as certain that God, who is the perfect Being, exists as any theorem of geometry could possibly be."

More than anything else, it was Descartes' certainty that won him so many eager disciples, first in France and then all over Europe. In a gesture of real intellectual magnificence, he had seized upon the very doubts that tormented his contemporaries and had made them the basis of his philosophical system. Then he had gone on to demonstrate how doubt could lead to unquestionable truth. After generations of religious conflict and philosophical dispute, Descartes promised answers that all reasonable men could accept. The key was clarity of thought and impeccable logic.

A century later, Descartes was to become one of the public heroes of the Enlightenment, but even in his own day he was by no means a philosopher's philosopher. Any literate man or woman could follow and appreciate his lucid, simply written arguments, and many did. In fact, Cartesian thought had its greatest impact upon an audience of amateurs, rather than upon professional scholars. Inevitably, in this process, it lost much of its subtlety and technical brilliance. Reduced to a number of catch phrases such as "systematic doubt" and "clear and distinct ideas," and to an unbounded faith in the power of reason, Cartesian thought passed into the popular domain as "the geometric spirit."

The geometric spirit dominated the intellectual and artistic life of France in the second half of the 17th Century. One of its most faithful advocates was Bernard Le Bovier de Fontenelle, who lived to be 100 and was one of the favorite philosophers of the French court. Fontenelle's graceful treatises on scientific subjects, written in the form of "digressions" and "conversations," helped to explain to fashionable ladies such matters as Copernican theory. Of the geometric spirit, Fontenelle observed that it improved almost anything to which it was applied, being "not so attached to geometry that it cannot be disentangled and carried over into other areas of knowledge. A work on morals, on politics, on criticism, perhaps even on eloquence, will be better, all other things being equal, if it is written by the hand of a geometer."

Under the impact of this new spirit, a new style of art emerged. The grandeur of Baroque still remained, and so did the emotional content and the technical virtuosity. But these were now contained within orderly, disciplined forms. Just as the French King had tamed his rebellious nobles and bent them to his will, so French artists tamed the human passions and presented them in a lucid, rational style. Many of the elements of the new style were Classical in origin, and the style came in fact to be called Classicism.

Like all major stylistic changes, this one occurred gradually, over a period of at least a generation. If a moment could be picked when the balance shifted from an art of movement and tension to one of order and clarity, that moment would probably be when Louis XIV rejected Bernini's plan for the rebuilding of the Louvre. The winning design, submitted by two Frenchmen, Claude Perrault and Louis Le Vau, was a model of Classical regularity and proportion. Its chaste fluted columns, simple, evenly spaced windows and severe angular pediments had almost nothing in common with the ornate and complex design submitted by Bernini. Louis' rejection of the Italian architect, the greatest Baroque artist of the day, also marks the moment when the artistic supremacy of Europe passed from Rome to Paris.

The most spectacular example of the new style was unquestionably Versailles, the royal palace designed for Louis by Le Vau and his successor, Jules Hardouin Mansart. Somber and symmetrical on the outside, richly sumptuous on the inside, Versailles creates the impression of enormous vitality held in check by a rational and stable order. Nothing could have symbolized more perfectly the lifework of the Sun King.

Under Louis' watchful eye, every aspect of French culture was to be governed by elaborate rules. The French language, for example, was finally codified during Louis' reign with the publication of the great French dictionary. This work, prepared by the "Forty Immortals," the members of the French Academy, was begun in 1638—a year after René Descartes published his "Discourse on Method." It took 56 years to complete. The Academy's lengthy deliberations prompted one wit to write:

Six months they've been engaged on F;
Oh, that my fate will guarantee
That I should keep alive to G.

A POET'S CALL TO ORDER

The arbiter of literary taste during the reign of Louis XIV was the court poet Nicolas Boileau, a champion of reason and restraint. Some samples of his pithy advice to writers, from *The Art of Poetry*, appear below.

Most writers mounted on a resty muse,
Extravagant and senseless objects choose;
They think they err, if in their verse they fall
On any thought that's plain or natural.
Fly this excess; and let Italians be
Vain authors of false glittering poetry.

All that is needless carefully avoid;
The mind once satisfied is quickly cloyed.

Take time for thinking; never work in haste;
And value not yourself for writing fast;
A rapid poem, with such fury writ,
Shows want of judgment, not abounding wit.

Polish, repolish, every color lay,
And sometimes add, but oftener take away.

Choose not your tale of accidents too full,
Too much variety may make it dull.
Achilles' rage alone, when wrought with skill,
Abundantly does a whole Iliad fill.

Your actors must by reason be controlled;
Let young men speak like young, old men like old.
Observe the town and study well the court,
For thither various characters resort.

Choose a sure judge to censure what you write,
Whose reason leads, and knowledge gives you light.

Let not your only business be to write;
Be virtuous, just, and in your friends delight.
'Tis not enough your poems be admired,
But strive your conversation be desired.

The Academy's famous dictionary was far more than a simple listing of words with their derivations and meanings. It was a selective catalog of *proper* words and expressions. Colloquialisms, slang, usages that seemed grotesque or too vivid were rigidly excluded. The dictionary was an attempt—and a remarkably successful one—to refine and mold the French language.

What the Academy did for language, the poet Nicolas Boileau did for letters. Boileau was one of the Four Friends, *la Société des Quatre Amis*, the most famous literary figures of the day; the others were the poet La Fontaine and the playwrights Racine and Molière. Boileau was probably the least gifted of the four, but he was much admired by the King. When first summoned to read his works at court, Boileau had wisely elected to recite some hitherto unpublished lines honoring The Grand Monarch. "Remember," said the pleased King, "I have always an hour a week for you when you care to come."

With Louis' active support, Boileau became the supreme arbiter of French literary taste. A true follower of Descartes, he worshiped reason and undertook to make literature conform to its rules. "Love reason, then," he told his contemporaries in *The Art of Poetry*, "that your writings may always draw from her alone both their splendor and their worth." From the moment of its publication in 1674, the book imposed the Classical virtues of order, simplicity and restraint upon French literature.

It is customary to believe that creativity and order are somehow contradictory, that art inevitably suffers when subjected to rules and regulations and official patronage. In the case of 17th Century France, quite the opposite was true; French culture flourished under Louis XIV as never before or since. Apparently, under the right circumstances, discipline of style and taste can stimulate an artist, challenging him to reach new heights of accomplishment. "Imagination in a Poet," said John Dryden, the first great English exponent of the new Classical style, "is a faculty so Wild and Lawless, that, like a High-ranging Spaniel it must have cloggs tied to it, lest it out-run the Judgement. . . . But certainly that which most regulates the Fancy, and gives the Judgement its busiest Employment, is likely to bring forth the richest and clearest Thoughts."

Racine, the French playwright whose tragic dramas are the culmination of the great era of French tragedy, wrote his plays in strict accordance with Boileau's rules—and yet they are plays of the most intense and concentrated emotion. Unlike the works of Shakespeare, which roam over improbable distances of time and place, Racine's dramas observe the so-called "Classical unities." Each play deals with a single action, taking place in a single locality, within the confines of a single day. Again unlike Shakespeare, who dilutes even his greatest tragedies with interludes of comedy or gentle lyricism, Racine keeps his tragedy pure. All his characters are regal or noble, all the language is lofty, all the behavior is of aristocratic society.

With nothing left to focus upon except the inner life of the characters, the drama of a Racine play is in the confrontation of the characters with their fate. Underneath the faultless perfection of their surface, his plays seethe and smolder with passion. Racine's characters have been likened to wild beasts pacing back and forth behind the bars of their cages, their words piercing like daggers through the fluid grace of his poetry. The women for whom his finest plays are named—Andromaque, Bérénice, Iphigénie, Phèdre—are women consumed by a love that cannot be fulfilled; it is their fate, and they know it. And yet, they continue to defy fate, even though they know that the order that governs their lives makes appeasement of passion impossible. Miraculously, the structure of Racine's

plays is the counterpart of their themes. Both the characters and the plays move according to predetermined form—and in both cases the form intensifies the meaning.

Racine's tremendous dramas were worthy of the great King who was their patron, and Louis was pleased to have inspired them. But the King's real favorites were the brilliant satirical comedies of Jean Baptiste Poquelin, better known as Molière. Like Shakespeare, Molière was not just a writer of plays, but a complete man of the theater; it was his whole world. At 21, he sold his hereditary right to the position of *valet tapissier de chambre du roi*, which carried with it the privilege of making the King's bed, and used the money to found a theatrical company. The company's leading lady, Madeleine Béjart, soon became his mistress. Nineteen years later Molière married a young woman whose name also was Béjart, Armande Béjart, and who was either Madeleine's daughter or younger sister—the records do not say.

At first, Molière's company was a resounding failure. He was unable to compete with the two existing theater companies in Paris and, despite the fact that he served as producer, director, stage manager, author and actor, was unable to remain solvent. Three times he was arrested for debt, and once he was briefly thrown into debtors' prison—until his father came forward to pay up his son's bills. In 1646, after three years of unsuccessful struggle in Paris, Molière took his troupe off to the provinces. There they remained for 12 years, touring from town to town, eking out a living while they perfected their art.

In 1658, the company returned to the capital and managed to win the patronage of the King's brother, Philippe d'Orléans. Philippe, who was known at court as "Monsieur," arranged for the "Troupe de Monsieur" to perform before the King: Molière, who fancied himself a great tragedian, chose to present as the main feature of the evening Corneille's tragedy, *Nicomède.* It was not a great success. Happily, he had thought to follow it with a short farce of his own composition, *Le Docteur Amoureux.* Louis was enchanted and the Troupe de Monsieur was immediately established in the theater world of Paris.

Molière continued to write, produce and act in tragedies as well as comedies, but his real genius, apparent to everyone but him, was for the latter. During the remaining 15 years of his life he turned out a series of comic masterpieces.

The Cartesian spirit is as evident in these comedies as it is in the tragedies of Racine. Molière is concerned not with particular human beings, but with pure types of human folly and weakness. Stripping away unnecessary details of time, place or circumstance, he concentrates on the essence of the Snob, the Miser, the Hypocrite, the Cuckold. With enormous wit and devastating clarity, he analyzes human nature and society, and makes men laugh at their own absurdity. There is Harpagon, the Miser *(L'Avare),* who has such a dislike of the word "giving" that he cannot even bring himself to say, "I give you good morning"; there is Tartuffe, the sanctimonious hypocrite, who explains that it is all right for him to seduce his benefactor's wife because "the immorality of the action [is rectified by] the purity of the intention"; there is Philamente, one of *Les Femmes Savantes,* who fires her maid for using a word condemned by the Academy; there is Monsieur Jourdain, *Le Bourgeois Gentilhomme,* surrounded by his fencing master, his music master, his dancing master, his philosopher, his tailor. Here, for example, is M. Jourdain making the astonishing discovery that all his life he has unwittingly been speaking "prose:"

PHILOSOPHER. *Because, my dear sir, if you want to express yourself at all there's only verse or prose. . . .*

M. JOURDAIN. *And talking, as I am now, which is that?*
PHILOSOPHER. *That is prose.*
M. JOURDAIN. *You mean to say that when I say "Nicole, fetch me my slippers" or "Give me my night-cap" that's prose?*
PHILOSOPHER. *Certainly, sir.*
M. JOURDAIN. *Well, my goodness! Here I've been talking prose for forty years and never known it, and mighty grateful I am to you for telling me!*

Entranced by his discovery, M. Jourdain goes off to parade his new knowledge before his long-suffering wife:

M. JOURDAIN. *I'm ashamed of your ignorance. For example, do you know what you are doing—what you are talking at this very moment?*
MME. JOURDAIN. *I'm talking plain common sense—you ought to be mending your ways.*
M. JOURDAIN. *That's not what I mean. What I'm asking is what sort of speech are you using?*
MME. JOURDAIN. *Speech! I'm not making a speech. But what I'm saying makes sense and that's more than can be said for your goings on.*
M. JOURDAIN. *I'm not talking about that. I'm asking what I am talking now. The words I am using—what are they?*
MME. JOURDAIN. *Stuff and nonsense!*
M. JOURDAIN. *Not at all! The words we are both using. What are they?*
MME. JOURDAIN. *Well, what on earth are they?*
M. JOURDAIN. *What are they called?*
MME. JOURDAIN. *Call them what you like.*
M. JOURDAIN. *They are prose, you ignorant creature!*
MME. JOURDAIN. *Prose?*
M. JOURDAIN. *Yes, prose! Everything that's prose isn't verse and everything that isn't verse is prose. Now you see what it is to be a scholar!*

Inevitably, Molière's sharp eye and barbed pen angered his victims. *Tartuffe,* his greatest play, so enraged pious Parisians that one vicar declared that

MOLIÈRE IN COSTUME, *acting in his satirical play, "The Doctor in Spite of Himself," took the main part, that of a woodcutter who passed as a doctor by speaking impressive Latin gibberish. In this play Molière mocked the quack doctors common to the era; in others he poked fun at all levels of society.*

Molière "should be burned at the stake as a foretaste of the fires of hell." But Louis XIV, Molière's most faithful admirer, was always there to protect him. *Tartuffe*, in fact, was first presented at one of the lavish royal entertainments that were so much a part of life at the court of the Sun King. This particular entertainment was called "The Pleasures of the Enchanted Isle," and it was organized and directed by Molière—who often served his patron in this fashion. The "Pleasures" took place in the palace and gardens of Versailles, in settings lit by hundreds of torches and chandeliers holding 4,000 candles. It lasted for a whole week in May of 1664, and presented the King and his courtiers with a dazzling succession of tournaments, ballets, operas, concerts, plays and feasts.

Tartuffe, Molière's own contribution to the festivities, closes with a speech that can only have been intended to describe Louis himself: "We live under a prince who is an enemy to fraud, a prince whose eyes penetrate into the heart, and whom all the art of imposters cannot deceive." Order and Reason were personified in the Sun King; all the genius of the mightiest nation in Christendom was marshaled to glorify the greatest monarch of the age. No wonder the rest of Europe, dazzled by the spectacle of Louis at Versailles, soon followed suit. Just as the armies of Louis had overawed his neighbors, and as his absolutism had become the model for kings everywhere, so French culture and the geometric spirit swept everything before it. In England, John Dryden was inspired to rewrite the plays of Shakespeare so that they might live up to the new standards of clarity and decorum; on the continent, a German scholar named Christian Thomasius solemnly composed a *Discourse on the Form in which one should imitate the French.*

Despite this apparently monumental victory for reason and order, there were signs that Cartesian thought and the geometric spirit did not satisfy

125

everyone. One of the most eloquent opponents to the deification of reason was himself a scientist, the noted mathematician Blaise Pascal. Pascal had written an important treatise on conic sections before he was 20, and had also invented an adding machine—to help his father, a tax collector, at his work. Later, he conducted a series of famous experiments with the barometer, proving that the instrument could be used for forecasting weather, and—at the instigation of a dice-throwing friend —did much of the preliminary research for what eventually became known to mathematicians as the laws of probability.

At the age of 31, however, Pascal had a mystical experience that profoundly altered the few remaining years of his life. On the night of November 23, 1654, he was seated in his room reading the Bible when suddenly he had a vision. It lasted, he afterwards calculated, "from about half-past ten until about half-past twelve," and filled him with great joy. When it was over, he wrote it down on a piece of parchment and had it sewn inside his coat, so that it would always be with him. Thereafter, until his death in 1662, Pascal devoted his life to the study of religion as passionately as he had once devoted it to science. "Speaking frankly," he wrote a friend, "I find geometry the noblest exercise of the mind, yet I know it to be so useless that I see no difference between a geometer and a clever artisan. I call it the loveliest occupation in the world, but only an occupation. . . . I am now engaged on studies so remote from these that I should find it difficult to remember what they were all about."

Pascal rejected the cold perfection of Descartes' universe. "I cannot forgive Descartes," he wrote. "He would gladly, in all his philosophy, have left God out altogether." Pascal thought that Descartes had left no place for feeling, for emotions, for love. It was only through love that man could comprehend God, and this was a kind of knowledge that had nothing to do with reason. "The heart has its reasons," he declared in his most famous utterance, "of which reason knows nothing."

To Pascal, the most wonderful and moving thing about man was not his reason, but his consciousness of himself. "Man is but a reed," he wrote in his *Pensées*, "the most feeble thing in nature; but he is a thinking reed. The entire universe need not arm itself to crush him; a vapor, a drop of water, suffice to kill him. But if the universe were to crush him, man would still be nobler than that which killed him, because he knows that he is dying, and of its victory the universe knows nothing."

Reason, Pascal was saying in effect, was not enough. Cartesian thought, with its emphasis on logic and order, left too many things unanswered. In the last years of the reign of Louis XIV there were similar doubts about the order the Sun King had imposed on France. Louis had used the immense power of his office to bring peace and prosperity to his country; his bureaucrats, his army, his courtiers and his artists all worked together to create in France the veritable apotheosis of order. But now this order seemed to threaten the very things it was designed to preserve—the peace, the stability, the social values.

In 1685, Louis revoked the Edict of Nantes and openly persecuted Protestants, not because they threatened France but because it was an affront to the King to have so many subjects adhering to a religion different from his own. Similarly, he persisted in his military aggressions against France's neighbors even when those actions no longer served the interests of France in any conceivable way. Louis' pursuit of order became an insatiable thirst for power. There was a lesson to be learned from this. Absolutism brings order but it also invites despotism, and therefore needs to be checked. Eventually France was to learn this lesson—but it was England that learned it first.

GENTLEMEN REVELERS, *in "The Festivals of Bacchus," ride on stage in the theater of the Palais Royal as a Miser (center) is hauled off by servants.*

THE BIRTH OF BALLET

Modern ballet arose largely from the 17th Century French court's passion for dancing and amateur theatricals. Several nights a week might be devoted to such entertainments, and the aristocratic performers spent days perfecting their roles. An essential part of every nobleman's training, these performances, characterized by elaborate costumes and fantastic sets, were gradually formalized into the modern art of choreography. One of the most fervent amateurs was young King Louis XIV himself, who played scores of roles and set up the first permanent ballet school, l'Académie Royale de la Danse.

When only 12 the precocious King appeared in *The Festivals of Bacchus*, a ballet in 30 scenes celebrating the Greek god of wine. As a series of contemporary sketches shows, spoilsports were banished in the opening scene *(above)*, making way for the mirthful antics of the worshipers of wine, women and song.

A rollicking procession of masked and merry tipplers

THE DEVOTEES OF WINE *make their appearances in the ballet. From left to right: a musician; a jester seeking the step he has lost through drunkenness; a crippled beggar, impoverish*

Like most court ballets, *The Festivals of Bacchus* was composed of many short scenes of dancing, singing and spoken dialogue loosely organized on a central theme. The dialogue in the balloons is translated from the actual script of the ballet. The young King and his gentlemen amateurs joined professional performers in putting on the comic and dramatic masks used for all the parts, including those of female characters and of buffoons *(below)*. As he grew older and more self-important, however, Louis would represent only gods, kings and heroes. At 30 he abandoned the stage, partly because he heard his nickname—"The Ballet King."

rough drink; a bibulous knight; a tipsy courtier; a town crier, announcing the Festivals; a barrel-chested swordsman; a reveler dressed in wine mugs; and the Festivals' host.

Rakes, Greek divinities and medieval knights

> OF ALL THE MAGIC TRICKS OF LOVE,
> THE NEATEST ANY LOVER'S KNOWN
> IS DEFTLY AND WITH PERFECT GRACE
> TO TAKE A HEART AND GIVE HIS OWN.

The Three Graces

Godenot

BEHOLD A PRINCE SO SWEET AND MILD
THAT EVEN WHEN HE WAS A CHILD
HIS PLAYMATES ALWAYS WERE THE GRACES.
LET'S RENDER HIM EACH WHIM UNTIL HE'S
CONVINCED WE LOVE THE KING OF LILIES
WHO HOLDS OUR HEARTS IN SILKEN TRACES.

MY DEATHLESS LOVE WILL DIE
AN EARLY DEATH
IF, SCORNING ME, YOU STAY
A FAITHFUL WIFE;
WHY SHOULD YOUR HUSBAND HOARD
YOUR LOVING CHARMS,
WHILE I GET NONE, GROW GRAY, AND
SPOIL MY LIFE?

The second stage set of the *Festivals* showed the Knights of the Round Table *(left)* in Bacchus' palace, feasting and watching magicians make birds and rabbits appear. Scenes like this were typical of the carefree anachronisms of court ballets. French audiences thought nothing of mixing in with the three Greek Graces a fanciful squire at arms, an amorous pirate, a farcical Spanish character named Godenot and a character in contemporary French dress called "The Good Hostess"—all cynically discussing the wiles of courtly love.

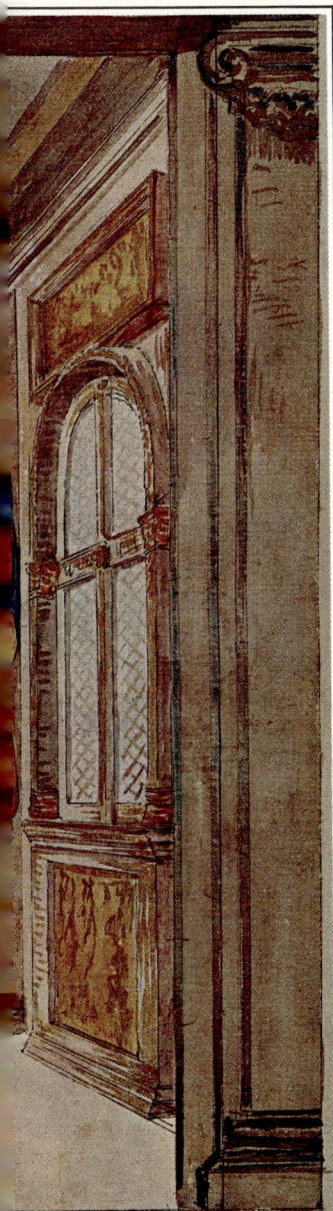

Squire at Arms

I'VE SAILED THE SEVEN SEAS
CAPTURING RICH BOOTIES
THAT MULTIPLY MY GAINS.
BUT I WOULD TRADE MY RICHES FOR A PRIZE
ESTEEMED ABOVE ALL OTHERS IN MEN'S EYES:
FREEDOM FROM LOVE,
   SWEET FREEDOM FROM LOVE'S PAINS.

The Good Hostess

Pirate

SPARKLING AND BRIGHT, I KNOW THAT THERE ARE FEW
GALLANTS WHOSE FLAMES CAN MATCH MY ARDENT FIRE.
I MUST CONFESS THAT I ALONE IMBUE
A TENDER MAIDEN'S HEART WITH TRUE DESIRE.

The Man of Fire

Fire, ice, phantoms and creatures of the night

I TAKE A STEP TOWARD SPRING, THAW AND SHED THE RIME

THAT HELD ME YOUNG AND FROZEN TILL THE TIME

WHEN I WOULD WIN ALL WOMEN, PUT ALL MEN TO SHAME.

THE TIME'S ARRIVED; I'M WARMING TO THE GAME!

The Man of Ice

The third act of the *Festivals* was dedicated to Bacchus' follower, the God of Sleep. The visions, sprites and elements attending him *(above)* were cast with subtle allusions to the actors: the young King, who was just becoming interested in girls, played the melting Man of Ice; the Duc de Candalle, a famous lady-killer of the day, played the torrid Man of Fire.

The bizarre pageantry of the feast of wine

TOASTING HIS MERRY RETAINERS, *Bacchus straddles a wine cask. The small figure at top left is one of the god's childhood nurses. Below her is a winemaker; to the right is Autum*

The French courtiers, who devoted much money and care to their everyday dress, spared no effort in preparing costumes for the stage. Bacchus and his attendants were festooned with grapes; his musicians wore animal heads, alluding to Bacchus' role as a wild woodland god. Autumn, symbolizing the harvest and vintage time, came covered with garlands and wheat. The men who played Bacchus' wet nurses stuffed their costumes appropriately.

holding a cornucopia. The larger figures are musicians. The old man on the donkey at top right is Silenus, Bacchus' tutor; at the left is Lethe, the River of Forgetfulness.

The Grand Finale: a visit from Apollo

In the last tableau of Louis' bacchanalian ballet, Apollo, the patron deity of poetry and music, appeared enthroned on a sunburst *(right)* surrounded by the nine Muses, the goddesses who reigned over the arts. Besides offering Apollo *(above)* an opportunity for flattering the King, the scene gave the stage designers a chance to show their skills. The actors, who went through several costume changes, were seated on platforms that were suspended by pulleys from the ceiling and concealed from the audience's view by clouds made of painted flats and gauze. As a grand finale, Apollo and his maidens were slowly cranked up to the stage loft and disappeared, to the admiring delight of all.

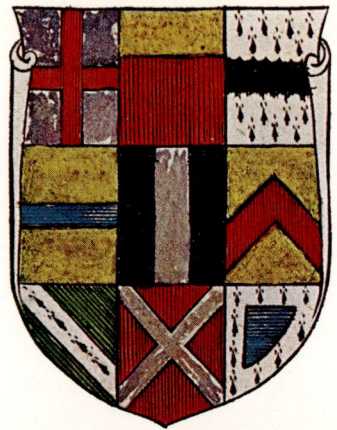

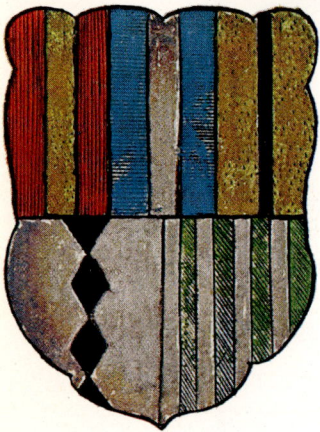

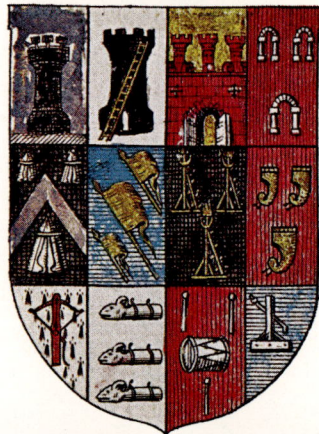

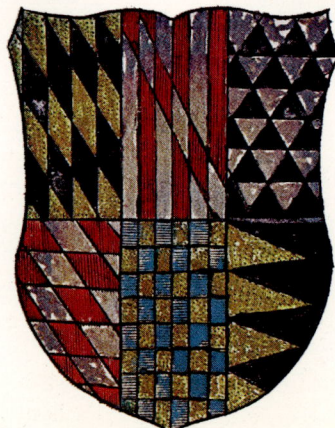

7
ROYALTY VERSUS PARLIAMENT

During the last decades of the 17th Century, while absolutism triumphed nearly everywhere on the continent of Europe, England established a new kind of political order, called constitutionalism. The new order was born only after a century of turmoil and bloodshed, but it seemed to offer in return immunity from the twin perils of anarchy and despotism. It protected the rights of the people against arbitrary acts of government, and it did this, miraculously, without destroying the government's power to deal with its problems at home and its enemies abroad. The English were the first to learn how to tame Leviathan, the modern state, and make it their servant rather than their master. Their reward for this achievement was an era of domestic tranquillity and of unprecedented influence in world politics.

None of this was designed or foreseen. The new order was finally established after the Glorious Revolution of 1688, but the book that justified that revolution—John Locke's *Two Treatises on Civil Government*—did not appear until the revolution was over. In fact, the revolution was simply the spontaneous culmination of a long and complicated series of events that began with the coronation of James I, the first Stuart King of England, in 1603. The history of England between James's accession and the exile of his grandson, James II, 85 years later, has all the familiar elements of the age— clashing religions, decaying political traditions, the rise of new social and economic forces, the intertwining of domestic and foreign affairs in the conduct of state. But all of this is pervaded by the indefinable force of human personality. The key to English history in the 17th Century lies in the character and personality of its first four Stuart Kings.

When the great Queen Elizabeth lay dying in 1603, she was asked to name her heir and replied characteristically that no one but a king should succeed her. The man she chose was James VI of Scotland, son of her cousin the ill-starred Mary Queen of Scots. It was a popular choice. James was known to be a learned monarch, and he had a legitimate claim to the English crown. England was also pleased to note that his acceptance of Protestantism seemed beyond question: in 1587, when Parliament had condemned his Catholic mother to

SIGNS OF NOBILITY, *these engravings show devices that could appear on gentlemen's coats of arms. A man named Lyons might pick a lion; to make his shield unique, he might place it over a cross on a red background. Crossbows, drums and catapults were often used to recall military feats.*

death, James had tactfully limited himself to a few formal protests.

As James made his way from Edinburgh to London in April 1603, amidst general rejoicing, one trivial event went almost unnoticed. A man accused of theft was brought before the King, and James ordered him hanged immediately, without trial. It was an example of a disregard for law on the King's part that was soon to plunge England into the gravest constitutional struggle of its history. At issue in this struggle were the relative rights of the King and Parliament—an issue not especially new nor even especially English, but complicated in this case by the nature of the government that James had inherited from Elizabeth. The Queen had been concerned with the substance of power, rather than its appearance. She was quite content to let Parliament think that it ruled, so long as it did what she wanted. Through a combination of feminine wiles and unsurpassed political skill, she made herself one of England's most effective monarchs—but she left her successor a Parliament filled with a sense of its own importance, and determined to play an active part in the government of the Kingdom. James had no intention of sharing his power, either in appearance or in substance. Never was a ruler less suited to the role in which history cast him.

Sully, the French statesman, called the English King "the most learned fool in Christendom," and James was indeed a born pedant. He relished elaborate disputations over some fine point in theology or political philosophy. While still King of Scotland, he had pontificated, in a treatise on the *Trew Law of Free Monarchies*, on the divine right of kings. To James, "free monarchy" meant a monarchy free of all earthly restraints: a king, he was fond of reminding Parliament, was "the supremest thing on earth."

But for all his intellectual pretensions, James was a weakling in action. He was utterly convinced of the correctness of his policies, but completely incapable of carrying them out. He was rigid where he should have been flexible, and vacillating where he should have been firm. He had a special fondness for handsome young men, two of whom exercised an enormous and unfortunate influence over him—Robert Carr, whom he made Earl of Somerset, and George Villiers, who succeeded Somerset as favorite and became Duke of Buckingham.

James's pedantry and stubbornness might have been assets in some situations, but the situation in 17th Century England was not one of them. When James came to the throne, the respective rights of the King and Parliament were not clearly defined, and the making of laws required the concurrent action of both. Each also had certain powers traditionally its own. The King, for example, controlled foreign policy and had the right, through an authority called the "royal prerogative," to act outside the law or even against the law in case of emergency. No one could say exactly what the limits of the royal prerogative were, but it was a constant temptation to kings, and a constant anxiety to their subjects.

Parliament's special powers had to do with control of the country's purse strings. Although the King, as an extensive landholder in England and also as the beneficiary of certain feudal duties, possessed an independent income for the day-to-day expenses of the crown, he had to go to Parliament for any additional funds—because only Parliament could levy taxes. In theory, this should have worked very well. In fact, by the beginning of the 17th Century the King's own sources of revenue were inadequate to his needs. Queen Elizabeth, deeply in debt, had sold some of the crown lands, and steady inflation had reduced the value of the rest. James and his successors were in the position of pensioners living on a fixed income; year by year

A Catalogue of the severall Sects and Opinions in England and other Nations.
With a briefe Rehearsall of their false and dangerous Tenents.

87

One Evins a Welch man was lately committed to New-gate for saying hee was Christ

Iesuit

Hee rs one blasphemously
That he was christ did say
Such spirits more foretold
To rise ith latter dayes

Arminian Arian Adamite Libertin

Ante scripturian Soule Sleeper Anabaptist Familist Seeker Divorcer

the amount became less and less adequate. As the crown's financial needs increased, so did the power of Parliament. Every time the King asked Parliament for money, Parliament exacted certain royal concessions. The situation could scarcely have been more unstable.

The crisis, when it came, was precipitated by religion. England was officially Protestant. The Church of England, established a century before by Henry VIII in his break with Roman Catholicism, was a state church headed by the King. But it represented a curious sort of compromise. Although its doctrine was Protestant, its rites and organization were not. Anglican bishops presided over dioceses, just as the Catholic bishops did, and many Anglican churches celebrated mass. Inevitably, the Church of England came under attack from both sides. Devout and fanatical Protestant sects who called themselves Puritans and believed that the Church had strayed too far from the piety and saintliness of early Christianity, demanded that it be purified of such "Popish" practices as the use of the Cross in baptism and the use of the ring in the marriage ceremony. On the other hand, many Roman Catholic Englishmen remained loyal to their faith despite systematic persecution, and dreamed of one day returning England to the Roman Catholic fold.

Caught between these extremes, James chose to defend the Church of England. He believed, quite correctly, that the fate of the English monarchy was tied to the fate of the Anglican Church: the strength of one depended upon the survival of the other. "No bishop, no king," said James succinctly, and set out to extend the authority of both. Of the two forces arrayed against him, James's Puritan enemies were in much the better position to act. They were strongly represented in Parliament, where they added their dissenting religious opinions to an already existing political hostility to the

King. For a time the skirmishes between King and Parliament were minor, confined to such matters as the King's use of his royal prerogative to impose new duties on imported currants. After the start of the Thirty Years' War, the situation became more serious.

Protestant England had been delighted in 1613 when James I gave his daughter Elizabeth in marriage to the Elector Palatine, Frederick V. It was outraged when, five years later, at the very outset of the war between Catholic and Protestant Germany, James turned around and proposed to marry his son Charles to the Catholic Infanta of Spain. In spite of English resistance to this strange alliance, James pursued it for years. To placate his royal relatives-to-be, he even arranged for the execution of Sir Walter Raleigh, Spain's arch-foe.

In 1621 the House of Commons demanded that James abandon his plans for this marriage. It also demanded that he become the head of a great Protestant military alliance against the Habsburg powers, one of which, of course, was Spain. In reply, James instructed Parliament to stop meddling in foreign policy, which was the King's business. But Parliament would not be silent. Instead, it entered a Grand Protestation in its journal. James's response was quick and brutal: he dissolved Parliament, arrested three of the leading members of Commons, and, calling for the journal, ripped out the offending Protestation.

Two years later James made peace with Parliament and in 1624 went to war against Spain—after the Spanish Infanta had insolently turned down his son. He even sent an army to help the Protestant princes in their war against the Habsburgs in Germany. But he never really resolved the issues between the King and Parliament, and in fact he never really tried.

It has been said that James steered the ship of state straight for the rocks, but left his son to wreck it. In the 24 years of his reign, Charles I did precisely that. Charles ascended the throne in 1625, inheriting from his father a hostile Parliament and a hopeless war against Spain. The new King was even less suited to the needs of his people and his time than the old one. Where James had been stubborn and dogmatic, Charles was petty and weak willed. He lacked any understanding of the broad issues of the day, and was even more prone than his father to fall under the influence of inept and unscrupulous favorites. Guided more by emotion and prejudice than by reason, he was devious with opponents and disloyal to his friends. Like his father, he believed in absolutism and the divine right of kings. But in Charles's case this belief was accompanied by an even more bitter hatred of Puritans and a considerable sympathy for Roman Catholicism.

Within four years of his coronation, Charles had created an irreparable breach between himself and his subjects. The war against Spain had been badly mismanaged, and he had somehow contrived to involve England in war against France at the same time. The cost of fighting simultaneously the two greatest powers in Christendom was more than the royal purse could bear. Charles was forced to turn to Parliament for money, but Parliament was not disposed to be generous. It resented the King's attempts to impose new taxes and duties without Parliamentary approval; it was fearful of his obvious sympathy for Roman Catholics; it hated his inept advisor, the Duke of Buckingham.

Three times in four years, when Parliament presumed to discuss these matters, Charles dismissed it and arrested its leaders. In 1629, when Charles once again summoned Parliament to ask it for money, the body immediately turned its attention to religion, and protested heatedly against the introduction of "papist" practices into the Church of England. This time, when the King tried to adjourn Parliament, the Speaker was held forcibly in his seat while Parliament passed by acclamation three resolutions. The first said that anyone who tampered with England's established Protestantism was an enemy of the state; the second said that anyone who attempted to impose taxes without the consent of Parliament was an enemy of the state; the third said that anyone who paid such illegally imposed taxes was a traitor to England. With this resounding act of defiance, Parliament voted to adjourn.

By this time Charles had had enough. Recognizing that he could not get along with Parliament, he resolved to get along without it. For 11 years, between 1629 and 1640, he ruled virtually as an autocrat. His chief problem was, of course, money. With no Parliament to vote taxes, he was forced to spend less and find ways to get more. Sometimes he was driven to extremes of ingenuity. He fined citizens eligible for knighthood for *not* becoming knights, pawned the royal jewels, sold trading monopolies in various fields of commerce, and extended the special "ship money" tax, used to support the royal navy, from port cities to the entire country. By one means or another he managed to make ends meet, and he might have gone on indefinitely in this fashion if it had not been for one thing: religion.

In 1637, on the advice of the Archbishop of Canterbury, Charles decided to impose the doctrine and organization of the Church of England upon his Scottish subjects. The Scots, most of whom were Presbyterians, swore to resist him to the death. Charles was in no mood to compromise, and prepared to raise an army. For this, however, he needed money—no less, in fact, than one million pounds. It could come only from Parliament. On April 13, 1640, this body met for the first time in 11 years—with results that could have been foreseen by anyone less blind than Charles. Parliament insisted upon taking up its grievances, and within three

weeks the King imperiously dismissed it. This was the famous Short Parliament. A few months later, finding himself in even more desperate straits—with a Scottish army occupying the northern counties of England—Charles again summoned Parliament into session.

This Parliament, which met on November 3, 1640, continued to sit in one form or another for 13 years, and became known as the Long Parliament. It is also known as the Parliament that presided over the destruction of the English monarchy. It deprived the King of his right to dissolve any Parliament without its consent; passed an act requiring the King to call Parliament every three years; abolished the "prerogative courts" to which the King turned for legal support; and declared all taxes imposed without Parliamentary consent to be null and void. The King, desperately in need of Parliament's financial help, assented to all of these measures. He balked, however, when Parliament proposed to undermine the Church of England by doing away with its bishoprics and abolishing the Book of Common Prayer.

By March 1642, relations between the King and Parliament had deteriorated so badly that the King, fearing violence to himself or his Queen, moved his court from London to York. There, in June, he received Parliament's ultimatum, the "Nineteen Propositions" that would, in effect, have given Parliament complete control of the army, the Church and the state. The King, in return, would have been given more money. Despite the promise of adequate revenue, Charles rejected the Propositions out of hand. Thereafter, events moved swiftly to a climax. On July 12, Parliament voted to raise an army; on August 22, the King raised the royal standard at Nottingham and called upon his loyal followers to join him; England's first civil war had begun.

At first the two sides were rather evenly matched. The King had the support of most of the aristocracy, while Parliament's support came from the merchants and small landowners; the west of England and Wales tended to be royalist, the east and south were for Parliament. But the division by class and geography was actually less important than the differences in ideology: the war was fought primarily over religion and politics. The King's supporters, called Cavaliers because of their dashing appearance, believed in the monarchy and the Church of England. Parliament's champions, called Roundheads because of their short-cropped hair, wanted to limit or destroy the monarchy and to replace the Church of England with either of two alternatives. One group favored a national church based on Presbyterian forms; another favored independent Puritan congregations.

The first two years of the war produced no appreciable advantage for either side. By the end of 1643, the King's forces controlled three quarters of the country, but early in 1644 Parliament signed a treaty with Scotland that brought Scottish arms to its aid. Partly because of this, but far more through the efforts of one man, the balance soon began to swing decisively toward the Roundheads. The man was Oliver Cromwell, one of the most remarkable figures in the history of the 17th Century.

Cromwell was born in 1599 in East Anglia, and lived the life of an ordinary country gentleman of modest means until the war made him famous. In 1628 and again in 1640, he was elected to Parliament, where he gained a modest name for himself as a leader of the Puritan cause. His unsuspected genius for military matters became apparent only shortly after the start of the war.

Cromwell organized and trained an army in his native district that became the backbone of the Parliamentary forces. In July 1644, this army crushed the King's army at the Battle of Marston Moor, the first decisive encounter of the war. After Marston Moor, the defeated general gave Cromwell's troops the name of "Ironsides" because, he said, they could not be "broken or divided." Soon Cromwell, as lieutenant-general of all the Parliamentary forces, was converting them all into "Ironsides." This was the nucleus of the New Model Army that took to the field in the spring of 1645 and was to prove virtually invincible.

The secret of Cromwell's genius lay in an extraordinary combination of humility and arrogance, of tolerance and uncompromising firmness. He was utterly convinced that he was doing God's will, and utterly convinced that God knew it. After his victory at the Battle of Naseby in June 1645, he wrote: "I can say this of Naseby: that when I saw the enemy draw up and march in gallant order toward us, and we a company of poor, ignorant men . . . I could not . . . but smile out to God in praises, in assurance of victory, because God would, by things that are not, bring to naught things that are. Of which I had great assurance. And God did it."

By communicating this sense of divine mission to his troops, Cromwell forged an army that fought passionately for a cause, rather than for pay or spoils. By failing to communicate his own deep tolerance of other men's beliefs, he also forged an army of fanatics. This was Cromwell's great tragedy.

After the Battle of Naseby, Charles surrendered —but he surrendered to the Scots, thinking that the Presbyterians would treat him more leniently than Cromwell's Puritans. Also, he hoped that his enemies would quarrel among themselves—and this was precisely what happened. Faced with the task of rebuilding England's political and religious structure, they became hopelessly divided. Most of the members of Parliament were for a limited monarchy and a national Presbyterian Church. But Cromwell's New Model Army wanted neither a King nor a national church, and refused to compromise.

While Parliament and the army wrangled, Charles secretly concluded a treaty with Scotland, promis-

GRIM MEMENTOS of the execution of England's Charles I for high treason are his bloody silk shirt and a death warrant signed by leaders of the Puritan rebellion. Among the authorizing signatures, each followed by its owner's seal, is that of Oliver Cromwell (first column, third from top). The warrant is dated 1648, according to England's Old Style calendar; modern dating sets the execution in 1649.

ing to establish a national Presbyterian Church. Then, with the support of Scottish armies, he embarked on a second civil war. Cromwell, who had been undecided about the future of the monarchy, quickly made up his mind. Declaring that further negotiation with Charles would be "to meddle with an accursed thing," he led the New Model Army against the royalist Scottish forces, and crushed them at the Battle of Preston in August 1648. Thereafter the reins of government were firmly in Puritan hands. The 140 Presbyterian members of Parliament were expelled, and a "Rump" Parliament of 60 Puritans ruled England.

On December 13, 1648, this Rump Parliament voted to try the King for high treason. The trial of Charles I began on January 20, 1649, and on January 27 the court handed down its sentence: "that he, the said Charles Stuart, as tyrant, traitor, murderer, and public enemy to the good people of this nation, shall be put to death by the severing of his head from his body." On January 30, Charles met his fate with a dignity and a regal demeanor often lacking in his 24 years upon the throne.

For the next 11 years, England was without a King. As Cromwell had declared at Charles's trial, "We will cut off the King's head with the crown on it." During this period, power remained in the hands of the army, and the army was controlled, until his death, by Oliver Cromwell. The story of this strange, melancholy interlude in English history is the story of Cromwell's futile attempts to bring stability and a measure of religious freedom to his country. The force that ultimately defeated him was the fanaticism of his own Puritan followers. Determined to root out heresy and godlessness, and to establish what they called a "rule of the Saints" based on the Biblical laws of Moses, these men had no patience with constitutional government or the rule of law. England was once again threatened by tyranny—a tyranny of Saints.

Cromwell did everything in his power to control them. In 1653, at his behest, Parliament adopted England's first and only written constitution, the Instrument of Government. It established a Lord Protector, Cromwell, and an executive body called the Council of State—and it guaranteed England a wide degree of religious freedom. But the Puritan Parliaments elected under the Instrument were unwilling to abide by its terms. More and more, Cromwell had to rely on military power to preserve some degree of order and freedom. Unable to find any solid basis on which to build a constitutional government, he finally ruled virtually as a dictator.

Cromwell's death in 1658 made a return to monarchy inevitable. England was tired of radicalism and fanaticism, of rule by "Saints" and Model Army major-generals. It longed to return to the comfortable traditions of king, Church and Parliament. Consequently when Charles II, living in exile in Europe, promised to rule as a limited monarch, England welcomed him home.

On May 29, 1660, Charles entered a jubilant London. "This day," wrote John Evelyn breathlessly, "came his Majesty, Charles the Second to London, after a sad and long exile and calamitous suffering both of the King and the Church, being 17 years. This was also his birthday, and with a triumph of above 20,000 horse and foot [soldiers], brandishing their swords, and shouting with inexpressible joy; the ways strewd with flowers, the bells ringing, the streets hung with tapestry, fountains running with wine; the Mayor, Aldermen, and all the companies in their liveries, chains of gold, and banners. Lords and Nobles, clad in cloth of silver, gold and velvet; the windows and balconies, all set with ladies; trumpets, music, and myriads of people flocking even so far as from Rochester, so as they were seven hours in passing the city, even from two in the afternoon 'til nine at night. I stood in the Strand and beheld it, and blessed God."

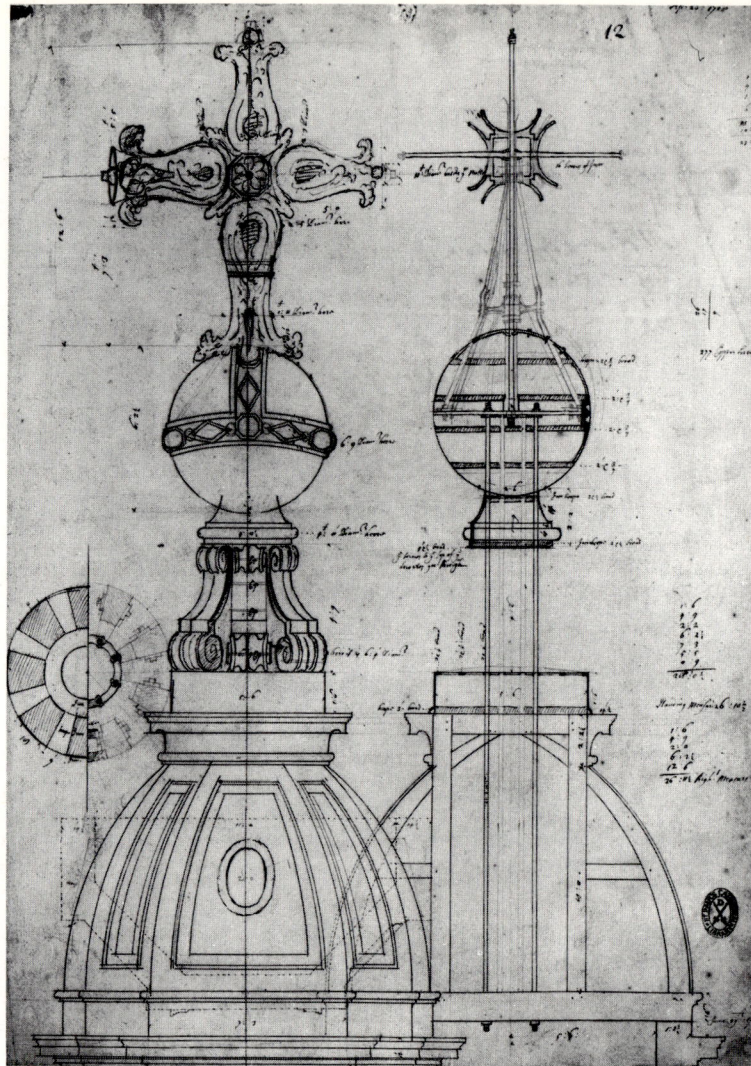

AN ORB AND CROSS for *St. Paul's Cathedral* were *Sir Christopher Wren's finishing touches for the church that he built to replace a previous structure destroyed in London's Great Fire of 1666. Wren's sketches include the design for the ornament atop the church, of which the upper 40 feet is seen here with a cutaway view showing its internal framework and a small floor plan of its midsection.*

The restoration of Charles II was more than a political event. With it, the whole tone of English life changed. The young King had spent a good part of his exile in France, and had brought back with him a taste and style shaped by the French court. Soon the drab, grim seriousness of the Puritan era gave way to lighthearted elegance. Courtiers dressed in sumptuous clothes and wore enormous wigs, danced to French airs and admired the latest of the King's dazzling succession of mistresses. The most famous of these, the irrepressible Nell Gwyn, enlivened London with her beauty and wit. Once, when a jeering crowd mistook Nell for her Catholic rival, Nell leaned from her coach and cried, "Be silent, good people; I am the *Protestant* whore!"

Restoration London was a different world from the London of Cromwell in every way; even the physical appearance of the city changed. After the Great Fire of 1666 destroyed two thirds of its buildings, the architect who supervised its rebuilding, Sir Christopher Wren, gave London a new elegance—and 52 beautiful churches, one of which is England's great Baroque cathedral, St. Paul's. Literature flourished and the theaters, once banned as sinful and godless, reopened. Englishmen roared at the bawdy comedies of William Wycherly and William Congreve, and at the satirical verse of John Dryden and Samuel Butler. If occasionally there was a voice from the Puritan past, such as was raised by the pious John Bunyan of *Pilgrim's Progress*, it was seldom heard in the rollicking court of Charles II.

And yet, beneath the glittering surface, all was not well. Charles II, like his father and grandfather, believed in the divine right of kings and in absolute monarchy. In addition, he possessed in full measure the diplomatic and political skills they so conspicuously lacked. Instead of making himself sole ruler of his realm by force of arms and dogmatic assertion, Charles proposed to use guile and political skill. To achieve this, Charles mastered two arts that

had baffled his father and grandfather: he devised ways of getting along with Parliament and ways of getting along without it. The first he achieved by seeing to it that Parliament always contained a substantial number of men who would support his views. He used every device at his disposal to gain their allegiance, from persuasion to bribery and blackmail. These supporters of the monarchy came to be known as Tories, and they formed the nucleus of England's first real political party.

Getting along without Parliament was somewhat more difficult, since it involved the problem of getting along without money. But Charles was imaginative, and he soon solved this, too. He discovered that there was another person in Europe equally anxious not to have Parliament meet. That person was Louis XIV, who feared that Parliament's anti-Catholic sentiment would lead it to demand war with France. Out of this bizarre community of interests came the secret Treaty of Dover. Under its terms, Louis regularly supplied Charles with substantial sums of money in return for Charles's agreement not to call Parliament into session except when required to by law. Charles also promised Louis that he would become a Catholic, and announce his conversion at the first politic moment.

Although the terms of this treaty remained secret, vague suspicions began to circulate through the country. Once again, it seemed, Protestant Englishmen were faced with the twin specters of absolutism and Catholicism. In 1678 these fears coalesced around the figure of one man, a charlatan named Titus Oates, who claimed he had been present at a Jesuit meeting in London that had plotted the conquest of England. The revelation of Oates's "Popish Plot," which in fact Oates had simply invented, precipitated a nationwide hysteria. Scores of innocent Catholics were tortured and killed before the frenzy died down.

The real danger to England lay not in the imaginary conspiracies of priests, but in the machinations of Charles II and his heir. To meet these dangers an opposition party arose. Its members, known as Whigs, were devoted to constitutionalism, limited monarchy and freedom of religion for all Christians except Roman Catholics—whom the Whigs considered agents of a foreign power. Their greatest spokesman was John Locke, whose *Two Treatises on Civil Government* and *Letters on Toleration* became the bible not only of the Whig cause, but—in the following century—of the American Revolution.

Despite uprisings and opposition, Charles II managed, with the help of the Tories and the money of Louis XIV, to steer the ship of state without wrecking it. It was an impressive performance; only a man with Charles's special gifts could have done it. In 1685, when Charles died, his brother James succeeded him—and the fate of absolutism in England was finally sealed.

The brief reign of James II was, quite simply, a disaster. Even before he came to the throne, James had announced his intention of reinstating Catholicism, and of ruling England without interference from Parliament. Once in power, he quickly made it clear that these were not idle threats. Within months, in open defiance of Parliament, he had begun to fill the army and navy with Catholic officers. The Whigs were driven almost to the verge of rebellion, and the Tories, torn by conflicting loyalties, did not know which side to support. Finally, because James was old and without male heirs, they decided to put up with him. Then, on June 10, 1688, to the consternation of the Tories and the horror of the Whigs, James became the father of a son. The prospect of hereditary Catholic monarchy stretched before them—and this was unthinkable. James and his infant son had finally united Protestant England in a common cause.

On June 30, seven Whig and Tory leaders sent a letter to William of Orange, leader of the Protestant Netherlands and husband of Mary, James's Protestant daughter by his first wife. The letter invited William to come to England with his army and protect the English people against their King. William accepted, and by the end of October had completed his preparations; his ships lay in the Dutch ports, awaiting a favorable wind. On November 1, it came, the famous "Protestant Wind," carrying William's fleet to the coast of Devon and trapping the fleet of James II in the Thames.

Four days later William's army landed on English soil. Its banners bore the motto of the House of Orange, "I will maintain," to which had been added, for the occasion, "the Liberties of England and the Protestant Religion." When news of the landing reached London, James's army and government abandoned him and James eventually fled to France. The Glorious Revolution, as it came to be called, had been won without firing a shot.

The significance of the Revolution, however, was not in the drama of the immediate events, but in their aftermath. Early in 1689 a special Parliament convened to establish a new government for England. It began by passing a Declaration of Rights, laying down the terms by which England was to be governed. Upon William and Mary's acceptance of these terms, they became King and Queen of England, and England became the first modern state to be governed by a regular system of constitutional law. The force of this law derived from the people, and although the system was not a democracy, it did represent an overwhelming majority of the people whose opinions counted in 17th Century politics—the nobility, the property owners, the wealthy merchants. For the next 25 years the enormous strength of this new form of government was to be demonstrated in a succession of wars that pitted England against the century's supreme example of absolutist government: the France of Louis XIV.

All along Thames Street, where I did view several places, and so up by London Wall, by Blackfriars, to Ludgate; and thence to Bridewell....Homewards, and took up a boy that had a lanthorn, that was picking up of rags, and got him to light me home, and had great discourse with him how he could get sometimes three or four bushels of rags in a day, and got 3d. a bushel for them, and what and how many ways there are for poor children to get their livings honestly....So to bed, to be up betimes by the help of a 'larum watch, which by chance I borrowed from my watchmaker today.

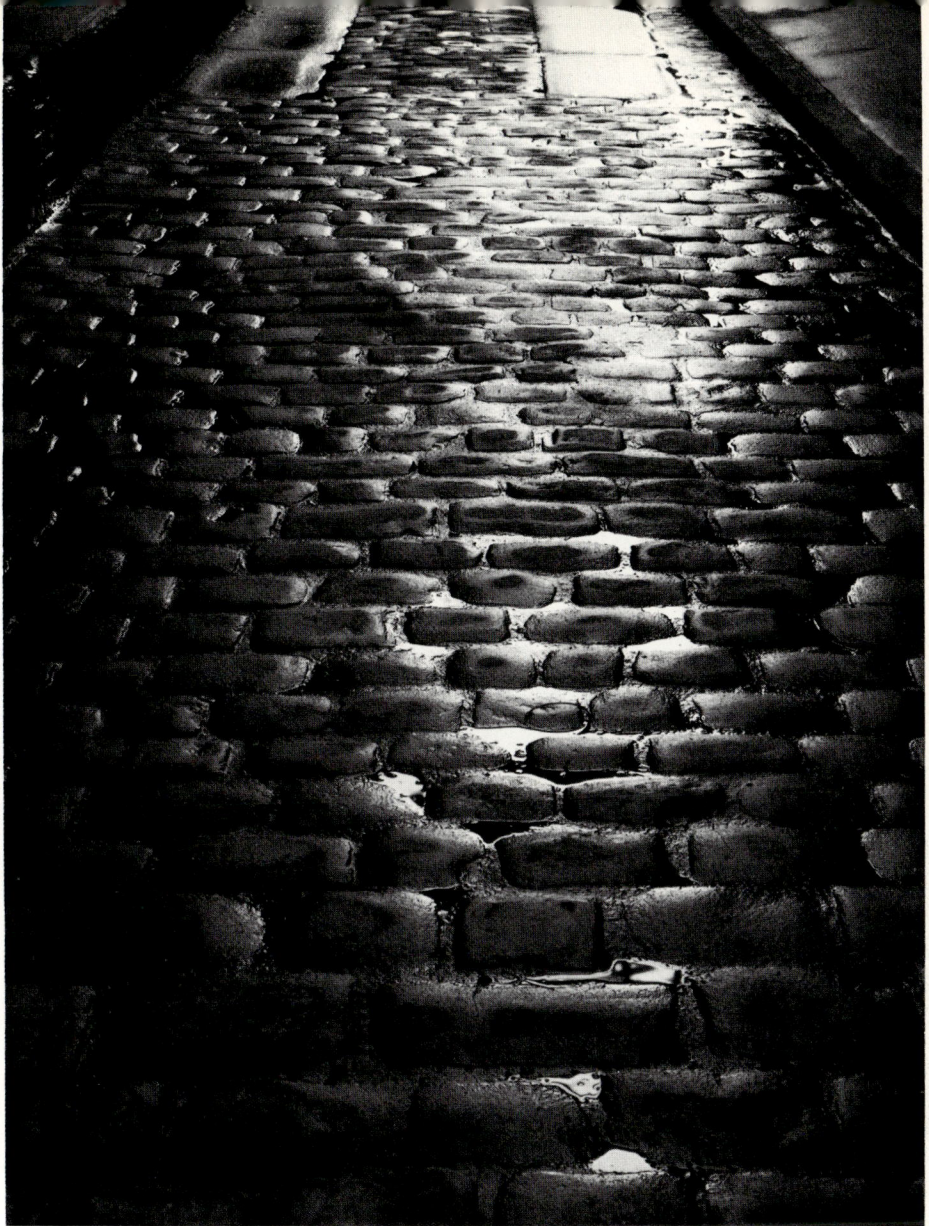

IN NARROW, COBBLED STREETS LIKE THIS, PEPYS GATHERED WHAT HE CALLED THE "TALK OF THE TOWN."

SAMUEL PEPYS'S LONDON

London in the 1660s was a lusty, brawling city, the storm center as well as the capital of Restoration England. Here was the place to observe the myriad forces that were transforming England from a largely medieval state into a modern power. And here lived one of the most celebrated observers of all time: Samuel Pepys, whose 1,250,000-word diary—sampled here in excerpts—recorded not only such memorable events as the Great Fire and the Plague of 1665, but also such revealing personal details as his pride in keeping a good house and table. Pepys, the ambitious, well-educated son of a tailor, broadened his horizons as he rose to Secretary of the Admiralty, but his delight remained in the busy streets, the gossip-filled taverns and the ribald court life of the city he knew and loved.

A STROLL IN THE PARK

To the Park, where I saw how far they had proceeded in the Pall-mall, and in making a river through the Park...which is now every day more and more pleasant. Here meeting with Laud Crisp, I took him to the further end, and sat under a tree, and there sang some songs.

A HOME IN GOOD ORDER

Home, and there find all things in readiness for a good dinner. By and by come my guests, and very good company, and a most neat and excellent, but dear, dinner. Lord! to see with what way they looked upon all my fine plate was pleasant; for I made the best show I could, to take down the pride of Mrs. Clerke who thinks herself very great.

To Westminster Abbey, where we saw Dr. Frewen translated to the Archbishopric of York. Here I saw the Bishops of Winchester, Bangor, Rochester, Bath and Wells, and Salisbury, in King Henry VII's chapel. But Lord: how people did look upon them as strange creatures, and few with any kind of love or respect.

THE TOMB OF HENRY VII IN WESTMINSTER ABBEY, WHERE KINGS AND CLERGY WE.

ALTED. PEPYS WAS CRITICAL OF BOTH.

TRACERY WINDOW, WESTMINSTER HALL, WHERE PEPYS WATCHED CHARLES II CELEBRATING HIS CORONATION.

A FEAST FOR A KING

*R*ound *the Abbey to Westminster Hall, all the way within rails, and 10,000 people with the ground covered with blue cloth. And the King came in with his crown on, and his sceptre in his hand. And many fine ceremonies there was of the Heralds leading up people before him, and bowing; and three lords coming before the courses on horseback, and staying so all dinnertime. I went from table to table to see the Bishops and all others at their dinner, and was infinitely pleased with it.*

To Lambeth to dinner with the Archbishop of Canterbury; a noble house with good pictures and furniture and exceeding great cheer....My cousin Roger told us that the Archbishop do keep a wench, and that he is as very a wencher as can be, which is one of the most astonishing things that I have heard of.

THE PLAGUE

*It frightened me indeed to see so many graves
lie so high upon the churchyard...Lord! what a sad time it is to
see no boats upon the river; and grass grows all up and down
White Hall court, and nobody but poor wretches in the streets! The
Duke showed us the number of the plague this week; it is
increased about 600....To bed, troubled, how to put my things and
estate in order, in case it should please God to call me away.*

PEPYS WENT TO THE CHURCH OF ST. KATHERINE CREE, AMONG OTHERS, TO COMPARE THE SERMONS.

ON A SUNDAY

Creed and I abroad, and called at several churches; and it is a wonder to see, and by that to guess the ill temper of the city at this time, either to religion in general, or to the King, that in some churches there was hardly ten people, and those poor people.

A NIGHT AT COURT

To White Hall into the ball this night before the King. They danced the Branle. After that, the King led a lady a single Coranto. Then to country dances, the King leading the first, which he called for, which was, says he, "Cuckolds all awry," the old dance of England. When the King dances, all the ladies in the room and the Queen herself, stand up.

STEEPLE OF ALL HALLOWS CHURCH, BARKING, NEAR PEPYS'S HOME.

THE GREAT FIRE

Up to the top of Barking steeple, and there saw the saddest sight of desolation that I ever saw: everywhere great fires, oil-cellars, and brimstone, and other things burning....Saw the fire grow...a most horrid, malicious, bloody flame and a horrid noise it made, and the cracking of houses at their ruin...And Lord! to see how the streets and the highways are crowded with people running.

AN OUTING ON THE RIVER

About eight o'clock, having got some bottles of wine and beer, and neats' tongues, we went to our barge at the Tower and so set out for the Hope, all the way down playing at cards and other sports, spending our time pretty merry. Embarked again for home; and so to cards and other sports till we came to Greenwich, and there to an alehouse, and so to the barge again, having shown them the King's pleasure-boat: and so home, bringing night home with us.

THE GOOD LIFE

*A*way to the Bear,
in Drury Lane, and there bespoke
a dish of meat; and in the meantime
sat and sung; and by and by
dined with mighty pleasure and
excellent meat, one little dish
enough for all, and a good wine,
and all for 8s…To my office. Home
to dinner. We had a fricasee
of rabbits and chickens, a leg of
mutton boiled, three carps in a dish,
a great dish of a side of lamb,
a dish of roasted pigeons, a dish of
four lobsters, three tarts, a lamprey
pie (a most rare pie), a dish of
anchovies, a good wine of several sorts,
and all things mighty noble and to
my great content….Lord! to see how
I am treated, that come from so
mean a beginning, is matter of wonder
to me. But it is God's mercy to me
and His blessing upon my
taking pains and being punctual.

DINNER: A SUBJECT DEAR TO SAMUEL PEPYS'S HEART.

8

A WORLD IN BALANCE

The Age of Kings ended, as it had begun, in conflict. But the wars that brought the 17th Century to a close were radically different from the one that had marked its beginning. The business of warfare was still killing, but the techniques of killing had changed and so had the character and aims of the belligerents. The Thirty Years' War had been fought out between royal dynasties or religious confederations; the wars of the late 17th Century were fought out between the representatives of a new sort of political unit, the territorial state.

These wars raged from Ireland in the west to Russia in the east, from Sweden in the north to Italy in the south. Every country in Europe was involved, directly or indirectly, in what was in effect a single cataclysmic struggle. At stake were the lands of three declining empires—the Spanish, the Swedish and the Turkish. Also at stake, and far more important, were the relative positions of the new territorial states. Each was fighting to extend its boundaries, to secure its frontiers, to gain overseas territories and a share in the world's trade. Out of their conflict emerged the broad outlines of an international order that was to endure down to the 20th Century.

The leading figure in this sprawling drama was, as might be expected, the Sun King. Secure in his authority, and with the mightiest and best-organized army in Christendom, Louis XIV set out coldly and deliberately to dominate Europe. Three times between 1667 and 1688 he loosed his army against his neighbors to the north and east. In 1667, in the War of Devolution, he attempted to seize the Spanish Netherlands; in 1672, in the Dutch War, he moved against the Dutch republic to the north; and in 1688, in the War of the League of Augsburg, he sent his armies eastward to seize strategic positions along the Rhine. Louis was stopped from further aggression only by alliances that included virtually every country in Western Europe; there was no ruler who did not fear him.

Louis' arch-enemy was the Habsburg ruler of the Holy Roman Empire, Leopold I, grandson of Ferdinand II, the Emperor whose ambitious plans for his Empire had touched off the Thirty Years' War. Significantly, Leopold no longer thought of that Empire as a viable political unit. Instead of trying

A PROPHECY FOR EUROPE *was intimated in this 1658 Rembrandt etching, which shows a statue displaced by the Phoenix, the mythical bird said to rise reborn from its own ashes. Half a century later the conflagrations that consumed the Age of Kings had given birth to a new European order.*

to revitalize it, he devoted himself to the task of turning his family holdings in Central and Eastern Europe into a modern and more centrally organized state. It was a job of enormous proportions, but Leopold was remarkably successful. The Habsburg lands, when he came to power in 1658, embraced most of Austria, Hungary and Bohemia—a territory containing a bewildering variety of languages and religions, local privileges and local customs. Nevertheless, Leopold established an effective administrative structure, run from Vienna, and made his court the focus of his country's intellectual and economic life.

His success was all the more impressive because Austria was under constant threat of attack from France on the west and Turkey on the east. Like the double-headed eagle on the crest of the House of Habsburg, Leopold faced in two directions—and Louis XIV conspired with Kara Mustafa, the Grand Vizier, to make sure that the double harassment continued. But Louis' strategy ultimately failed—because it was too successful. In 1682, encouraged by Louis and by a disgruntled Hungarian nobility, Mustafa assembled an army of 200,000 men, enormous for its day, and prepared to march up the Danube valley into Hungary and Austria. In fact, Mustafa proposed to capture Vienna itself.

Leopold's outnumbered army fell back helplessly before this onslaught, and on July 14, 1683, Vienna was surrounded. The city held out for two months, and then, just as it was on the verge of being starved into submission, a rescuing army appeared. It was led by Charles of Lorraine, an imperial prince whose duchy had fallen into French hands, and by John Sobieski, the King of Poland. This army became the nucleus of the army of the Holy League, an alliance that united Poland, Austria and the republic of Venice in a war to drive the infidel Turks from Europe. Lavishly supported by the papal treasury, and swelled by volunteers from every country in Europe, even France, the Holy League finally succeeded in annihilating the Turkish army at the Battle of Zenta, in Serbia, in 1697. At the signing of the Treaty of Karlowitz in January 1699, Leopold's possession of Hungary, Transylvania, Croatia and Slavonia was assured, and the Emperor was freed to turn his undivided attention westward—to France, and to Louis XIV.

At the same time, another new territorial state was also preparing to move against Louis: the principality of Brandenburg-Prussia, soon to become the kingdom of Prussia. Brandenburg-Prussia had come into being in 1618, when the Hohenzollern Elector of Brandenburg inherited the fief of Prussia. Although its birth happened to coincide with the start of the Thirty Years' War, it did not figure prominently in that war, and in fact showed little promise of ever becoming important in any way at all. It was a small realm, geographically divided, with no notable natural resources and a sparse population. But under the leadership of Frederick William, known as the Great Elector, Brandenburg-Prussia was transformed.

Frederick William, who ruled from 1640 to 1688, was one of the great state-builders of the 17th Century. His methods, peculiarly his own, were to have profound consequences for Germany as well as the rest of Europe; the Great Elector built a state around a standing army. Faced with more than the usual number of divisive forces in his widely scattered lands, Frederick William used his military organization, the Commissariat of War, as the basis of his civil administration. The army and the government were virtually one. With this splendid organization, and a fighting force that by 1678 numbered some 45,000 men, Frederick William played an increasingly important role in European politics. He took advantage of the century's constant wars by selling his support first to one side, then to the other, and his son, the relatively ineffectual Frederick III, followed his example. In 1701, in exchange for joining the Grand Alliance against Louis XIV, Frederick III gained himself the title of Frederick I, King of Prussia. Out of the chaos of Germany at the close of the Thirty Years' War, a modern state had emerged to join the powers of Europe.

At the same time England too began to play a major role in the power structure of Europe. After nearly a century of domestic strife, the country's Glorious Revolution had at last established a new and stable political order, and had brought to the throne the Dutch leader, William III, of the house of Orange, a leader in the resistance to Louis XIV. England's interests on the continent were threefold: to prevent James II and his heirs, supported by Louis XIV, from regaining the English crown; to protect and expand England's overseas trade, particularly in the New World; and to prevent the rise of a European power strong enough to challenge England's position.

When the reckless policies of Louis XIV united English public opinion in favor of war against France, England's new constitutional government got its first test of strength. Its merits were quickly apparent. Backed by a Parliament that spoke for all the influential elements in English society, William III could draw upon the resources of his country more effectively than any other sovereign of his time. Parliament voted him funds not only by raising taxes, but also by borrowing money from the newly established Bank of England. William thus got more money, and got it faster, than he could ever have raised through taxation alone—and England got its first national debt, a sign not of weakness, but of the people's confidence in their government.

The last of the great territorial states to enter the arena of European politics at the end of the 17th Century was Russia, and it arrived there largely through the efforts of one man, Czar Peter the Great. Peter came to power in 1689. A giant of a man, with an energy and temper to match, he was utterly dedicated to the task of transforming his vast and primitive realm into a modern state, and involved himself personally in the project. Convinced that Russia's only hope lay in copying the technology and administrative techniques of the West, Peter toured Europe for more than a year, visiting factories, hospitals, government offices, museums and universities. For a time he even worked as a shipwright in a Dutch shipyard.

In 1698 Peter returned to Russia, determined to put what he had learned into practice. His campaign to modernize and Westernize Russia included political, economic, educational and military reforms—and even reforms in dress. Like Louis XIV, Peter understood the importance of appearances. He announced that no one should enter his presence wearing a beard, the badge of old Russia, and personally shaved a number of his courtiers to emphasize the point. He also outlawed the wearing of the traditional long Russian robe. Peter was convinced that Russia needed direct communication with Europe, a "window on the West." But his natural route to the West lay through the Baltic Sea, which was practically a Swedish lake. Under the leadership of the famous Gustavus Adolphus and his able successors, Charles X and Charles XI, Sweden had carved out a considerable empire for itself along the Baltic shores, and it guarded that empire jealously with its armies. To break Sweden's hold upon the Baltic, Peter formed a secret alliance in 1699 with Denmark and Poland against Charles XII of Sweden. The following year the three nations launched what came to be known as the Great Northern War.

If the allies expected an easy victory over Sweden, they were quickly disillusioned; Charles was more than a match for the combined might of his foes. By August 1700, Denmark was defeated and had withdrawn from the alliance, and Charles had turned his attention eastward to confront Russia. On November 30, at Narva, with an army of only 8,000 men, he completely routed a Russian army of 40,000—and then spent the remainder of a pleasant winter in snowball fights and elk hunts while his troops rested. In the spring, he invaded Poland.

During the next seven years, while the Swedish army fought its way across Poland and down into Central Europe, Peter put together another Russian army. The disaster at Narva shocked him but did not deter him from his goal. When Charles turned northward again, Peter was waiting for him with a new army of 100,000 men armed with modern weapons—and a Russian navy. In the spring of 1709, the Swedish army, weakened by the ordeal of a Russian winter, was finally defeated at the Battle of Poltava—and Peter secured his "window on the West."

In the same year, another decisive battle was helping to determine the course of another great conflict. At Malplaquet, in the north of France, an Anglo-Dutch army under the Duke of Marlborough and a Habsburg army under Eugene of Savoy defeated the French army in the bloodiest battle of the War of the Spanish Succession. Like the Great Northern War, the War of the Spanish Succession had begun a decade before, and it too was a dramatic climax to the Age of Kings: out of its battles and diplomatic maneuvers emerged the modern system of power politics.

On November 1, 1700, the last Habsburg King of Spain died. Within months, the nations of Europe were fighting over his vast and far-flung possessions—in Spain, in the Spanish Netherlands, in Sicily, Naples and Milan, in the New World.

Charles II of Spain, the most grotesque monarch of the 17th Century, had been a travesty of a king. Generations of royal intermarriage had culminated in Charles in a creature so defective in mind and body as to be scarcely even a man. He was born in 1661, the product of his father's old age, and his brief life consisted chiefly of a passage from prolonged infancy to premature senility. He was not weaned until he was five, could not walk until he was 10, and was considered to be too feeble for the rigors of education. In Charles, the famous Habsburg chin reached such massive proportions that he was unable to chew, and his tongue was so large that he was barely able to speak. Lame, epileptic, bald at the age of 35, Charles suffered one further disability, politically more significant than all the rest: he was impotent.

The Spanish King's physical inability to beget an heir was common knowledge throughout Europe, and a subject of the most intense concern. When he died, who would inherit his throne? Who would rule over the Spanish possessions in the Netherlands and the New World, in Sicily, Naples and Milan? The answer would profoundly affect the European balance of power, and statesmen were not prepared to sit idly by while a degenerate monarch made the decision. Even while Charles was still alive, negotiations were under way to settle the Spanish succession.

The two principal claimants, in terms of power and hereditary right, were Louis XIV of France and Leopold I of Austria. Both claims were based on ties to Philip III of Spain, grandfather of the unfortunate Charles, and both splendidly illustrate the dynastic complexity of the age. Philip had had two daughters; the elder was the mother of Louis XIV, the younger, the mother of Leopold. A generation later, Philip's son, Philip IV, had also had two daughters; the elder had married Louis XIV, the younger had married Leopold.

Louis' claim to the throne of Spain was based on the fact that his mother and his wife were the older sisters of Leopold's mother and wife. Leopold's claim was based on the fact that Louis' wife had explicitly renounced her right to the Spanish throne when she married Louis. Yes, replied Louis' supporters, but the renunciation had been made on the condition that France was to receive, instead, a dowry of 500,000 gold crowns—and the dowry had never been paid. Therefore the renunciation was invalid.

The arguments might have gone on indefinitely, delving ever more deeply into the intricacies of dynastic succession, but soon the realities of power politics pushed them aside. The simple fact was that control of Spain by either France or Austria was intolerable to the rest of Europe; it raised the spectre of a Bourbon or Habsburg super-state. Mindful of these fears, both Louis and Leopold had, in fact, put forward their claims indirectly— Louis through Philippe d'Anjou, his grandson; Leopold through the Archduke Charles, his son. But these maneuvers satisfied no one. Some other solution would have to be found.

Fortunately, there was a third hereditary claimant, the very young Prince Joseph Ferdinand of Bavaria. The seven-year-old prince was the great-grandson of Philip IV of Spain. He was also, as it happened, the grandson of Leopold of Austria— through Leopold's marriage to the Spanish princess, Margaret Theresa. But Prince Joseph Ferdinand had no claim upon the Austrian crown, and therefore posed no threat to the European balance of power. Accordingly, on October 11, 1698, France, England and Holland signed a treaty, agreeing to recognize Joseph Ferdinand as the heir to the Spanish throne and all the Spanish lands except those in Italy. These were to be divided between France and Austria, as compensation for relinquishing their claims to the throne. France was to get Naples and Sicily; Austria would get Milan.

Within four months, this seemingly reasonable treaty was a dead letter. Leopold rejected it imme-

A WISE MONARCH IN THE EAST

As Europe's Age of Kings drew to a close with the emergence of a new international order, the Chinese emperor K'ang Hsi was consolidating what was soon to become the wealthiest, largest and most populous empire in the world. Unlike Louis XIV's France, bankrupt from a succession of wars, China was entering a period of unequaled prosperity under its new ruler, who expanded his country's borders to include Tibet and Formosa, and instituted programs of trade and public works.

The second of the great Manchu monarchs who replaced the corrupt Mings, K'ang Hsi, like Louis, became an energetic champion of industry and the arts. He subsidized the manufacture of exquisite porcelain vases and dishes and commissioned the compilation of both a 40,000-character dictionary and an encyclopedia that embraced the whole of Chinese knowledge. Through these and other actions during his long reign (1661-1722), K'ang Hsi laid the foundations for more than a century of prosperity and learning.

diately, declaring that he meant to press the claim of his son. A month later, Charles II himself, unwilling to countenance the division of his lands, drew up a will leaving all of his empire, including the Italian possessions, to the young Bavarian prince. Then, in February 1699, Joseph Ferdinand unexpectedly died. Everything was right back where it had started—except that now there was no third alternative.

The death of the young prince set off a veritable frenzy of diplomatic negotiation and intrigue. While Leopold stubbornly continued to press the claims of his son, the Archduke Charles, representatives of France, England and the Netherlands met to draw up a second treaty. According to its terms the Spanish crown, and the Spanish possessions in the Netherlands and the Americas, were to be awarded to the Archduke Charles, and the Spanish holdings in Italy were to go to France. The generosity of Louis XIV in agreeing to these terms was remarkable; even more remarkable was the greed of Leopold in rejecting them.

All through the summer Europe waited for Charles II's reactions, while diplomats pressed him from all sides. The Austrians urged him to be mindful of the sacredness of his Habsburg family ties. The French pointed out their military superiority, and suggested that Leopold might not be able to defend his son's possessions. The Pope, Innocent XII, supported France, but only on condition that the French claimant, Philippe d'Anjou, renounce his right to the throne of France. The Spanish nobility, anxious to preserve the Spanish empire intact, also backed this proposal, and at their insistence, on October 2, 1700, Charles II named Philippe his heir. A month later, Charles died.

His death placed Louis XIV in a peculiar position. On the one hand, Louis was party to a treaty that gave the bulk of the Spanish empire to the Austrian claimant; on the other, he was the grand-father of the young man chosen to inherit the whole thing. No matter which tie he elected to honor, he would almost certainly be involved in a war—for Leopold, having accepted neither the treaty nor the will of Charles II, would only accede to either by force. Louis could thus fight for the treaty and gain Naples, Sicily and Milan for himself, or he could fight to win the whole empire for his grandson. After some hesitation, he chose to seek the greater prize.

In February 1701, Philippe d'Anjou was proclaimed Philip V of Spain, and immediately renounced forever any dynastic claim to the throne of France. But the Spanish ambassador, kneeling before him at Versailles, was heard to murmur a sentence that confirmed the worst suspicions of every statesman in Europe: *"Il n'y a plus de Pyrénées*—There are no more Pyrenees." Were all the negotiations and treaties of the past two years to end in the dreaded union of France and Spain? Would Louis XIV, who had seemed so reasonable and circumspect while Charles II lived, now revert to his aggressive ways and, with Spain on his side, dream of even greater conquests? The fate of Europe hung upon his decision.

It was immediately apparent that Louis would have to take up arms against Leopold, but it was also apparent that Louis could count on the support, or at least the neutrality, of England and Holland simply by avoiding any move that seemed to threaten their territory or trade. Both countries had accepted Philippe as King of Spain, and both had indicated a desire to live at peace with France. With a modicum of discretion, Louis could have assured that peace. Instead, as early as February 1701 Louis embarked on a series of moves that might have been specifically designed to arouse the hostility of the English and Dutch. Acting as though the Spanish possessions in the Netherlands were in fact French, he sent an army into them to take over a string of fortresses garrisoned, according to a treaty arrangement, by the Dutch. He claimed that he was doing this temporarily, until Spanish troops could take over—but it was widely recognized as the first step in the annexation of the Spanish Netherlands.

Even more serious, Louis attempted to win for France the trading privileges enjoyed by English and Dutch merchants in Spain and the Spanish colonies. French ships took over the profitable slave trade between Africa and the Spanish possessions in South America, and England was to admit in 1716 that "the preservation of the commerce between the kingdom of Great Britain and Spain was one of the chief motives that induced our two royal predecessors to enter the late, long, expensive war." When Louis, in June 1701, arranged an alliance between France, Spain and Portugal that threatened to exclude England and Holland from the entire Mediterranean, it was more than those two nations could endure.

In July, negotiations were begun to forge a Grand Alliance against the Sun King; on September 7, 1701, the alliance became a reality. England, Holland and Austria agreed to fight for Leopold's right to Spain's European possessions, and for the security of English and Dutch territories and trade. The British Parliament had already voted to recruit a navy of 30,000 men and to raise £2,700,000 for the common effort. Leopold's army, under the brilliant general Eugene of Savoy, was prepared to invade Italy. Soon every state in Germany except Bavaria and the principality of Cologne joined the Alliance, and the War of the Spanish Succession had begun.

The events of this war proved that Louis XIV had at last overstepped the bounds of military and political reality. Despite the vast forces at his disposal—a French army of some 400,000 men, plus the armies of his two allies, Spain and Bavaria—

Louis was no match for the combined might of his enemies. In the west, John Churchill, Duke of Marlborough, conquered the lower Rhine with an Anglo-Dutch army, and threatened the French forces in the Spanish Netherlands. In the south, the army of Eugene of Savoy harassed a French force three times its size.

Meanwhile, Louis had decided, with characteristic boldness, to strike directly at the heart of his Austrian enemy. In 1703 he dispatched a French army eastward through the Black Forest to join the army of his Bavarian allies and march on Vienna. But Marlborough thwarted his plan. With enormous skill and daring, the English general brought his forces from the lower Rhine to the upper Danube in time to join the army of Eugene of Savoy at the town of Blenheim, in Bavaria. There, on August 13, 1704, the French suffered their first great military defeat. It was soon followed by others—at Ramillies in 1706, at Oudenarde in 1708, both in the Spanish Netherlands.

At the same time, Louis' diplomatic and financial positions were also weakening. Portugal, never really a willing member of the French-Spanish accord, had deserted Louis in 1703 to join the Grand Alliance. And it was increasingly apparent that the French people and the French economy, after 20 years of nearly continuous warfare, were on the verge of collapse. By 1708 Louis was ready to make peace, even though the terms offered by his enemies were harsh. He agreed to recognize Leopold's son as the King of Spain, to recognize Queen Anne as the legitimate monarch of England and give up his support of the Stuart pretender, to surrender all claim to the Spanish colonies and relinquish all captured Habsburg possessions, to destroy the French naval base at Dunkirk.

One condition, however, he refused to accept: he would not help his enemies drive his grandson out of Spain. On this point negotiations collapsed, and hostilities began again. Louis issued a ringing manifesto, calling upon the French people to gather themselves for a new effort, and the response was magnificent. Men flocked to join the army, and money flowed in to replenish the royal treasury. In the face of the humiliating peace terms, Frenchmen stood with their King.

In September 1709, the opposing armies again met in battle, at Malplaquet. When it was over, Marlborough and Eugene of Savoy had vanquished the French, but 40,000 men lay dead or wounded in the space of 10 square miles. Both sides were so horrified at the cost that once again there was talk of peace. This time the terms were even steeper. Louis' enemies insisted that France should not only agree to, but actually lead the campaign to drive Philip V from Spain.

Again the Sun King refused, and again the war continued. But now the arrogance of the Grand Alliance seemed about to be punished. In 1710 the Whig government in England was overthrown— partly out of popular revulsion to the holocaust at Malplaquet—and a Tory government, controlled by Marlborough's enemies, replaced it. The change gravely weakened England's commitment to the Grand Alliance. A year later, the Austrian Emperor died, and Archduke Charles—the allies' candidate for the Spanish throne—succeeded him, placing the allies in an untenable position. If they persisted in their avowed goal, they would create precisely the situation they had originally joined to prevent —the union of the Spanish throne with one of the great powers of Europe.

These changes, plus a French victory in the Battle of Denain in 1712, disposed the allies to be more realistic in their peace terms. Negotiations were reopened, and in 1713 the Peace of Utrecht was signed. By its terms, Philippe d'Anjou, the Bourbon Prince, was recognized as Philip V of Spain, but was required to renounce his claim to the throne of France. England received Gibraltar and the Mediterranean island of Minorca, assuring it access to the inland sea, and the French territories of Newfoundland and Nova Scotia in the New World. England also got the coveted *asiento*, the shipping rights to the lucrative slave trade between Africa and Latin America. Austria received the Spanish Netherlands, Milan, Sardinia and Naples. The Dutch got the right once again to garrison the forts along the border between France and what was now the "Austrian" Netherlands. Louis XIV recognized the Protestant succession to the English throne, and all of Europe recognized Frederick I as King of the sovereign state of Prussia.

The Peace of Utrecht brought to Europe not just an end to conflict, but the outlines of a new system of European states. It was a system governed by balance of power, within which each sovereign, independent, secular state could—and did—vie for power and wealth. Each state ruthlessly pursued its own interests, but all were bound up together in a larger European order that regulated their actions and set limits on their ambitions.

The 17th Century, an Age of Kings, and also an age of grandeur and of genius, marks one of the great turning points in human history: it inherited a world of tension and conflict, of superstition and anarchy; it bequeathed to posterity a world of order and reason based upon the power of the modern state and the authority of modern science. The century had begun with John Donne lamenting the loss of all coherence, of all just relations. It ended with Gottfried Wilhelm Leibniz, the last of its great philosophers, demonstrating that this was "the best of all possible worlds." Although Leibniz was making a metaphysical point, men interpreted him to mean that the world was perfect—and accepted the premise as valid. Few men would have done so in 1600. This is perhaps the best measure of the achievement of the Age of Kings.

THE ORDER OF THE DAY

As the Age of Kings marched to a close, Europe settled into in a new era of comparative order and stability. Nowhere was the new spirit more vividly reflected than in the field of military science. Large standing armies of disciplined professional soldiers largely replaced the freewheeling mercenaries of earlier days; battle tactics and training methods were refined and formalized. To make sure that nothing was left to chance, scores of illustrated manuals methodically described procedures for handling new weapons such as the flintlock, shown below being fired by an imperial infantryman at the German command "Feuer!"

WELL-DRILLED SPECIALISTS

STANDARD BEARER

INFANTRYMAN THROWING GRENADE

AUSTRIAN GRENADIER

Organization and discipline were the passwords to victory in Europe's new armies. The most powerful fighting force of the century, the army of France, owed its effectiveness to the genius of Louis XIV's war minister, the Marquis de Louvois. A stern administrator, Louvois believed that war should be waged by the book. He set up Europe's first military supply system, pay scales and formal chain of command.

French soldiers were rigorously trained to be specialists in weapons like the hand grenade and bayonet *(engravings below and left)*; for the first time many regiments proudly wore uniforms of regulation color and cut. So effective were the French reforms that most other nations in Europe copied them, and armies were gradually transformed from ragtag conglomerations of hirelings into organized fighting machines.

MUSKETEER FIXING BAYONET

PIKEMAN WITH PIKE AND SWORD

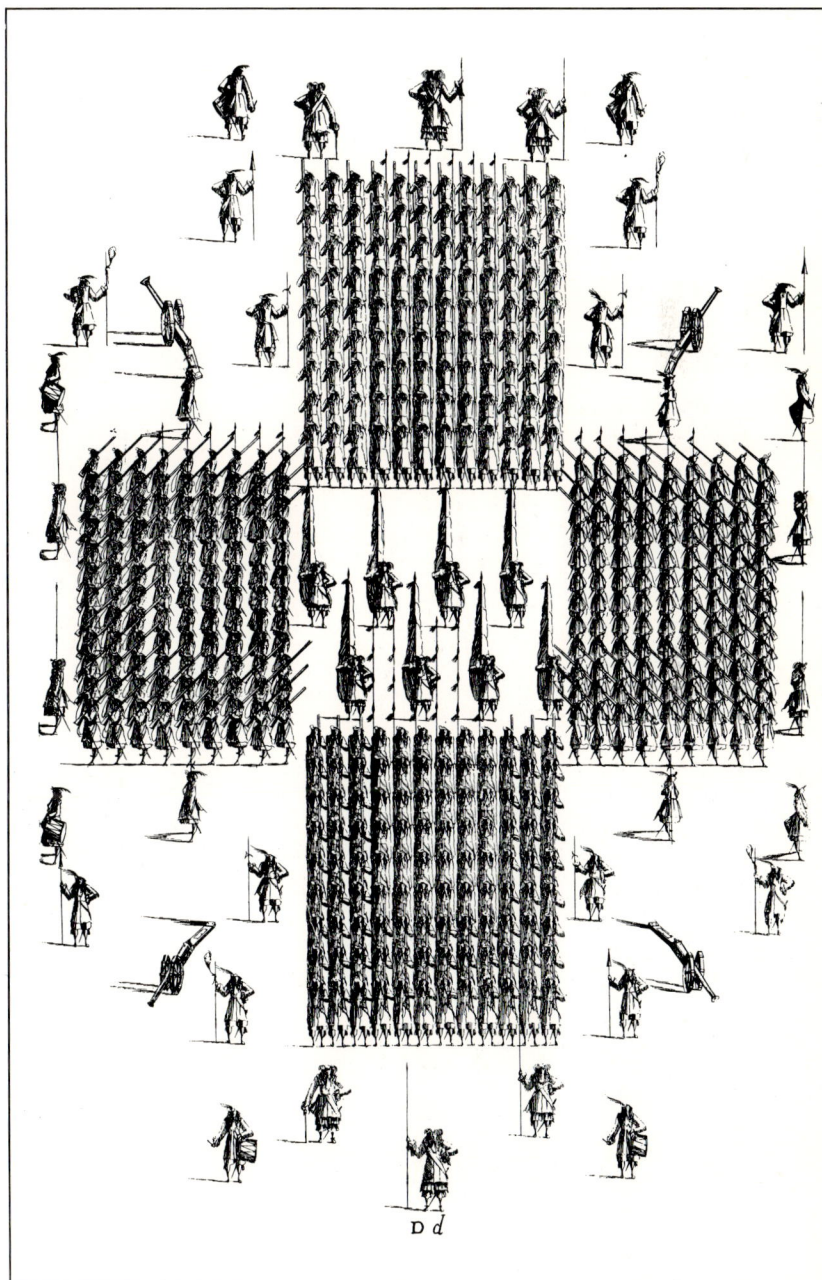

D d

PARADING THEIR SKILLS, *infantrymen stand at attention in a defensive formation shown in an Italian training manual. Pikemen and musketeers are deployed to form a hollow cross with standard-bearers in the center, officers, drummers and cannoneers outside. Relentless drilling in such exercises led to high precision in actual battle maneuvers.*

THE FLINTLOCK: A FORMIDABLE WEAPON

The European foot soldier, made more effective by training and discipline, gained still greater striking power from improved firearms. Early muskets, which had to be touched off by a piece of burning cord, were unwieldy devices, hard to aim, dangerous to fire and time-consuming to reload. But with the new flintlock *(below)*, a man could get off as many as six shots a minute—with some assurance that his weapon would not blow up in his face.

In battle tactics based on this firepower, long ranks of soldiers marched abreast toward the enemy, delivering massed volleys on command. To ensure precision, intricate drills were perfected for firing and reloading. In one step, soldiers used their teeth to open the paper capsules that held the powder for each shot, and no man was recruited as a musketeer unless he had a strong bite.

FIRING BY THE NUMBERS, *a musketeer raises his flintlock (top left), cocks and fires it, and then reloads by packing powder and ball through the muzzle with a ramrod. In the firing mechanism (opposite page), a hammer holding a piece of flint produced a spark by hitting a hinged, L-shaped steel arm. The impact knocked the arm forward, exposing a pinch of gunpowder held in a shallow pan. The spark ignited the gunpowder, which flared through a tiny hole in the barrel to set off the larger charge inside.*

A HARDER-HITTING ARTILLERY

In the early days of the 17th Century, artillery was still decidedly a hit-or-miss affair. Gunners were often private journeymen who cast their own cannons and hired themselves out to the highest bidder—sometimes switching sides in the middle of a battle. But gradually regulations were tightened, guns were cast in foundries to standardized sizes, and artillery was incorporated into the regular army. Cannons were developed for specific tasks, from the small, highly mobile anti-personnel gun shown at right to the 3,000-pound giants illustrated below, used for blasting holes in fortresses.

TENDING SIEGE GUNS, *a cannoneer (top) fires his piece by holding a lit fuse on a long pole to a touch-hole in the barrel, while others (center) pour water down the barrel to douse remnants of burning wadding before reloading with powder and shot. A third cannon overheated by too much firing is cooled by water-soaked sheepskins.*

STOUT WARSHIPS FOR THE SEA

As more efficient armies lined up for battle on land, refurbished navies sought to gain control of the seas. During the second half of the 17th Century, the British and the Dutch, Europe's two greatest seafaring powers, fought three naval wars against each other for control of overseas commerce. Under Charles II, the British started a major shipbuilding program, founded naval academies to train professional officers, and issued manuals of tactics that helped move their ships to later victories with spit-and-polish precision.

The French, jealous of Britain's maritime prowess, launched a naval program of their own. Jean Baptiste Colbert, Louis XIV's minister for finance and trade, renovated France's dilapidated ports, built dockyards, founded training schools and published the *Atlas de Colbert*, a shipbuilding manual that became the bible of French shipwrights. Colbert's moves were so effective that France's navy increased from only 20 vessels in 1661 to 270 warships by 1677.

A FLOATING FORTRESS, *a 190-foot French ship of the line is shown in scale model form, stripped of hull planking on one side to reveal its massive wooden skeleton. Gunports on the far side indicate positions of some of the ship's 104 cannon. Wood from some 2,000 oak trees was needed to build vessels of this size, the largest of the century.*

THE BIRTH OF A BATTLESHIP, *depicted in Colbert's "Atlas," outlines techniques for launching vessels like this 84-gun man-of-war. Ships were built near the water's edge, then hauled by block and tackle down greased timbers at high tide.*

With the precision of toy soldiers, imperial pikemen fix their weapons through holes in a rail.

The rank behind will cross these pikes to construct a barrier behind which to change the guard.

CHRONOLOGY: *A listing of significant events during the Age of Kings*

Arts and Science

1600	Johannes Kepler becomes Tycho Brahe's assistant in his observatory at Prague
1603	The century's first scientific society, *Accademia dei Lincei*, is formed in Rome
1606	Rembrandt van Rijn is born in Leiden
1607	Claudio Monteverdi, "Beethoven of the Baroque," produces his first opera, *Orfeo*
1609	Kepler publishes *Astronomia Nova*, containing two famous laws about the orbits of planets
1610	Galileo publishes *The Starry Messenger*, announcing his telescopic discoveries
1611	John Donne writes "An Anatomie of the World," criticizing the "new philosophy"
1616	The notion of a sun-centered planetary system is condemned by the Catholic Inquisition
1619	Kepler publishes *De Harmonice Mundi*, explaining "celestial harmonics"
1620	Francis Bacon publishes *Novum Organum*, expounding a new method of learning
1622	Jean Baptiste Poquelin, later renowned as the playwright Molière, is born in Paris
1623	Gianlorenzo Bernini, at age 25, creates his great Baroque statue, *David*
1623	Velasquez becomes court painter to Philip IV of Spain
1628	William Harvey publishes his treatise on the circulation of the blood
1629	Bernini is appointed official architect in charge of St. Peter's
1632	Galileo publishes the *Dialogue on the Two Chief Systems of the World*
1632	Anthony van Dyck becomes court painter to Charles I of England
1633	Galileo is forced by the Inquisition to recant his heretical ideas
1635	The French Academy is founded by Richelieu to purify French language and literature
1637	Pierre Corneille's first tragedy, *Le Cid*, is performed
1637	René Descartes' *Discourse on Method* appears, enunciating his universe based on reason
1638	Galileo's *Discourses on Two New Sciences* is published
1639	Jean Racine, French classical dramatist, is born at La Ferté-Milon
1641	Descartes' *Meditations* appear, arguing the superiority of the mind over the senses
1642	Rembrandt paints *The Night Watch*, the group portrait of a Dutch shooting company
1642	Sir Isaac Newton is born
1643	Evangelista Torricelli, Italian physicist, invents the barometer
1645	Pascal perfects his *pascaline*, the world's first calculating machine
1646	Gottfried Wilhelm Leibniz, German mathematician and philosopher, is born
1647	Johannes Hevelius publishes *Selenographia*, an illustrated study of the moon

Politics and Society

1603	James I, son of Mary Queen of Scots, succeeds Queen Elizabeth I as monarch of England
1605	The Gunpowder Plot, a conspiracy to blow up James I and the English Parliament, is discovered and frustrated
1608	Protestant Union of German princes is formed
1609	The Catholic League is founded by Maximilian of Bavaria
1610	Henry IV of France is assassinated by a religious fanatic
1611	Gustavus Adolphus succeeds his father Charles IX as King of Sweden
1613	Michael Romanov is chosen Czar of Russia, beginning the dynasty that ruled until 1917
1618	Brandenburg and Prussia are united under one ruler
1618	Protestant Bohemians revolt against Catholic Ferdinand; the Thirty Years' War begins
1619	Protestant Bohemians elect Frederick V, a Calvinist, their King; the deposed King Ferdinand is elected Holy Roman Emperor
1620	Army of the Catholic League routs forces of Frederick V in the Battle of the White Mountain
1621	England's House of Commons enters Protestation against James I in its journal; James rips it out
1624	Richelieu is made Louis XIII's chief minister
1625	King Christian IV of Denmark enters the Thirty Years' War on the Protestant side; Wallenstein creates an army for Emperor Ferdinand
1626	Army of the Catholic League defeats Christian IV in the Battle of Lutter
1628	Parliament adopts the Petition of Right, asking the King to suspend his use of the royal prerogative
1629	Emperor Ferdinand issues the Edict of Restitution, returning all lands seized from the Catholic Church since 1555
1630	Gustavus Adolphus of Sweden enters the Thirty Years' War to aid German Protestants
1631	Gustavus Adolphus defeats Catholic League's army at the Battle of Breitenfeld in the first significant Protestant victory of the war
1632	The Swedish army defeats Wallenstein's army in the Battle of Lützen, but Gustavus is killed
1635	Peace of Prague ends the third phase of the Thirty Years' War; France declares war on the Habsburgs
1637	Ferdinand dies and is succeeded as Holy Roman Emperor by his son
1637	Charles I of England attempts to impose the Anglican Church on Scotland
1638	Louis XIV is born to Louis XIII and Anne of Austria
1640	Frederick William, the Great Elector, begins his 48-year rule in Brandenburg-Prussia
1642	England's Long Parliament presents its Nineteen Propositions, designed to transfer sovereignty from King to Parliament; Charles rejects them and civil war erupts
1642	Richelieu dies and Cardinal Mazarin succeeds him as chief minister of France
1643	Louis XIII dies and is succeeded by five-year-old Louis XIV under the regency of his mother
1644	Oliver Cromwell's army defeats Royalists in the Battle of Marston Moor, winning his first decisive victory for the Parliamentarians
1645	Cromwell's victory at the Battle of Naseby ends England's first civil war
1646	Charles I surrenders himself to the Scots

1650	René Descartes dies in Stockholm
1651	Thomas Hobbes publishes *The Leviathan*, his political treatise on the nature of the state
1652	Italian composer Jean Baptiste Lully enters the service of Louis XIV
1654	Pascal has a vision of God and turns from mathematics to religion
1654	Otto von Guericke demonstrates the existence and force of atmospheric pressure
1656	James Harrington completes *Oceana*, his concept of a utopian commonwealth
1659	*Les Précieuses Ridicules*, Molière's first comedy of manners, is performed
1660	Von Guericke invents the first rotating electrical generator
1661	Robert Boyle publishes *The Sceptical Chymist* and formulates his famous law of gases
1665	Bernini visits Paris and carves a bust of Louis XIV
1665	English physicist Robert Hooke publishes *Micrographia*, describing cells in plant tissues
1666	Jean Baptiste Colbert, Louis XIV's chief adviser, founds the French Academy of Sciences
1667	John Milton publishes *Paradise Lost*
1667	Racine writes *Andromaque*, the play that established him as the equal of Corneille
1668	Jean de la Fontaine publishes the first of his sophisticated *Fables* and becomes the most widely read author in France
1670	Pascal's *Pensées*, attacking Cartesian thought, are published posthumously
1672	Jean Baptiste Lully, court composer to Louis XIV, founds the Royal Academy of Music
1674	Nicolas Boileau publishes *The Art of Poetry*, codifying French literary style
1674	Dutch microscopist Anton van Leeuwenhoek gives the first accurate description of red blood corpuscles
1678	Samuel Butler completes *Hudibras*, his epic mocking Puritanism
1682	John Dryden's political satire, *Absalom and Achitophel*, is completed
1682	Edmund Halley observes the comet now called by his name
1685	Johann Sebastian Bach is born in Eisenach; George Frideric Handel is born in Halle
1687	Newton publishes *Philosophiae Naturalis Principia Mathematica*, in which he announces the Law of Universal Gravitation
1689	John Locke's *Letters on Toleration* are published, defending religious liberty
1690	Locke's *Two Treatises on Civil Government* appears, and is used in defense of England's Glorious Revolution
1694	The French Academy issues the first edition of its dictionary
1694	François Marie Arouet, later known as Voltaire, is born in Paris
1700	William Congreve writes *The Way of the World*, the greatest Restoration comedy
1711	Sir Christopher Wren's St. Paul's Cathedral is officially completed
1714	Leibniz publishes *Monadology*, expounding his famous theory that the universe is made up of particles called "monads"

1652	England and the Dutch Republic begin the first of three Anglo-Dutch wars for control of overseas commerce
1653	England's first and only written constitution makes Cromwell Lord Protector of the English Commonwealth; the Long Parliament is dissolved
1654	Queen Christina of Sweden abdicates and is succeeded by Charles X
1655	Charles X attacks Poland, to make the Baltic a "Swedish lake"
1660	Treaty of Oliva ends Swedish-Polish hostilities; neighboring Prussia is recognized as a sovereign state
1660	Charles II begins his reign as King of England, restoring the monarchy
1661	Mazarin dies and Louis XIV begins his personal rule
1665	Philip IV of Spain dies and is succeeded by his son Charles II, a sickly monarch who becomes the last of the Spanish Habsburg kings
1665	The Great Plague of London kills more than 60,000 people
1666	London's Great Fire destroys two thirds of the city
1667	Louis XIV begins the War of Devolution against the Spanish Netherlands, to seize them for France
1668	The Triple Alliance is formed by English, Dutch and Swedes against Louis XIV's aggression in the Spanish Netherlands
1670	Treaty of Dover secretly allies Louis XIV and England's Charles II
1672	Charles II and Louis XIV join in war on Dutch
1674	England withdraws from the Dutch War
1678	Peace of Nijmegen brings the Dutch War to a close; France acquires Franche-Comté
1682	Louis XIV moves court into the newly remodeled Palace of Versailles
1683	Turks invade Habsburg lands in Eastern Europe and lay siege to Vienna
1685	Edict of Nantes, granting French Huguenots religious liberty, is revoked by Louis XIV
1688	Parliamentary enemies of James II invite William of Orange to invade England
1689	Declaration of Rights establishes England's constitutional government; William and Mary are declared rulers of England
1694	Queen Mary of England dies of smallpox
1694	Bank of England is founded, to lend money to the government
1699	Treaty of Karlowitz ends the Holy League's war with the Turks
1700	Great Northern War breaks out between Sweden and alliance of Poland, Denmark and Russia; Swedes overwhelm Russians at the Battle of Narva
1701	Grand Alliance unites England, Holland and Austria against policies of Louis XIV
1701	War of the Spanish Succession begins, pitting France against the Grand Alliance
1704	French forces are routed by an Anglo-Dutch army under Marlborough at the Battle of Blenheim
1709	Russian army crushes Charles XII of Sweden at the Battle of Poltava
1713	Peace of Utrecht ends the War of the Spanish Succession and establishes a new order in Europe
1715	Louis XIV dies after a 72-year reign in France

BIBLIOGRAPHY

These books were selected during the preparation of this volume for their interest and authority, and for their usefulness to readers seeking additional information on specific points. An asterisk (*) marks works available in both hard-cover and paperback editions; a dagger (†) indicates availability only in paperback.

GENERAL READING

†Ashley, Maurice, *England in the Seventeenth Century.* 3rd ed. Penguin Books, 1961.
Clark, Sir George, *The Later Stuarts 1660-1714.* 2nd ed. Oxford University Press, 1956.
*Clark, Sir George, *The Seventeenth Century.* 2nd ed. Oxford University Press, 1947.
Davies, Godfrey, *The Early Stuarts 1603-1660.* 2nd ed. Oxford University Press, 1959.
Durant, Will and Ariel, *The Age of Louis XIV.* Simon and Schuster, 1963.
Durant, Will and Ariel, *The Age of Reason Begins.* Simon and Schuster, 1961.
*Fay, Sidney B., and Klaus Epstein, *The Rise of Brandenburg-Prussia, to 1786.* Holt, Rinehart and Winston, 1964.
*Friedrich, Carl J., *The Age of the Baroque 1610-1660.* Harper & Row, 1952.
†Friedrich, Carl J., and Charles Blitzer, *The Age of Power.* Cornell University Press, 1957.
Holborn, Hajo, *A History of Modern Germany: 1648-1840.* Alfred A. Knopf, 1964.
†Lewis, W. H., *The Splendid Century: Life in the France of Louis XIV.* Anchor, 1957.
*Nussbaum, Frederick L., *The Triumph of Science and Reason 1660-1685.* Harper & Row, 1953.
*Ogg, David, *Europe in the Seventeenth Century.* 8th ed. Macmillan, 1960.
*Rowen, Herbert H., *A History of Early Modern Europe 1500-1815.* Bobbs-Merrill, 1966.
*Trevelyan, G. M., *England under the Stuarts.* 21st ed. Barnes & Noble, 1949.
*Wedgwood, C. V., *The Thirty Years War.* Anchor Books, 1961.
*Wolf, John B., *The Emergence of the Great Powers 1685-1715.* Harper & Row, 1951.

BIOGRAPHY

Baldinucci, Filippo, *The Life of Bernini.* Transl. by Catherine Enggass. Pennsylvania State University Press, 1966.
†Bishop, Morris, *Blaise Pascal.* Dell, 1966.
Cronin, Vincent, *Louis XIV.* Houghton Mifflin, 1965.
*Geymonat, Ludovico, *Galileo Galilei.* Transl. by Stillman Drake. McGraw-Hill, 1965.
†Huxley, Aldous, *Grey Eminence: A Study in Religion and Politics.* Harper & Row, 1966.
Lewis, W. H., *Louis XIV: An Informal Portrait.* Harcourt, Brace and World, 1959.
Mitford, Nancy, *The Sun King.* London, Hamish Hamilton, 1966.
Roberts, Michael, *Gustavus Adolphus: A History of Sweden 1611-1632.* 2 vols. Barnes & Noble, 1958.
Watson, Francis, *Wallenstein, Soldier under Saturn.* Appleton-Century-Crofts, 1938.

THOUGHT AND CULTURE

Cook, Albert S., *The Art of Poetry: The Poetical Treatises of Horace, Vida, and Boileau.* Transl. by Howes, Pitt and Soame. G. E. Stechert, 1926.
*Descartes, René, *Philosophical Writings.* Transl. by Norman Kemp Smith. Modern Library, 1958.
Evelyn, John, *The Diary of John Evelyn.* Everyman's Library, 1966.
*Grimmelshausen, J., *Simplicius Simplicissimus.* Transl. by George Schulz-Behrend. Library of Liberal Arts, 1965.
*Hobbes, Thomas, *The Leviathan.* Everyman's Library, 1950.
McKinney, Howard D., and W. R. Anderson, *Music in History: The Evolution of an Art.* American Book Company, 1966.
*Molière, Jean Baptiste, *The Misanthrope and Other Plays.* Transl. by John Wood. Penguin, 1959.
*Molière, Jean Baptiste, *The Miser and Other Plays.* Transl. by John Wood. Penguin, 1962.
*Pascal, Blaise, *Pensées* and *The Provincial Letters.* Transl. by W. F. Trotter and Thomas M'Crie. Modern Library, 1941.
*Pepys, Samuel, *The Diary of Samuel Pepys.* 3 vols. Ed. by John Warrington. Everyman's Library, 1953.
Ziegler, Gilette, ed., *At the Court of Versailles: Eyewitness Reports from the Reign of Louis XIV.* Transl. by Simon Watson Taylor. E. P. Dutton, 1966.

ART AND ARCHITECTURE

*Bazin, Germain, *Baroque and Rococo Art.* Transl. by Jonathan Griffin. Frederick A. Praeger, 1964.
Bechtel, Edwin De T., *Jacques Callot.* George Braziller, 1955.
Kitson, Michael, *The Age of Baroque.* McGraw-Hill, 1966.
Rosenberg, Jakob, *Rembrandt: Life and Work.* Rev. ed. Phaidon Publishers, 1964.
*Tapié, Victor L., *The Age of Grandeur: Baroque Art and Architecture.* Transl. by A. Ross Williamson. Frederick A. Praeger, 1961.
Wittkower, Rudolph, *Art and Architecture in Italy 1600-1750.* 2nd ed. Penguin, 1965.
Wittkower, Rudolph, *Gian Lorenzo Bernini: The Sculptor of the Roman Baroque.* 2nd ed. Phaidon Publishers, 1966.

SCIENCE AND TECHNOLOGY

*Boas, Marie, *The Scientific Renaissance 1450-1630.* Harper & Row, 1962.
*Butterfield, Herbert, *The Origins of Modern Science 1300-1800.* Macmillan, 1957.
*De Santillana, Giorgio, *The Crime of Galileo.* University of Chicago Press, 1955.
†Hall, A. R., *The Scientific Revolution 1500-1800.* 2nd ed. Beacon Press, 1962.
*Koestler, Arthur, *The Sleepwalkers.* The Macmillan Company, 1959.
*Singer, Charles, *A Short History of Scientific Ideas to 1900.* Oxford University Press, 1959.
†Toulmin, Stephen and June Goodfield, *The Fabric of the Heavens: The Development of Astronomy and Dynamics.* Harper & Row, 1962.
*Wolf, A., *A History of Science, Technology and Philosophy in the 16th & 17th Centuries.* 2 vols. Harper & Row, 1959.

ART INFORMATION AND PICTURE CREDITS

The sources for the illustrations in this book are set forth below. Descriptive notes on the works of art are included. Credits for pictures positioned from left to right are separated by semicolons, from top to bottom by dashes. Photographers' names that follow a descriptive note appear in parentheses. Abbreviations include "c." for century and "ca." for circa.

Cover—Detail from *Défaite du Comte de Marsin au Canal de Bruges*, tapestry designed by Charles Le Brun, Tapisserie des Gobelins, 1665-1680, Musée de Versailles (Dmitri Kessel). 8-9—Map by Willem Janszoon Blaeu from *Theatrum Orbis Terrarum sive Atlas Novus*, 1635, American Geographical Society, New York (Lee Boltin).

CHAPTER 1: 10—*Marriage Banquet of Leopold I and Margaret Theresa* by Jan Thomas, oil, 1666, Kunsthistorisches Museum, Vienna (Erich Lessing from Magnum). 14-15—Engravings of trades by Nicolas de Larmessin, late 17th c., New York Public Library, Print Division. 19-29—Playing cards made for King Charles I, by the Worshipful Company of Makers of Playing Cards, inlaid silk, ca. 1628, courtesy Katharine Gregory, New York (Robert S. Crandall). 20—*Louis XIV* by Henri Testelin, oil on canvas, 17th c., Musée de Versailles (Robert Doisneau from Rapho Guillumette).—*Gustavus Adolphus, King of Sweden* by Henry Bolland, oil, 1631, Verwaltung der Staatlichen Schlösser und Gärten, Berlin. 21—*Emperor Leopold I*, attributed to Jan Thomas, oil, ca. 1686, Kunsthistorisches Museum, Vienna (Erich Lessing from Magnum)—*William III of Orange* by Caspar Netscher, oil, 17th c., Staatliche Museen, Berlin. 22—*Madame de Maintenon* by Pierre Mignard, oil, 17th c., Musée de Versailles (Giraudon); *Bishop Bossuet* by Hyacinthe Rigaud, oil, 17th c., Louvre, Paris (Giraudon)—*Archbishop Fénelon* by Joseph Vivien, oil, 17th c., Musée de Versailles (Robert Doisneau from Rapho Guillumette); *Cardinal Richelieu* by Philippe de Champaigne, oil, ca. 1750, Musée Condé, Chantilly (Giraudon).—*Cardinal Mazarin* by Philippe de Champaigne, oil, ca. 1750, Musée Condé, Chantilly (Giraudon).—*Louis, Grand Dauphin* by Hyacinthe Rigaud, oil, 17th c. Staatliche Museen, Berlin; *Le Grand Condé* by David Teniers le Jeune, oil, 17th c., Musée Condé, Chantilly (Giraudon). 23—*Marie de' Medici* by Scifione Pulzone, oil, late 16th c., Pitti Palace, Florence (Scala).—*Jean Baptiste Colbert* by Nicholas Robert, oil, 17th c., Bibliothèque du Muséum d'Histoire Naturelle, Paris (Giraudon).—*Madame de Sévigné* by Ferdinand Elle, oil, 17th c., Musée de Versailles (Robert Doisneau from Rapho Guillumette); *Nicolas Fouquet* by French School of the 17th c., Musée de Versailles (Giraudon).—*Louise de la Vallière* by French School of the 17th c., oil, 17th c., Musée de Versailles (Robert Doisneau from Rapho Guillumette). 24—*Albrecht von Wallenstein* by Anthony van Dyck, grisaille, 17th c., Bayerische Staatsgemäldesammlungen Munich (Foto Blauel); *Maximilian I of Bavaria* by Nicholas Prugger, oil, 17th c., Alte Pinakothek, Munich (Foto Blauel); *Count Johann Tilly* by Anthony van Dyck, grisaille, 17th c., Staatsgemäldesammlungen Munich (Foto Blauel).—*Empress Margaret Theresa*, attributed to Jan Thomas, oil, ca. 1668, Kunsthistorisches Museum, Vienna (Erich Lessing from Magnum); *Eleanor of Neuburg* by J.F.V. Douven, oil, 17th c., Alte Pinakothek, Munich (Walter Sanders). 25—*Emperor Ferdinand II*, artist unknown, oil on canvas, ca. 1618, Kunsthistorisches Museum, Vienna (Erich Lessing from Magnum); *Maria of Bavaria* by Josef Heintz, oil, 1604, Kunsthistorisches Museum, Vienna (Erich Lessing from Magnum)—*Emperor Ferdinand III* by Jan van den Hoecke, oil, early 17th c., Kunsthistorisches Museum, Vienna (Erich Lessing from Magnum); *Maria Anna of Spain with her oldest son*, artist unknown, oil, 17th c., Kunsthistorisches Museum, Vienna (Erich Lessing from Magnum); *Philip IV of Spain* by Diego Velasquez, oil, 17th c., Prado Museum, Madrid (Scala)—*Don Balthasar Carlos* by Diego Velasquez, oil, 17th c., Prado Museum, Madrid (Fernand Bourges and Robert Kafka). 26—*Oliver Cromwell* by Robert Walker, oil, ca. 1655, courtesy National Portrait Gallery, London (Larry Burrows); Mary Stuart, detail from *William II and Mary Stuart* by Anthony van Dyck, oil, 17th c., Rijksmuseum, Amsterdam—*Lucy Walter* by Sir Godfrey Kneller, oil, 17th c., courtesy the Duke of Buccleuch and Queensbury K.T., G.C.V.O. (Eric Schaal)—Henriette, detail from *Children of Charles I* by Anthony van Dyck, oil, 17th c., Galleria Sabauda, Turin (Pierre Boulat); *Charles I of England on Horseback* by pupil of Anthony van Dyck, oil, 17th c., Alte Pinakothek, Munich (Walter Sanders). 27—*Queen Anne of England*, artist unknown, oil, 17th c., Bayerische Staatsgemäldesammlungen, Munich (Walter Sanders); *John Churchill, Duke of Marlborough* by John Riley, ca. 1704, courtesy the Earl Spencer, Northampton, England (Larry Burrows).—*Nell Gwyn* by Sir Peter Lely, oil, 1671, The Bower Collection, Chiddingstone Castle, Kent (Eric Schaal); *Catherine of Braganza* by Dirk Stoop, oil, 1662, National Portrait Gallery, London (Larry Burrows); *Barbara Villiers*, by Sir Peter Lely, courtesy The Ditchley Foundation, England, oil, 17th c. (Larry Burrows)—*Charles II of England*, in the style of Sir Peter Lely, oil, 1689, courtesy Collection of the Duke of Portland (Eric Schaal); *James II of England*, in the style of Van Dyck, oil, 17th c., courtesy Alba Collection, Spain (Frank Lerner). 28—*Frederick the Winter King* by Willem van Honthorst, oil, 17th c., Verwaltung der Staatlichen Schlösser und Gärten, Berlin; *Ernst von Mansfeld* by Robert van Voerst after Van Dyck, copper etching, 17th c., Landesmuseum, Brunswick (Robert Lackenbach from Black Star); *Elizabeth Stuart* by disciple of Michiel Janszoon van Mierevelt, oil, ca. 1615, Niedersächsisches Landesmuseum, Hannover (Robert Lackenbach from Black Star).—*Frederick William, the Great Elector* by Matthaeus Merian the Younger, oil, 17th c., Staatliche Museen, Berlin; *Louise Henriette* by Willem van Honthorst, oil on canvas, 17th c., Staatliche Museen, Berlin; *General George von Derfflinger*, artist unknown, oil, ca. 1670, Staatliche Museen, Berlin.—*Christina of Sweden as a child* by Jakob Henrik Elbfas, oil, 17th c., National Museum, Stockholm (Derek Bayes); *Frederick I of Prussia* attributed to Gideon Romandon, oil, 1695, Verwaltung der Staatlichen Schlösser und Gärten, Berlin (Walter Steinkopf); *Sophie Charlotte* by Friedrich Wilhelm Weidemann, oil, 17th c., Staatliche Museen, Berlin. 29—*King Christian IV* by Pieter Isaacsz, oil, ca. 1620, Frederiksborg Museet, Denmark; *Count Axel Oxenstierna* by Jakob Henrik Elbfas, oil, 1626, *Schloss Bad Homburg von der Höhe*, Hessen, Germany (Robert Lackenbach from Black Star)—*Charles X* by Sébastien Bourdon, oil, 1652-1653, National Museum, Stockholm—*Mary Stuart* by Willem van Honthorst, oil, 1677, Staatliche Museen, Berlin (Robert Lackenbach from Black

Star); *William II of Orange* by Willem van Honthorst, oil, 17th c., Staatliche Museen, Berlin.

CHAPTER 2: 30—*Head of Dying Warrior* by Andreas Schlüter, stone, 1696, Zeughaus, Berlin (Deutsche Fotothek, Dresden). 32—Map by Rafael D. Palacios. 39—The Bettmann Archive. 43-53—Illustrations from *Misères et Malheurs de la Guerre* by Jacques Callot, engravings, 1633, courtesy William H. Schab, Rare Books and Prints, New York.

CHAPTER 3: 54—Photograph by Henri Dauman. 56—The Mansell Collection, London. 60—Inlaid desk with clock, school of André-Charles Boulle, wood, tortoise shell and brass, ca. 1715, Louvre, Paris (Photo Bulloz). 61—Pedestal Clock by André-Charles Boulle and Jacques Thuret, oak with tortoise shell, gilt, bronze, brass and engraved pewter, ca. 1700, Metropolitan Museum of Art, New York, Rogers Fund 1958; side table, wood with mosaic marble top, 17th c., Louvre, Paris (H. Roger Viollet)—armchair, gilded walnut covered with red velvet, ca. 1690, Metropolitan Museum of Art, New York, gift of J. Pierpont Morgan 1917—Chest of drawers, in the style of André-Charles Boulle, wood with metal, ebony and tortoise shell, ca. 1700, Louvre, Paris (Giraudon). 63—Detail from *Défaite du Comte de Marsin au Canal de Bruges*, tapestry designed by Charles Le Brun, Tapisserie des Gobelins, 1665-1680, Musée de Versailles (Dmitri Kessel). 64-65—*Entrevue de Louis XIV et de Philippe IV dans l'Ile des Faisans*, tapestry designed by Charles Le Brun, Tapisserie des Gobelins, 1665-1680, Gobelin Museum, Paris; *Baptême de Dauphin à St. Germain en Laye*, tapestry designed by Charles Le Brun, Tapisserie des Gobelins, 17th c., Musée de Versailles (Dmitri Kessel). 66-67—*L'Entrée du roi à Dunkerque*, tapestry designed by Charles Le Brun, Tapisserie des Gobelins, 17th c., Musée de Versailles (Dmitri Kessel). 68—Detail from *Audience Donñee par le roi au Cardinal Chigi*, tapestry designed by Charles Le Brun, Tapisserie des Gobelins, 1665-1680, Musée de Versailles (Dmitri Kessel). 69—Detail from *Renouvellement d'Alliance avec les Suisses*, tapestry designed by Charles Le Brun, Tapisserie des Gobelins, 1665-1680, Musée de Versailles (Dmitri Kessel). 70-71—Detail from *Le Mois de Juin vu de Fontainebleau*, tapestry designed by Charles Le Brun, Tapisserie des Gobelins, 1668, Mobilier National, Paris (Dmitri Kessel)—detail from *Le Mois de Janvier, representation de l'Opéra au Louvre*, tapestry designed by Charles Le Brun, Tapisserie des Gobelins, 1668, Mobilier National, Paris (Dmitri Kessel). 72—Detail from *Le Roi visitant la manufacture des Gobelins*, tapestry designed by Charles Le Brun, Tapisserie des Gobelins, 1665-1680, Musée de Versailles (Dmitri Kessel). 73—*Construction de l'Hôtel des Invalides*, tapestry designed by Pierre Dulin, Tapisserie des Gobelins, 1716, Mobilier National, Paris (Dmitri Kessel). 74-75—*Le Triomphe d'Alexandre*, tapestry designed by Charles Le Brun, and Louis Testelin, Tapisserie des Gobelins, 1664, Mobilier National, Paris (Dmitri Kessel).

CHAPTER 4: 76—St. Athanasius, detail from *Catheda Petri* by Gianlorenzo Bernini, gilt bronze, 1663, St. Peter's Basilica, Rome (Dmitri Kessel). 79—*Bust of Louis XIV* by Gianlorenzo Bernini, marble, 1665, Musée de Versailles (Pierre Boulat). 80—*Lady with a Lute* by Jan Vermeer, oil, 17th c., Metropolitan Museum of Art, New York, bequest of Colis P. Huntington, 1925 (Frank Lerner); *Syndics of the Cloth Drapers' Guild* by Rembrandt van Rijn, oil, 1662, Rijksmuseum, Amsterdam—*The Night Watch* by Rembrandt van Rijn, oil, 1642, Rijksmuseum, Amsterdam; *Lady With a Fan* or *Portrait of Agatha Bas* by Rembrandt van Rijn, oil, 1641, Buckingham Palace, London, copyright reserved; *Saul and David* by Rembrandt van Rijn, oil, ca. 1655, Mauritshuis, The Hague—*The Merry Lute Player* by Frans Hals, oil, 1625-1627, private collection; *Charles I of England* by Anthony van Dyck, oil, 1633, courtesy of the Earl of Warwick (Eric Schaal); *Philip IV of Spain* by Diego Velasquez, oil, 1634, Prado Museum, Madrid (Scala); *Louis XIV* by Hyacinthe Rigaud, oil, 1701, Louvre, Paris (Scala)—*Andromeda Liberated by Perseus* by Peter Paul Rubens, oil, 1639-1640, Prado, Madrid (Lee Boltin); detail from the *Fountain of the Four Rivers* by Gianlorenzo Bernini, stone, 1648-1651, Piazza Navona, Rome (Dmitri Kessel). 85—Detail from *Bust of Gabriele Fonseca* by Gianlorenzo Bernini, marble, 1668-1675, Fonseca Chapel, San Lorenzo in Lucina, Rome (Leonard von Matt from Rapho Guillumette). 86-87—*Apollo and Daphne* by Gianlorenzo Bernini, marble, 1622-1625, Galleria Borghese, Rome (Leonard von Matt from Rapho Guillumette); Detail from *Pluto and Proserpina* by Gianlorenzo Bernini, marble, 1621-1622, Galleria Borghese, Rome (Leonard von Matt from Rapho Guillumette). 88—Detail from *David* by Gianlorenzo Bernini, marble, 1623, Galleria Borghese, Rome (Leonard von Matt from Rapho Guillumette). 89—Detail from *Daniel* by Gianlorenzo Bernini, marble, 1655-1657, Chigi Chapel, Santa Maria del Popolo, Rome (Leonard von Matt from Rapho Guillumette). 90-91—*Constantine the Great* by Gianlorenzo Bernini, marble, 1654-1670, Scala Regia, Vatican City (Leonard von Matt from Rapho Guillumette). 92-93—*The Ecstasy of St. Teresa* and two details from the same by Gianlorenzo Bernini, marble and gilded wood, 1645-1652, Cornaro Chapel, Santa Maria della Vittoria, Rome (Alinari). 94-95—*The Glory* by Gianlorenzo Bernini, marble, bronze, gilt, stucco and glass, 1657-1666, St. Peter's Basilica, Vatican City (Leonard von Matt from Rapho Guillumette).

CHAPTER 5: 96—Drawings of the moon from notes for *Sidereus Nuncius* by Galileo Galilei, 1610, Biblioteca Nazionale, Florence (Paola Tosi). 99—From *Harmonice Mundi, Libri V*, 1619, Burndy Library, Norwalk, Connecticut (Lee Boltin). 104—Anatomy of a Horse from *Della Cavalleria* by George Lohneyss, 1624, New York Public Library, The Spencer Collection. 107—Sir Isaac Newton, engraving after portrait by Godfrey Kneller, New York Public Library, Picture Collection; diagram from *Philosophia Naturalis Principia Mathematica* by Sir Isaac Newton, 1687, Burndy Library, Norwalk, Connecticut (Lee Boltin). 108-109—Left: engraving of an eye, The Bettmann Archive—Anton van Leeuwenhoek's microscope, The Bettmann Archive; microscopic view of wood from *Arcana Naturae* by Anton van Leeuwenhoek, 1696, Burndy Library, Norwalk, Connecticut (Lee Boltin). Right: microscope and light condenser from *Micrographia* by Robert Hooke, 1665, Burndy Library, Norwalk, Connecticut (Lee Boltin)—microscopic view of fly's eye from *Micrographia* by Robert Hooke, 1665, Burndy Library, Norwalk, Connecticut (Lee Boltin); microscope designed by Robert Hooke, The Science Museum, London (Derek Bayes). 110—*Blaise Pascal*, New York Public Library, Picture Collection; calculating machine designed by Pascal, courtesy IBM, New York (Lee Boltin)—Otto von Guericke, Burndy Library, Norwalk, Connecticut (Lee Boltin)—bronze hemispheres, Deutsches Museum, Munich (Robert Lackenbach from Black Star)—horses from the Duke of Newcastle's *General System of Horsemanship*, New York Public Library, Print Division. 111—Diagram of pendulum clock from *Opera Geometrica Varia*, collected works of Christian Huygens, 1724, Burndy Library, Norwalk, Connecticut (Lee Boltin); back of antique clock, courtesy Dr. Peter D. Guggenheim, New York—Christian Huygens, Burndy Library, Norwalk, Connecticut (Lee Boltin); dial face of antique clock, courtesy Dr. Peter D. Guggenheim, New York (Lee Boltin); Huygens's experimental cycloid pendulum, Conservatoire des Arts et Métiers, Paris (Eddy Van Der Veen). 112—Portrait of Nicolaus Steno (The Bettmann Archive)—diagram from *De Solido Intra Solidum Naturalitur Contentum* by Nicolaus Steno, 1669, Burndy Library, Norwalk, Connecticut (Lee Boltin). 113—Crosscut of trunk of loblolly pine, The American Museum of Natural History, New York (Alex Rota); diagram from *Opera Omnia*, collected works of Marcello Malpighi, 1687, Burndy Library, Norwalk, Connecticut (Lee Boltin)—diagram from *Opera Omnia*, collected works of Marcello Malpighi, 1687, Burndy Library, Norwalk, Connecticut (Lee Boltin); Marcello Malpighi, oil, 1682, courtesy Dr. Michael Pijoan, New Mexico (Art Taylor)—diagram from *Opera Omnia*, collected works of Marcello Malpighi, 1687, Burndy Library, Norwalk, Connecticut (Lee Boltin). 114—Diagram from *Machina Coelestis* by Johannes Hevelius, 1673, Burndy Library, Norwalk, Connecticut (Lee Boltin); diagram from *Selenographia* by Johannes Hevelius, 1647, Burndy Library, Norwalk, Connecticut (Lee Boltin). Background: moon map from *Selenographia* by Johannes Hevelius, 1647, Burndy Library, Norwalk, Connecticut (Lee Boltin). 115—Left: Edmund Halley, New York Public Library, Picture Collection. Background, table from *A Synopsis of the Astronomy of Comets* by Edmund Halley, 1705, Burndy Library, Norwalk, Connecticut (Lee Boltin). Right: Zodiacal sign from *Arati Solensis Phaenomena et Prognostica* by Theodorus Graminaeus, 1569, courtesy Simone Gossner, New York (Herbert Orth). Background, photograph from Smithsonian Astrophysical Observatory, Cambridge, Massachusetts.

CHAPTER 6: 116—Design for a Parterre from "Nouveaux Livres de Parterres" in *Oeuvre de Sr. Marot Contenant Plusieurs Pensées Utilles aux Architectes, Peintres, Sculpteurs, Orfeuves, Jardiniers, et Autres; le Tout en Faveur de Ceux Qui S'Appliquent aux Beaux Arts* by Daniel Marot, 1712, New York Public Library, Print Division (Lee Boltin). 120—Plan for the Louvre, by Gianlorenzo Bernini, 1664 (George Silk)—New York Public Library, Print Division. 125—Bibliothèque Nationale, Paris (H. Roger Viollet). 127-137—Illustrations from *Ballet du Roy des Festes de Bacchus*, watercolor, 1651, Bibliothèque Nationale, Paris.

CHAPTER 7: 138—Heraldic shields from pack of English playing cards, by Richard Blome, 17th c., courtesy Collection of Mr. Albert Field, New York (Robert S. Crandall). 141—From Jackdaw Publications Ltd., courtesy of the British Museum, London. 145—London Museum (Radio Times Hulton Picture Library). 146—Design for St. Paul's Cathedral by Christopher Wren, 1708, by courtesy of the Dean and Chapter of St. Paul's Cathedral, London (Larry Burrows). 149-163—Photographs by Evelyn Hofer. 152-3—By Courtesy of the Dean and Chapter, Westminster Abbey.

CHAPTER 8: 164—*The Phoenix*, by Rembrandt van Rijn, etching, 1658, courtesy Klipstein and Kornfeld, Bern (Albert Winkler). 169—New York Public Library, Oriental Division (Frank Lerner). 173—From *Das Kriegs-Exerzitum des Infanterieregiments Ulysses Grafen Browne*, hand-colored pen and ink drawing, Heeresgschichtliches Museum, Vienna (Erich Lessing from Magnum). 174—From *L'Art Militaire François* by Pierre Giffart, 1696, courtesy Anne S.K. Brown Military Collection, Providence (Lee Boltin); Grenadier, ca. 1710, Heeresgeschichtliches Museum, Vienna (Erich Lessing from Magnum). 175—From *L'Art Militaire François* by Pierre Giffart, 1696, courtesy Anne S.K. Brown Military Collection, Providence (Lee Boltin); from *Precetti Militari* by Francesco Marzioli, 1683, New York Public Library, The Spencer Collection. 176-177—From *Military Exercises: 1730* by J. J. Wolrab, edited by S. James Gooding, Museum Restoration Service, Ontario—courtesy Collection Jean Brunon, Marseilles (Erich Lessing from Magnum). 178-179—From *Les Travaux de Mars ou L'Art de la Guerre* by Allain M. Mallet, Paris, 1684, vol. 3., courtesy Anne S.K. Brown Military Collection, Providence (Lee Boltin); Musée de l'Armée, Paris (Erich Lessing from Magnum). 180-181—From *Atlas de Colbert* by Jean Baptiste Colbert, 1670-1680, Musée de la Marine, Paris (Erich Lessing from Magnum).—Musée de la Marine, Paris (Erich Lessing from Magnum). 182-183—From *Das Kriegs-Exerzitum des Infanterieregiments Ulysses Grafen Browne*, hand-colored pen and ink drawing, Heeresgschichtliches Museum, Vienna (Erich Lessing from Magnum).

ACKNOWLEDGMENTS

The editors of this book are particularly indebted to Herbert H. Rowen, Professor of History, Rutgers, The State University, New Brunswick, N.J.; Donald Posner, Associate Professor, Institute of Fine Arts, New York University; Frederick G. Kilgour, Yale University Library; Everard M. Upjohn, Professor of Art History, Columbia University; Helmut Nickel, Curator, Arms and Armor, The Metropolitan Museum of Art; Richard Kuehne, Director, U.S. Military Academy Library, West Point; Harold Peterson, Director, National Park Service, U.S. Dept. of the Interior; Bern Dibner, Director, and Adele Matthysse, Burndy Library, Norwalk, Conn.; Karl Kup, Curator of Prints, and Elizabeth Roth, New York Public Library; William Baker, naval architect, Curator, Hart Nautical Museum, Massachusetts Institute of Technology, Cambridge; Simone Gossner; Albert Field; Katharine Gregory; Jeremiah F. O'Sullivan, Professor of Medieval History, Fordham University; Sydney Horenstein, Scientific Assistant, American Museum of Natural History; Richard M. Klein, Curator of Plant Physiology, New York Botanical Garden; Edward J. Regan; Jean Adhémar, Conservateur en Chef, Cabinet des Éstampes, Bibliothèque Nationale, Paris; Marie-Christine Angebault, Assistante au Cabinet des Éstampes, Bibliothèque Nationale, Paris; Bernadette Brot, Inspecteur au Mobilier National, Paris; Jean Brunon, Marseille; Charlotte Jones, Chargé de Mission à la Conservation du Château de Versailles; François Le Monnier, Conservateur, Service Photographique and François Lesure, Conservateur au Département de la Musique, Bibliothèque Nationale, Paris; Colonel Dugue MacCarthy, Conservateur, and Colonel J. Wemaere, Conservateur, Musée de l'Armée, Paris; Nicholas Cooper, National Monuments Record, London; D. Pepys Whiteley, Pepys Library, Cambridge University; Kenneth Mills, Historical Building Survey, London; Cyril Hughes Hartman, London; Dr. Helmut Börch-Supan, Verwaltung der Staatlichen Schlösser und Gärten, Berlin; Hans-Heinrich Richter, Deutsche Fotothek, Dresden; Archiv Fuer Kunst und Geschichte, Berlin; Staatliche Museum zu Berlin, Gemaeldegalerie; Staatsbibliothek Berlin (Bildarchiv Handke); Alte Pinakothek, Munich; Maria Luisa Bonelli, Director, Museo di Storia della Scienza, Florence; Emanuele Casamassima, Director, Biblioteca Nazionale, Florence; Victor Velen, Florence; Johann Christoph von Allmayer-Beck, Direktor, Heeresgeschichtliches Museum, Vienna; Erwin M. Auer, Direktor, Kunsthistorisches Museum, Vienna; Lilly von Sauter, Schloss Ambros, Tirol.

INDEX

* This symbol in front of a page number indicates a photograph or painting of the subject mentioned.

A

Absolutism, 20, 62, 117, 125, 142, 147; in England, 15, 27, 147, 148; in France, 14, 15, 20, 22, 117, 125, 126, 148; as a 17th Century answer to the problem of order, 55-56; triumph of in Europe, 139
Académie Royale de la Danse, 127
Academy of France, compiles dictionary of the French language, 121-122
Acton, Lord, 62
Adriatic Sea, map 32
Advancement of Learning (Bacon), 105
Africa, 171, 172
Alexander the Great (French tapestry portrait), *74-75
All Hallows Church, Barking (London), *161
American Revolution, 148
Amusements and entertainments, card playing, 19; at the French court, *127-137. See also Ballet; Opera
"Anatomie of the World" (John Donne), quoted, 11
Anatomy, study of, 104, 113
Andromeda Liberated by Perseus (Rubens), *80
Anhalt, Christian von, 18, 33, 34
Anjou, Philippe d'. See Philip V of Spain
Anne, Queen of England, *27, 171
Architecture, Baroque, 81, 83
Ariadne (Monteverdi), 84
Aristocracy: coats of arms of, *138; corruption in France, 15; degrees of rank and power, 19; life at Versailles, 62; waning power of, 12
Aristotle, belief in theories of, 12
Armies: artillery, 178-179; first uniforms, 175; of France, 57-58, 175; grenadier, *174; infantry, *174, *175, 176, 177; mercenaries, 34-36, 43, 50, 52, 58, 173; musketeer, *175; New Model Army of England, 144, 145; pikemen, *175, *182-183; rise of professionalism in, 173, 174-178; specialists, *174; standard-bearer, *174; of Sweden, 40; training manual, *173
Arms: cannon, *178-179; firearms, *174, 176; flintlock, *173, 176, *177; musket, 34-35, 176; pike and sword, *175
Art: Baroque style, 13, 77-95, 93, 121. See also Bernini, Sculpture
Art of Poetry (Boileau), quoted, 122
Astronomy, 97-105. See also Galileo; Halley; Hevelius; Kepler
Atlantic Ocean, map 32
Atlas de Colbert (shipbuilding manual), 180
Atmospheric pressure, experiment in, *110
Austria, 16, 36, 39; joins the Holy League, 166; map 32; as part of Habsburg empire, 166; war with France, 68; and War of the Spanish Succession, 168-172
Austrian Netherlands. See Spanish Netherlands

B

Bacon, Francis, 11, 59; Advancement of Learning, 105; Novum Organum, 105
Balearic Islands, map 32
Ballet: beginnings of modern, 127; Festivals of Bacchus, *127-137; at the French court, 84, *127-137; performance of "Psyché" at the Louvre, *71
Baltic Sea, 40, 167; map 32
Bank of England, 167
Baroque style, 13; Bernini bust as supreme expression of, 77-78, 98; churches, 79; described in Chantelou's diary, 78; development of, 79; displaced by Clas-

sicism, 121; emphasis on communication, 79; expansion of social base and artistic range, 79, 81; as a new artistic order, 78-79; origin of term, 78; techniques of, 81; variant of in the Netherlands, 84. See also Bernini
Bavaria, 42, 171; map 32
Bavaria, Duke of. See Maximilian
Bedlam Hospital, 109
Béjart, Armande, 123
Béjart, Madeleine, 123
Bellarmine, Robert Cardinal, 103
Bernini, Gianlorenzo: bust of Louis XIV, 77-78, *79, 81, 82, 98; bust of Monsignor Montoya, 85; Daniel (detail), *89; David, 81, *88; design for the Louvre, 77, *120, 121; Fountain of the Four Rivers (detail), *80; genius of, 85; hands of Gabriele Fonseca, *85; realism in sculpture of, 89; religious art of, 85, 90-95; residence in Paris, 77, 78; St. Athanasius, *76; St. Peter's, 93, *94-95; St. Peter's chair, 77, 79, *94-95; St. Teresa, *92-93; sculpture, *76; statue of Constantine, *90-91; style of, 85
Bethlen Gabor, Prince, 34, 36
Blenheim, Battle of, 171
Blood circulation, Harvey's discovery of, 105-106, 113
Bohemia, 35; economic and political importance of, 31; government of, 31; Habsburgs' claim to, 42; hostility among the three estates, 31; map 32; nationalism in, 31, 32; as part of Habsburg empire, 166; Protestant-Catholic struggle, 31-32; Protestantism eradicated, 37; rebellion in, 32-33, 36, 37; religious struggle in, 31-32; revolt in, 25; scheme to elect a Protestant king, 18
Boileau, Nicolas, 122, 123; Art of Poetry, 122
Book of Common Prayer, 143
Bossuet, Bishop, portrait, *22
Bourbon dynasty, power of, 20; struggle with the Habsburgs, 39
Boyle, Robert, 105
Brahe, Tycho, 98-99, 100
Brandenburg, 28, 33, 166; map 32
Breitenfeld, battle at, 36, 40; map 32
Buckingham, Duke of, 140, 142
Bunyan, John, 147
Butler, Samuel, 147

C

Calculating machine, invention of, 110, 126
Calculus, as the foremost mathematical achievement of the 17th Century, 13; contribution by Newton, 107
Callot, Jacques (French artist), 43
Calvinism, 18, 33, 38, 42
Canterbury, Archbishop of, 154, 155
Cards. See Playing cards
Carlos, Don Baltasar, *25
Carr, Robert. See Somerset, Earl of
Cartesian thought. See Descartes
Catherine, Queen of England (wife of Charles II), *27
Catholic Church. See Roman Catholic Church
Catholic League, 18, 24, 36, 37, 38, 40
"Century of Louis the Great, The" (poem), 74
Chamlay, Marquis de (French topographer), 58
Chantelou (steward to Louis XIV), 78
Charles I, King of England: ascends throne, 142; character of, 142; death warrant, *145; dismisses Parliament, 142; execution of, 13, 26, 145; financial plight of, 143; imposes religious laws on Scotland, 143; moves court from London to York, 143; playing cards of, *19; portrait, *26;

*80, 81; proposed marriage with Spanish Infanta, 142; rules without Parliament for 11 years, 143; shirt worn at execution, *145; struggle with Parliament, 142-145; surrenders to the Scots, 144; treaty with Scotland, 144-145
Charles II, King of England: belief in absolutism, 147; character of, 147; connives with Louis XIV, 147; death, 148; develops the Navy, 180; mistresses of, *27; political acumen of, 147; portrait, *27; returns from exile, 146
Charles II, King of Spain, 25, 168, 170
Charles V, Holy Roman Emperor, 17
Charles X, King of Sweden, 167; portrait, *29
Charles XI, King of Sweden, 167
Charles XII, King of Sweden, 167, 168
Charles, Archduke of Austria, 169, 170, 172
Charles, Duke of Lorraine, rescues Vienna from the Turks, 166
Charles Emanuel, Duke of Savoy, 33, 34
Chemistry, 105
Chigi, Cardinal, *68
China, prosperity of under K'ang Hsi, 169
Christian IV, King of Denmark, 38; leads Protestant army in the Thirty Years' War, 36; portrait, *29
Christian, Prince of Brunswick, 38
Christina, Queen of Sweden: invites Descartes to Sweden, 118; portrait, *28
Churches and cathedrals: All Hallows, Barking (London), *161; Baroque style, 79; St. Katherine Cree (London), *158; St. Olave's, London, *156, *157; St. Paul's, London, *146, 147; St. Peter's, Rome, *76, 77, 93, 94-95; Westminster Abbey, London, *152-153
Churchill, John. See Marlborough, Duke of
Classicism, 121; Dryden as first English exponent, 123
Claudia of Austria, second wife of Leopold I, 24
Clavius, Father Christopher, S.J., 103
Clocks, Louis XIV style, *60, *61; pendulum, *111
Coats of arms, *138
Colbert, Jean Baptiste: Atlas de Colbert, 180; as coordinator of French economy, 57, 58-60; economic doctrine of, 59; naval program of, 180; portrait, *23
Cologne, 171; map 32
Cologne, Archbishop of, 16, 18
Condé, Prince de, *22
Congreve, William, 147
Constantine, Emperor, Bernini statue of, *90-91
Constitutionalism, 15-16, 139, 148
Copernicus, Nicholas, 98, 102, 103
Counter Reformation, 79
Croatia, 166
Cromwell, Oliver, 12; character of, 144; death, 146; final military defeat of the Royalists, 145; military genius of, 144; portrait, *26; rules England, 145-146; seizes control of English government, 13; signature, 145; suspends Parliament, 26
Czechs, in Bohemia, 31

D

Danube River, 18, 171
Danzig, 114
David (Bernini), 81 (detail), *88
Defenestration of Prague, 33
Denain, Battle of, 172
Denmark: alliance with Russia, 167; defeated in Great Northern War, 168; role in the Thirty Years' War, 36, map 32
Derfflinger, George von, portrait, *28-29
Descartes, René, 74; challenged by Pascal,

126; character of, 117-118; death of, 118; Discourse on Method, 119, 121; early life, 117; "I think, therefore I am," 119; invents coordinate geometry, 118; letter to Princess Elizabeth, 118; philosophy of, 118-121; settles in the Netherlands, 118; as a soldier, 117; system of logic, 119
Dessau, battle at, 38; map 32
Dialogue on the Two Chief Systems of the World (Galileo), 103, 104
Discourse on Method (Descartes), 119, 121
Discourses on Two New Sciences (Galileo), 105
Dissenters, religious, *141
Divorce, 140
Docteur Amoureux, Le (Molière), 124
Doctor in Spite of Himself, The (Molière), 125
Donauwörth, riot in, 18; map 32
Donne, John, 172; "Anatomie of the World," quoted, 11
Dresden, 84
Dryden, John, 147; as first English exponent of Classicism, 123; quoted, 123; rewrites Shakespeare's plays, 125
Dunkirk, 171; triumphal entry of Louis XIV, *66-67
Dutch War, 165
Dynamics, as a 17th Century creation, 13

E

Edict of Nantes, revoked by Louis XIV, 126
Edict of Restitution (1629), 36, 38, 39, 42; annulled, 41
Elbe River, 38
Eleanor of Neuburg (third wife of Leopold I), portrait, *24
Elector Palatine. See Frederick V
Elector of Saxony. See John George
Elizabeth I, Queen of England, 139, 140
Elizabeth Stuart (wife of Frederick of Bohemia, Elector Palatine), 33, 142; portrait, *28
England: absolutism under the Stuarts, 15; beginnings of modern democracy in, 16; civil war in, 26, 143-145; constitutionalism in, 15-16; Cromwell seizes control of government, 13; cultural renaissance of, 147; Declaration of Rights, 148; established Church of, 141, 143; establishes new political order, 139; expansion of overseas trade, 167; first and only written constitution, 146; first national debt, 167; Gunpowder Plot (1605), 13; Jesuits in, 140; map 32; monarchy restored, 146; plays a major role in Europe, 167; "Popish Plot," 147; Protestant-Catholic struggle under the Stuarts, 143-148; rise of the Whigs, 148; "Rump" Parliament, 145; sea power, 180; sends army to help the Protestant princes in Germany, 142; Short and Long Parliaments, 143; struggle between King and Parliament, 139, 140-145; Stuart rulers, *26-27; Toryism, 147, 148; treaties on the Spanish succession, 169, 170; under the Puritans, 145-146; under the Restoration, 147, 149; and the War of the Spanish Succession, 169-172; war with France, 142, 148, 167; war with Spain, 142
Enlightenment, the, 106
Entertainments. See Amusements
Ethics Demonstrated in the Geometric Manner (Spinoza), 106
Eugene of Savoy, 168, 171, 172
Eure River, 60
Europe: creativity in, 12-13; divisive forces in, 55; expanding commercial society of, 13; first international peace conference, 41-42; nationalism in, 58;

rent by political, religious and military conflicts, 12, 13; in 1618, *map 32*
Eurydice (Peri), 84
Evelyn, John, quoted, 146

F

Fénelon, Bishop, portrait, *22
Ferdinand II, Holy Roman Emperor, King of Bohemia, Archduke of Styria, allows Wallenstein to recruit an army, 38; chosen by Catholic princes to succeed Emperor, 18; death of, 41; demands to the German Electors, 39; dream of a united Catholic Germany, 38; Edict of Restitution, 36, 38, 39, 41, 42; elected King of Bohemia, 32; elected Holy Roman Emperor, 34, 36; implicated in Wallenstein's death, 41; as instigator of the Thirty Years' War, 165; plans subjugation of Germany, 37; portrait, *25; recalls Wallenstein, 40; regains Bohemian crown, 36; repressive rule of, 32
Ferdinand III, Holy Roman Emperor, portrait, *25
Festivals of Bacchus (ballet), *127-137
Feudalism, destruction of in 17th Century, 12
Flanders, 33, 36
Flintlock, development of, *173, 176; operation of, *177; used by Gustavus Adolphus, 40
Fontainebleau, palace of, 68, 71
Fontenelle, Bernard Le Bovier de, 121
Formosa, 169
Fountain of the Four Rivers (detail), Bernini, *80
Fouquet, Nicolas, portrait, *23
Four Friends. *See* Société des Quatre Amis
France: absolutism in, 14, 15, 22, 148; acquires holdings in the German Rhineland, 42; army of, 57-58, 175; bureaucracy in, 56, 57; codification of the language, 121-122; compilation of dictionary, 121-122; coordination of economy, 57, 58-60; crafts in, 60; decline of power, 169; defeated at Malplaquet, 168; destroyed by power of monarchy, 15; development of industry, 60; develops her navy, 180; the Fronde, 13; furniture making, 60; "geometric spirit," 121; Grand Dauphin, *22; guilds, 59, 60; *intendants,* 57, 58, 59; new order in, 57; reverence for the Classical period of ancient Greece, 74; role in the Thirty Years' War, 36, *map 32*; shipbuilding, 60; struggle against the Habsburgs, 33, 39, 41, 42; supports German fragmentation, 42; threatens Austria, 166; treaties on the Spanish succession, 169, 170; uniform commercial code laid down, 59; and War of the Spanish Succession, 168-172; wars with England, 142, 148, 167. *See also* Louis XIV
Franche-Comté, *map 32*
Frankfurt, 34
Frederick I of Prussia (Frederick III of Brandenburg), 14-15, 166-167, 172; portrait, *28
Frederick II, King of Denmark, builds observatory, 99
Frederick III, Elector of Brandenburg. *See* Frederick I of Prussia
Frederick V, King of Bohemia, Elector Palatine, 18, 40, 42; character of, 33; crowned King of Bohemia, 36; defeated at Battle of White Mountain, 36; elected King by Bohemian rebels, 34; flees to Dutch Republic, 36; loses support of Protestant rulers, 34; marriage of, 142; portrait, *28
Frederick William of Brandenburg (the Great Elector), 166-167; portrait, *28
Frederick William I, King of Prussia, 56
Friedland, 37, 42
Fronde, the, 13
Furniture, Louis XIV style, *60-61

G

Galilei, Galileo, 12; accused of heresy, 103-104; astronomical discoveries, 101-102; attacked by theologians, 102-103; *Dialogue on the Two Chief Systems of the World,* 103, 104; *Discourses on Two New Sciences,* 105; discovers law of the pendulum, 100-101; early life of, 100-101; invents the astronomical telescope, 101; mathematical studies, 101; recantation, 104; sketches of the moon, *96; *The Starry Messenger,* 101-102
Garden design, *116
Geology, 112
Geometry, 118, 126
Germany: constitutional rights subverted by Ferdinand, 38; decimation of population, 41; fragmentation of, 36, 42; invaded by Sweden, 40; invaded by Wallenstein's army, 38; Thirty Years' War in, 16, 38, 39, 40, 41, *map 32*; threatened with Catholic domination, 36; and the War of the Spanish Succession, 171. *See also* Holy Roman Empire
Gibraltar, 172
Glass making, in France, 60
Glorious Revolution of 1688, 26, 27, 139, 148, 167
Gobelins factory: establishment of, 60; Louis XIV inspects its products, *72; placed under state control by Louis XIV, 73; tapestries, *63, *66-67
Grand Alliance, the, 171, 172
Grand Dauphin of France (son of Louis XIV), baptism of, *65; portrait, *28
Gravitation, Law of, discovered by Newton, 106, 107
Great Elector. *See* Frederick William
Great Fire of London (1666), 109, 146, 147, 149
Great Northern War, 167-168
Greece, Classical period revered in France, 74
Greenwich, London, *160-161
Guericke, Otto von, *110
Guilds, in France, 59, 60
Gunpowder Plot (1605), 13
Gustavus Adolphus, King of Sweden, 28, 29, 40, 42, 118; absolutism, 20; army of, 57; assumes leadership of the Protestants, 36; builds an empire, 167; character of, 40; death of, 36, 41; defeats Wallenstein, 41; military conquests of, 21, 40; plans a Protestant confederation of central Europe, 40; portrait, *20; victory at Breitenfeld, 40
Gwyn, Nell, *27, 147

H

Habsburg dynasty: Austrian, 16, 41, *map 32*; challenged in Bohemia, 31, 32, 33; domination in Europe checked, 40; empire of in 1658, 166; German, 20; hereditary claim to kingdom of Bohemia, 42; as hereditary owners of the crown of the Holy Roman Empire, 16-17; imperils Sweden's Baltic trade, 33; intermarriage of, 11; last Habsburg King of Spain, 168; power of, 16, 20, 38, 39; power struggle with Louis XIV, 68; queens, 24; relations with France, 33, 41; Spanish, 20, *25, 36, 37, 38, 39, 41, *map 32*; struggle to retain power, 24; struggle with the Bourbons, 39; and War of the Spanish Succession, 168-172
Halley, Edmund, 107; portrait, *115; predicts return of comet, 115
Hals, Frans, 83; *The Merry Lute Player,* *80
Harrington, James, quoted, 14
Harvey, William, discovers the circulation of the blood, 105-106, 113
Henriette, Princess of England, *26
Henry IV, King of France, 84; murder of, 13
Henry VII, King of England, tomb of in Westminster Abbey, *152-153
Henry VIII, King of England, 141
Heurtebise, retreat from, 67
Hevelius, Johannes, 107; observatory of,

*114; *Selenographia,* 114; studies of the moon, *114
Hobbes, Thomas, *Leviathan,* 12, 55, 56, 106
Holland. *See* Netherlands
Holy League, 166
Holy Office of the Roman Catholic Church. *See* Inquisition
Holy Roman Empire: Catholic-Protestant struggle within, 33, *map 32*; conspiracy to elect a Protestant emperor, 33; crown of, 16-17; Electors of, 16, 31; at the end of the Thirty Years' War, 16, *map 32*; fragmentation of, 17-18; importance of Bohemia to, 31; military governments within, 17; nebulous boundaries of, 16; political entity of, 16; Reichstag, 17; religious faction in, 17, 18; rulers of, 16. *See also* Germany; Thirty Years' War
Hooke, Robert, character and work, 109; *Micrographia,* *109
Horsemanship, manual of, *104
Hradčany, castle, 32
Humanism, 11
Hungary, 16, 34, 166; *map 32*
Hus, Jan, 37
Huygens, Christian, *111

I

Innocent XII, Pope, 170
Inquisition, the (Holy Office of the Roman Catholic Church), 103, 104
Intendants, 57, 58, 59
Invalides, the, built by Louis XIV, *73
Ireland: *map 32*; war in, 165
Italy, 16, 169, 170, 171; as a Catholic stronghold, 12; opera in, 84; threatened by Louis XIV, 68; war in, 165

J

James I, King of England (James VI of Scotland), 33, 34, 38; ascends English throne, 139; character and personality, 139-140; defends Church of England, 141; favorites of, 140; struggles with Parliament, 140-142; treatise on the *Trew Law of Free Monarchies,* 140
James II, King of England, absolutism, 27; ascends throne, 148; deposition of, 26; disastrous reign of, 148; exiled, 139; flees to France, 148; portrait, *27; supported by Louis XIV, 167
James VI, King of Scotland. *See* James I, King of England
Jesuits, in England, 140
John George, Elector of Saxony, 34
Joseph Ferdinand, Prince of Bavaria, 169, 170

K

K'ang Hsi, Emperor of China, *169
Kara Mustafa, Grand Vizier of Turkey, besieges Vienna, 166; conspires with Louis XIV, 166
Kepler, Johannes, 37, 98, 99-100, 101, 102; casts Wallenstein's horoscope, 39; musical theme of the planets, *99; quoted, 102

L

La Fontaine, Jean de, 122
Lace making, in France, 60
Lady with a Fan (Rembrandt), *80, 81
Lady with a Lute (Vermeer), *80
Lambeth Palace, *154-155
La Vallière, Mlle. de, portrait, *23
Leeuwenhoek, Anton van, 107, 108
Leibniz, Gottfried Wilhelm, 172
Leipzig, 40
Lely, Sir Peter, 109
Leopold I of Austria, Holy Roman Emperor, 169, 170; as claimant to Spanish

throne, 168-169; portraits, *10, *21; as a skillful ruler, 20; transforms his empire into a modern state, 165-166; War of the Spanish Succession, 168, 169; wives of, *10, *24, 169
Le Tellier, Michel, Secretary of State for War, reorganizes French army, 57-58
Letters on Toleration (Locke), 148
Le Vau, Louis, 121
Leviathan (Hobbes), 12, 55, 56, 106
Locke, John, 148
London, *149-163; All Hallows Church, Barking, *161; as capital of Restoration England, 149; Great Fire of 1666, 109, 146, 147, 149; Greenwich, *160-161; rebuilt by Wren, 147; St. James's Park, *151; St. Katherine Cree (Church), *158; St. Olave's Church, *156, *157; St. Paul's Cathedral, *146, 147; Staple Inn, *150; Thames River, *160-161; Westminster Abbey, *152-153; Westminster Hall, *152; Westminster Palace, 13; White Hall, *158-159
Louis XIII, King of France, 39, 41, 56
Louis XIV, King of France, 12; absolutism under, 14, 15, 20, 22, 117, 125, 126, 148; achievements of his reign, 165; attempts to dominate Europe, 165; audience with Cardinal Chigi, *68; becomes absolute master of his kingdom, 57; Bernini's bust of, 77, *79, 81, 82, 98; and Bernini's plan for the Louvre, 77, 121; as a builder, 73; as claimant to Spanish throne, 168-169; conspires with Turks, 166; corruption of power, 62; court life, 22, 23, 60-61, 62, 70, 125; destructive use of power, 15; early reign of, 56; European enemies, 167; family life, 64-65; flowering of culture under, 14, 73, 121, 122; founds first ballet school, 127; grandmother of, *23; hunting, *70-71; "I am the State," 56; interest in amateur theatricals, 127, 129; last years of reign, 126; *Le Grand Siècle,* 117; love affairs, 61, 62; meeting with Swiss ambassadors, *69; meets his bride and his father-in-law, Philip IV of Spain, *64-65; military exploits of, 63, 67; mistresses of, *23; nickname, 129; as a patron of the arts, *72, *73; portraits, *20, *63, *80; power struggle with the Habsburgs, 68; as protector of Molière, 73, 125; Protestant caricature of, *56; pursuit of pleasure, 70-71; reign compared with Classical period of Greece, 74; relations with Charles II of England, 147, 148; relations with the Grand Dauphin, 22; resplendent reign of, 63; revokes Edict of Nantes, 126; self-glorification, 106; as a statesman, 68, 69; as symbol of the state, 60, 62; and War of the Spanish Succession, 168-172; wife of, *22
Louise Henrietta (wife of Frederick William, the Great Elector), portrait, *28
Louvois, Marquis de, 57-58, 175
Louvre, the, ballet performance at, *71; Bernini's plan for, 77, *120, 121; Louis XIV rebuilds, 73; rebuilt in the Classical style, 121; two façades, *120
Lully, Jean Baptiste, 62, 73, 84
Lutheranism, 17, 18, 33, 37, 38, 42
Lutter, battle at, 36, 38; *map 32*
Lützen, battle at, 36, 40; *map 32*
Luxembourg, Duc de, 62

M

Maintenon, Madame de, improves court morals, 22; portrait, *22
Mainz, *map 32*
Mainz, Archbishop of, 16, 18
Malpighi, Marcello, 106, 107; botanical investigations, *113; discovers capillary circulation in lungs, *113; portrait, *113
Malplaquet, Battle of, 168, 172
Manchu Dynasty, 169
Mannerism, 79
Mansart, Jules Hardouin, 121
Mansfeld, Ernst von, 33; ability as a commander, 35; defeated at Dessau, 38; deserts Frederick V, 34, 36; leads Protes-

tant army, 33; portrait, *28
Margaret Theresa, Princess of Spain (wife of Leopold I of Austria), *10, *24, 169
Maria of Bavaria, portrait, *25
Maria Anna of Spain (wife of Ferdinand III), portrait, *25
Marie Thérèse, Queen of France, meeting her future husband, *64-65
Marino, Giambattista, 86
Marlborough, Duke of, 67, 168, 171, 172; portrait, *27
Marston Moor, Battle of, 144
Martinet, Jean, Inspector-General of France, 58
Mary II, Queen of England, 148; portrait, *26
Mary Queen of Scots, 139
Mary Stuart (wife of Prince William II of Orange), *29
Mathematics, 98; calculus, 13, 107; Descartes' contributions to, 118; Galileo's studies, 101; geometry, 118, 126; Pascal's contributions to, 126
Matthias, Holy Roman Emperor, 18, 34
Maximilian, Duke of Bavaria, 34, 37, 38, 117; character of, 24; defeats Christian of Denmark, 38; forms Catholic League, 18; marches against Bohemia, 36; portrait, *24; rewarded by Ferdinand, 36
Mazarin, Cardinal, 56, 58; portrait, *22
Medici, Marie de', 84; portrait, *23
Medici family, 102
Mediterranean Sea, 171; map 32
Mercantilism, 59
Mercenary armies: conduct of, 43; English mercenary quoted, 50; in France; importance of in 17th Century, 34-36; replaced by professional armies, 173; treatment of at war's end, 52
Merchants and tradesmen: engravings, *14-15; prosperity of, 12
Merry Lute Player, The (Hals), *80
Michelangelo, 100
Micrographia (Hooke), *109
Microscopes, *108, *109
Milan, 168, 169, 170, 172; map 32
Military life. See Armies; Arms; Warfare
Milton, John, 12; Paradise Lost, quoted, 81-82, 98
Ming Dynasty, 169
Minorca, 172
Moldau River, 32
Molière, 12, 62, 122; Cartesian spirit in plays of, 124; in costume, *125; early life of, 123; founds theatrical company, 123; Le Bourgeois Gentilhomme, quoted, 124; Le Docteur Amoureux, 124; receives protection of Louis XIV, 73, 125; Tartuffe, 124-125
Monarchy: change in form during 17th Century, 56; power of in 17th Century Europe, 19, 20, 21
Monteverdi, Claudio, 84
Montoya, Monsignor, Bernini bust of, 85
Montpensier, Madame de, 84
Moselle River, 42
Münster, 41, 42; map 32
Music, of the Baroque period, 81, 84

N

Naples, 168, 169, 170, 172; map 32
Narrative of Personal Observations of the Four Wandering Satellites of Jupiter (Kepler), quoted, 102
Narva, Battle of, 168
Naseby, Battle of, 144
Navies, development of during 17th Century, 180
Netherlands, Dutch: aids German Protestants, 34; attacked by Louis XIV, 165; Baroque style in, 79, 81-83; Descartes moves to, 118; Frederick V flees to, 36; map 32; power of house of Orange in, 29; sea power, 180; and the War of the Spanish Succession, 170-172
Netherlands, Spanish, 16, 33; attacked by Louis XIV, 165; map 32; renamed Austrian Netherlands, 172; and the War of the Spanish Succession, 168, 170-172
New World, 168, 170, 171, 172

Newfoundland, 172
Newton, Isaac, 12, 100, *107; Law of Universal Gravitation, 106, 107; receives support from Halley, 115
Night Watch (Rembrandt), *80, 81
Nördlingen, Battle of, 36
North Sea, map 32
Norway, map 32
Nova Scotia, 172
Novum Organum (Bacon), 105

O

Oates, Titus, 147
Observatory: of Hevelius, *114; at Uraniborg, 99
On the Revolutions of the Heavenly Bodies (Copernicus), 98
Opera: of the Baroque period, 83-84; forbidden at French court during Lent, 22
Orange, house of, dominates politics in the Netherlands, 29; William III, 148, 167
Orléans, Philippe d', 62, 123; marriage, 26
Osnabrück, Westphalia, 41, 42; map 32
Ottoman Empire, map 32
Oudenarde, Battle of, 171
Oxenstierna, Count Axel, portrait, *29

P

Padua, 101
Painting: Baroque style, *80, 81. See also Art; Sculpture
Palaces: Fontainebleau, 68, 71; Lambeth, *154-155; Versailles, *54, 60, 61, 63, 65, 67, 70, 71, 74, 79, 117, 121, 125; White Hall, *158-159; Westminster, 13
Palatinate, 16, 18, 42; map 32
Paradise Lost (Milton), quoted, 81-82, 98
Paris, 60, 73
Pascal, Blaise, devotes life to study of religion, 126; experiments with barometer, 126; invents adding machine, 110, 126; Pensées, 126; portrait, *110
Paul V, Pope, 103
Peace conference, first international, 41-42
Peace of Augsburg, 17, 38
Peace of Prague, 36, 41
Peace of Utrecht, 172
Peace of Westphalia, 36, 42
Peasants: life of during the Thirty Years' War, 43, *48-49; unfair taxation of in France, 59, 60
Pepys, Samuel: character of, 149; extracts from diary, 149-163; house, 151; watches coronation of Charles II, 153
Peri, Jacopo, quoted, 84
Perrault, Claude, 121; Louvre colonnade, *128
Peter the Great, Czar of Russia, 167; defeats Sweden at Poltava, 168; hires French architect to design St. Petersburg, 14
Philip III, King of Spain, 168
Philip IV, King of Spain, 168, 169; portraits, *25, *64, *80, 83
Philip V of Spain (Philippe d'Anjou), 169, 170, 172
Philosophical ideas of the 17th Century, 11-12
Pilgrim's Progress (Bunyan), 147
Pisa, University of, 100, 101
Plague: in Germany during the Thirty Years' War, 41; of 1665, 149, 157
Plato, 74
Playing cards, decorated, *19-29
"Pleasures of the Enchanted Isle" (court entertainment), 125
Poetry, of the Baroque period, 81
Poland, 34, 40, 84; alliance with Russia, 167; invaded by Sweden, 168; joins the Holy League, 166; map 32; war with Sweden, 40
Political theory of the 17th Century, 13-16
Poltava, Battle of, 168
Pomerania, map 32
Poquelin, Jean Baptiste. See Molière
Portugal, 16; as a Catholic stronghold, 12;

joins Grand Alliance, 171; map 32
Prague, 32, 33, 34, 36, 37, 41, 84, 99; Defenestration, 33; map 32; surrenders to Catholic League army, 36
Presbyterianism, 143, 144, 145
Preston, Battle of, 145
Protestant Reformation, 11, 17
Protestant Union, 18, 33, 34
Protestantism: dream of pan-European Protestant alliance, 34; in England, 141, 143-148; harsh treatment of French Protestants by Louis XIV, 15, 126; rise of in Europe, 12, map 32; struggle with Catholics in Bohemia, 31, 34, 37, map 32
Prussia, 28, 33, 172; map 32. See also Brandenburg
"Psyché" (ballet composed for Louis XIV), *71
Ptolemy of Alexandria, 97-98, 103
Punch and Judy shows, 83
Puritanism, 26, 141, 144, 145-146

R

Racine, Jean, 73, 74, 122; Cartesian spirit in tragedies of, 124; Classical dramas of, 123; as member of the Four Friends, 122
Raleigh, Sir Walter, 142
Ramillies, Battle of, 171
Regensburg, 39
Reichstag (assembly of princes of the Holy Roman Empire), 17
Religious life: dissenters, *141. See also Presbyterianism; Protestantism; Puritanism; Roman Catholic Church
Rembrandt van Rijn, 12; etching, *164; Lady with a Fan, *80, 81; The Night Watch, *80, 81; preoccupation with personality, 82-83; Saul and David, *80, 83; Syndics of the Cloth Drapers' Guild, *80
Rhine River, 42, 171
Ricci, Ostilio, 101
Richelieu, Cardinal, 39; attitude to Gustavus Adolphus, 40; death of, 41; diminishes power of noblemen, 13; portrait, *22-23; wishes to sap Habsburg power, 39, 40
Rigaud, Hyacinthe, 83; Louis XIV, *80
Rolland, Romain, quoted, 83
Roman Catholic Church: attack upon Galileo, 103, 104; attempts to stem the tide of Protestantism, 79; continuing power of in the 17th Century, 12; encourages religious art, 78-79, 85, 93; extent in Europe in 1618, map 32; persecution of Catholics in England, 141, 147; plot to kill Protestant King of England (1605), 13. See also Catholic League
Rome, 85, 103. See also St. Peter's
Royal Society, of England, 108, 109
Rubens, Peter Paul, 83; Andromeda Liberated by Perseus, *80
Rudolph II, Holy Roman Emperor, 99
Russia, 14; alliance with Denmark and Poland, 167; emerges into European politics, 167; map 32; routed at Narva, 168; war in, 165; Westernization of, 167

S

St. James's Park, London, *151
St. Katherine Cree Church (London), *158
St. Olave's Church, London, *156, *157
St. Paul's Cathedral, London, 147; orb and cross, *146
St. Peter's, Rome, 77; Bernini sculptures, *76, 93, *94-95; St. Peter's chair, 77, 79, *94-95
St. Petersburg, 14
Saint-Simon, Duc de, quoted, 61-62
St. Teresa, Bernini statue, *92-93
Santa Maria Sopra Minerva (convent), 103
Sardinia, 172; map 32
Saul and David (Rembrandt), *80, 83
Savoy, map 32
Savoy, Duke of. See Charles Emanuel
Saxony, map 32
Saxony, Elector of, 16
Sceptical Chymist (Boyle), 105
Science and technology, 97-115; as an adjunct to French army reform, 58; begin-

nings of modern, 100; development of in 17th Century, 12, 13, 97, 98; free exchange of ideas, 105. See also Mathematics
Schlüter, Andreas, 31
Scotland, map 32; opposes Charles I's religious law, 143; supports Parliament in civil war in England, 144; treaty with Charles I, 144-145
Sculpture: Baroque, 81, 83; Constantine (Bernini), *90-91; Daniel (Bernini), *89; Daphne and Apollo (Bernini), *86; David (Bernini), *88; hands (Bernini), *85; Pluto and Proserpina (Bernini), *87; religious, 85, *90-91, *92-93, *94-95; St. Teresa (Bernini), *92-93; of subjects from the Greek myths (Bernini), *86-87; "warrior mask," *30
Selenographia (Hevelius), 114
Serbia, 166
Sévigné, Madame de, portrait of, *23
Shakespeare, William, 123, 125; Troilus and Cressida, quoted, 12
Shipbuilding, *180-181
Sicily, 168, 169, 170; map 32
Silesia, map 32
Simplicius Simplicissimus (character in novel), 46
Slave trade, 171, 172
Slavonia, 166
Sobieski, John, King of Poland, 166
Société des Quatre Amis, 122
Somerset, Earl of, 140
Sophie Charlotte, Princess (wife of Frederick I of Prussia), portrait, *28
Sophocles, 74
South America, 171, 172
Spain, 16, 33; as a Catholic stronghold, 12, map 32; decline of Empire, 165; truce with the United Provinces, 33; and War of the Spanish Succession, 168-172; war with England, 142
Spinoza, Baruch, Ethics Demonstrated in the Geometric Manner, 106
Starry Messenger, The (Galileo), 101-102
Steno, Nicolaus (Niels), geological studies, *112; portrait, *112
Stockholm, 118
Stuart dynasty, *26-27; absolutism under, 15; character and personality of Stuart Kings, 139; power of, 20
Styria, map 32
Sweden: awarded part of northern Germany under Peace of Westphalia, 42; Baltic empire, 167; Baltic trade imperiled by Habsburgs, 33; conducts separate negotiations with Habsburgs, 42; decline of Empire, 165; defeated at Poltava, 168; efficiency of army, 40; Great Northern War, 167-168; invades Germany, 40; map 32; role in the Thirty Years' War, 36; routs Russian army, 168; supports German fragmentation, 42; war in, 165
Switzerland: alliance with Louis XIV, 68; map 32; meeting of Swiss ambassadors with Louis XIV, *69
Syndics of the Cloth Drapers' Guild (Rembrandt), *80

T

Tapestries: scenes from the life of Louis XIV, *63-73; Triumphal Entry of Alexander the Great, *74-75. See also Gobelins factory
Taxation: in England, 142, 143; inequitable system in France, 59, 60
Telescope, 102, 114; invention of, 101; reflecting, 107
Thames River, *160-161
Theater: in the Baroque period, 83. See also Ballet; Molière; Opera; Racine
Thirty Years' War, 16, 31, 142; battle scene, *46-47; beginnings of, 25; Bohemian phase, 32-35; causes of, 18; central issue of, 39; change in character, 39; chronology, 36; Denmark's part in, 38; Europe on the eve of, map 32; execution of unruly soldiers, *50-51; horrors of, 43, 44, *48-49; last phase of, 41; lesson of, 55; looting, *48-49, 50;

mercenaries' role in, 35; military leaders, *24; *Miseries and Misfortunes of War* (etchings), *43; personalities of, *28-29; recruitment drives, *44-45; sacking a village, *48-49; as struggle between Habsburgs and Bourbons, 39; treatment of wounded, 47, *52; as a war between dynasties, 165

Thomasius, Christian, 125
Thurn, Count Heinrich Matthias, 33
Tibet, 169
Tilly, Count Johann, portrait, *24
Torelli, Giacomo, 83
Tory Party (England), 147, 148
Tradesmen, engravings, *14, *15
Transylvania, 166; *map* 32; rallies to Protestant cause, 34
Treatise on the *Trew Law of Free Monarchies* (James I of England), 140
Treaty of Dover, 147
Treaty of Karlowitz, 166
Treaty of Lübeck, 36
Tremblay, Father Joseph de, 39
Trier, *map* 32
Trier, Archbishop of, 16, 18
Troilus and Cressida (Shakespeare), quoted, 12
Turenne, Marshal, quoted, 58
Turkey: attacks Austria, 166; decline of Empire, 165; defeated by the Holy

League, 166; encroachment in Eastern Europe, 39
Two Treatises on Civil Government (Locke), 139, 148
Tyrol, *map* 32

U

United Provinces. See Dutch Netherlands
Universe, theories of, 12, 97-100, 101-102, 103, 120
University of Padua, 101
Uraniborg, observatory at, 99

V

Van Dyck, Anthony, 83; *Charles I of England*, *80, 81
Vatican: Bernini statue of Constantine, *90-91
Vauban, Marshal Sebastian, develops science of fortification, 58
Velasquez, Diego Rodriguez de Silva y, 12, 83; *Philip IV of Spain*, *80
Venice, 101; builds first opera house, 84; joins the Holy League, 166
Vermeer, Jan, 83; *Lady with a Lute*, *80

Versailles, 61, 63, 65, 67, 70, 71, 73, 170; building of, 60; as center of European culture, 62; description, 60; entertainments at, 125; as an example of Classicism, 121; gardens of, 117; huge size of, 79; life at, 61-62; Royal Chapel, *54; throne room, 74
Vienna, 33, 84; besieged by Turks, 166; as center of the Habsburg empire, 166; *map* 32
Villiers, Barbara, portrait, *27
Villiers, George. See Buckingham, Duke of
Voltaire: on the Holy Roman Empire, 16

W

Wallenstein, Albrecht von, 37-38; defeated by Gustavus, 41; dismissed by Ferdinand, 39; early life and character, 37; grim recruitment method of, 44; horoscope, 37-38, *39; marches against Germany, 38; murder of, 24, 41; physical description, 38; portrait, *24; recalled by Ferdinand, 40; rewarded for service in Thirty Years' War, 52
Walter, Lucy, portrait, *26
War of Devolution, 165
War of the League of Augsburg, 165
War of the Spanish Succession, 168-172

Warfare: changing nature of, 165; horrors of, 43, 44, *48-49; professionalism in, 34-35. See also Armies; Arms; Thirty Years' War
Weapons. See Arms
Wedgwood, C.V., quoted, 17
Westminster Abbey, London, tomb of Henry VII, *152-153
Westminster Hall, London, tracery window, *153
Westminster Palace, London, 13
Westphalia, 41, 42; *map* 32
Whig Party (England), 148
White Hall Palace (London), *158-159
White Mountain, Battle of the, 36
William II, Prince of Orange, portrait, *29
William III, King of England, Prince of Orange: ascends English throne, 29, 148; backed by Parliament, 167; invited to defend the English Protestant cause, 148; portrait, *21; as the preserver of English monarchy, 20
Women: at the court of Louis XIV, *23
Wren, Sir Christopher, 109, 146, 147
Wycherly, William, 147

Z

Zenta, Battle of, 166